THE GENESIS
OF THE
STALINIST
SOCIAL ORDER

PAVEL CAMPEANU

THE GENESIS

OF THE STALINIST SOCIAL ORDER

Translated by Michel Vale

M. E. Sharpe, Inc.
Armonk, New York and London, England

Published simultaneously as Vol. 18, No.1–2 of *International Journal
of Sociology*

Library of Congress Cataloging-in-Publication Data

Câmpeanu, Pavel.
    The genesis of the Stalinist social order / by Pavel Câmpeanu
        p.   cm.
    Translated from an unpublished French manuscript.
    ISBN 0-87332-420-X
    1. Communism—Soviet Union—History—20th century. 2. Soviet
Union—Economic policy—1917–   3. Bureaucracy—Soviet Union.
4. Stalin, Joseph, 1879-1953. I. Title.
HX313.C255 1988
306′.345′0947—dc19   88-26324
                                                              CIP

Printed in the United States of America

CONTENTS

THE GENESIS
OF THE
STALINIST
SOCIAL ORDER

I. FROM GENESIS TO REFORM

To what purpose is a study of the genesis of Stalinism, just at a time when hopes are grand that the world is about to witness its passing, according to Gorbachev's more or less explicit promises? The answer lies in the question. A deeper knowledge of the historical process which gave rise to Stalinist societies has never been so urgently necessary as today. Why? Because an evil cannot be effectively dealt with without a knowledge of how it came about. Because previous attempts to reform Stalinism have not led to its disappearance but to its rebirth as neo-Stalinism, and because its continued recurrence cannot be prevented unless the mechanisms of its birth are intimately known. Gorbachev himself has underscored this very point: it is by understanding the causes of the great errors—the tragic events of our history—that we will be able to draw lessons for the present, now that we want to renew society (from a talk January 8, 1988 to a meeting with managers of the mass media and the artists' unions). And, finally, because even while Stalin's present heir is doing battle with this encumbering heritage, at other places on the globe the genesis of Stalinism seems to be repeating itself, sometimes at the initiative of leaders who might have wished to avoid it. But a path cannot be avoided if its origins are not known. Russia was the first to embark upon this path, followed by China and North Korea in the 1950s, Cuba in the 1960s, and Vietnam in the 1970s, to take only these examples. The historical path of each of these revolutions was different, yet all had similar social consequences: the constitution of Stalinist-type societies. How is it possible for the Stalinist social order to be born from such dissimilar historical trajectories? A comparative analysis of the genesis and evolution of Stalinism in different countries and different epochs should provide some clues and is certainly necessary. But such an undertaking would have to be preceded by a less extensive, more in-depth study of the most revealing case—Russia, the first Stalinist society and hence the historical prototype for those that were to come later. The structural transformations that took place in Russia in the late 1920s would later be reproduced in most of their essential characteristics by every country that subsequently embarked on the same path, notwithstanding the various national traditions and cultural archetypes, the particular circumstances, and the individual actors involved.

The traditional penchant for drawing historical parallels must have a point of reference; for example, the Russian Revolution was, and still is, often compared with the French Revolution. Such parallels focus of course on similarities. Yet there were also indubitable differences between the two revolutions, and there is one in particular which seems crucial: namely, the contradiction which dominated the societies born of these revolutions. In postrevolutionary France this contradiction opposed the paroxysmal instability of power with the relative stability of ownership. In postrevolutionary Russia, the opposite was true: power was stable, and ownership was literally convulsed. At the manifest level—the outward march of events—power in France assumed a variety of forms at different times over the seven decades that followed 1789, being in turn Republican, Royal, and Imperial. But over the seventy years that have elapsed since the Russian Revolution, one type of power has maintained its dominion unchallenged, at least at the institutional level. Nothing comparable took place in France in either the twelve or the two hundred years following the storming of the Bastille. Indeed, not just France, but no other modern society prior to 1917 had experienced a destabilization of ownership of commensurate scope.

Thus the great singularity of the Russian Revolution, compared with all previous history, was the fate it reserved for ownership. It struck at the institution of ownership as such, not merely at one or another of its forms. Insofar as the Russian Revolution was unique in this respect, and this singularity is truly a defining characteristic, it may yield some valuable clues as to the nature of this social order. One could plausibly argue that, whereas in Revolutionary France it was ownership which was stable while power was unstable, with the former finally establishing its permanent dominion over the latter, in Soviet Russia the converse contradiction of stable power and unstable ownership led to the irreversible absorption of ownership by power.

These different historical itineraries reflect differences between the two social upheavals at their origins. The French Revolution erupted spontaneously and retained this character as it unfolded; conversely, the Russian Revolution may have been spontaneous in its eruption, but its subsequent course was guided by a strategy, which explains its anticipatory character. The immediate aim of the Russian Revolution was to transfer social ascendancy from an immature bourgeoisie to an immature proletariat and to quell the peasant appetite for private exploitation of the land; but the result was to destroy totally the entire previous, relatively unproductive system of ownership without establishing a viable alternative in its place. The state did not wither away, as forecast by Marxism; it grew stronger, and what withered away was ownership.

Destabilized ownership, born of an anticipatory revolution, was itself at the origin of what, for want of a better term, I shall call the Stalinist mode of production. Stalinism was premised not on the abolition of destabilized ownership, but on its radical modification, a modification that would enable it to become, within certain limits, economically functional. Essentially the various contending forms of ownership in postrevolutionary society were reduced to one specific form, an immutable monopoly, with absolute control over the nation's aggregate wealth. But the proprietary agent of this monopoly was not a class, nor a consolidated social stratum, nor the state, but an ultracentralized (even personalized) locus of power. The first anticapitalist industrialization in history was thus initiated on the basis of destabilized ownership, locked into a stability dearly purchased by the constraints of power, and carried ultimately to a virtual completion in a way that rigorously precluded any possibility of a restoration of private capitalism, but also all progress toward a transition to socialism as well.

The destabilization of ownership was only the outward expression of a general process of disintegration which ravaged the structures of postrevolutionary society. The anticipatory revolution had destroyed the existing structures without replacing them with others. It was the first revolution in history to give birth to a society for which destructuring was not a transitory but a chronic characteristic. The end product of this fundamental destructuring was the rigid structures of the Stalinist social order, which has since become a distinct international phenomenon capable not only of subsistence but also of proliferation. Throughout subsequent history revolutions which have tried to initiate belated industrialization based on the premature suppression of its natural agent have ultimately drifted toward the establishment of a social order of this or similar kind.

If this is the case, atemporal explanations which undertake to attribute the historical evolution of Cuba or, more recently, Nicaragua, to conspiracies devised in Moscow risk becoming so implausible that they lose even their credibility as propaganda. They ignore the real generating force of these deep-reaching historical processes, namely, the contemporary world system of imperialism.

In an attempt to understand these processes, my strategy will be to put aside the traditional descriptive histories of events and to look at how they transformed social and economic structures. All Stalinist-type societies have at least three structural elements in common: the first has to do with their immediate origins, namely, a victorious anticipatory, anticapitalist revolution; the second is the stage ushered in by victory, in which basic social relations, relations of ownership included, were utterly and irrevocably altered, with catastrophic consequences for all economic activity; the third is the absorption of the entire national patrimony by power, with the establishment of a global, ultracentralized monopoly on power and ownership that went on to become the effective agent of a kind of industrialization as alien to capitalism as it is to socialism.

In accordance with the above hypothesis, a description of the historical process leading to Stalinist society should begin with a description of anticipatory revolution. This is the topic developed in the preceding volume, *The Origins of Stalinism.* In this second volume I shall endeavor to describe the transformation of postrevolutionary Russia into the Stalinist social order, and, more specifically, the transformation of economically paralyzing, destabilized ownership into a global, ultracentralized monopoly with industrializing potential. Human factors and events aside, what created this potential was the emergence of a fitting social structure which enabled the monopoly to become functional within certain limits.

As remotely relevant as they may seem, these preliminary results directly concern a possible strategy for reform (which the Soviets believe they have). As long as reform sets its sights not on eradicating but merely on loosening this structure, and thus the monopoly, and on tempering their effects, it will perhaps be able to ameliorate Stalinism, but it will never to surmount it.

Before discovering how these two fundamental pillars of Stalinist societies can be eliminated, let us examine more closely the sources and processes which brought them into being.

II. IN SEARCH OF A STRUCTURE

1. Congenital disarticulation: syncretism

By anticipatory revolution I understand a desynchronization in the historical process unlike that imposed on it by the establishment of the world system of imperialism. Imperialism made the uneven development of the countries at its periphery the *sine qua non* of its existence. Once the division of the world into a center and a periphery became stabilized, historical desynchronization was transformed into an economic and political structure that embraced the entire world. Uneven development has assumed different forms in different places throughout the world, but its substance is everywhere the same: the possibility, or not, of industrialization. In the Western countries capitalism was the spark and driving force of industrialization at the national level. But on the world scale, as imperialism, it obstructed and even opposed it. Early in this century, nascent national capitalism in most of the backward countries, including Russia, was less interested in its industrializing mission than in the immediate advantages to be gained from a subaltern collaboration with the countries at the center.

But this class dilemma was no more than the expression of the antinomic predicament represented by the integration of these countries into the imperialist system. Their technological progress was slow, and this made it a matter of increasing urgency for them to overcome the industrial backwardness which their position in the imperialist system destined them perpetually to reproduce. Thus, growing underdevelopment and an equally growing need to overcome it—two tendencies born of the same process, but impelled in opposite directions—marked an unprecedented phenomenon: the reduplication of historical necessity. Reduced to mutually exclusive but equally plausible possibilities, historical necessity became antinomic and as such was more inclined to bring societies which it dominated to a standstill than to galvanize them into movement.

The more encumbered historical necessity is in its flow, the wider the range of historical possibility and hence of political strategies. Leninist strategy, centered on the possibility of replacing anti-industrial capitalism with pre-industrial socialism, was drawn up, put to the test, and, up to a point, confirmed within this general context. For my present purposes, the concept of antinomic necessity is useful for giving more clarity to the continuity in the historical arc that spans the imperialist system, Leninist-type (anticipatory) revolutions, and Stalinist-type societies.

Leninist strategy, at least in spirit, saw pre-industrial socialism as a transitory constraint rather than an ideal. Its true role was to open a new path to industrialization by changing its social agent. Shunned by a bourgeoisie floundering in underdevelopment, this role could only be assumed by the proletariat, despite its own underdevelopment. Leninist strategy can therefore be reduced to two fundamental propositions. First, the necessity of industrialization entailed the elimination of imperialist domination, which was preventing or distorting it. Second, to eliminate imperialist domination, it was necessary to remove its main internal pillar of support, a capitalist class incapable of accomplishing its historical mission. This path toward belated industrialization was the path of anticipatory revolution. The revolution achieved its anti-imperialist character by becoming anticipatorily anticapitalist. Dual necessity required dual satisfaction.

Under the pressures of the Civil War, the victorious revolution soon revealed its powers to transform, as well as the limits on those powers. With regard to the external world, it had created the conditions for freeing the country from imperialist rule, first and foremost by refusing to continue the war. Internally, its achievements were notably less coherent. Its potential for innovation found expression in the absolutely unprecedented feat of creating a class structure that included no possessing classes. However, this profound revolutionary change was limited in that it was accompanied by no comparable transformation in the forces of production. The two major obstacles to industrialization had been eliminated, but this was not sufficient. Born of antinomic necessity, postrevolutionary society inherited the antinomy of its parentage. Its predominately postcapitalist class structure had been imposed upon the productive forces without meshing with them, while its productive forces, still predominantly precapitalist, became merely more so. Thus was born a pre-industrial society of postcapitalist type which Stalinism would transform through the systematic application of extraeconomic constraints on anticapitalist industrial society.

The desynchronization of historical processes first imposed by the logic of imperialism and later inverted by the anticipatory revolution was in the end internalized by postrevolutionary society as a disarticulation between its new class structure, which was in advance of its time, and the old backward productive forces. The consequence of this direct leap from backwardness to historical anticipation obviously did not square with one of the key tenets of Marxist doctrine, namely, that there is a necessary correspondence between the character of the productive forces in a society and the character of the social relations dominating it.

But under certain conditions, this correspondence may break down. Engels gives a classical example of this in a letter to Tkachev: "Only when the social forces of production have attained a certain degree of development will it be possible to increase production sufficiently for the abolition of class differences to represent true progress, and to endure without causing an arrest or regression in the social mode of production." It was precisely this situation, set forth by Engels as a hypothetical possibility, which the anticipatory revolution made a reality. Engels' insight may be taken as a warning: any attempt to restructure class relations without regard for the state of productive forces runs the risk of causing an arrest or regression which will affect not simply one or another sphere of social life, but the mode of production as a whole.

Moreover, anticipatory revolution not only breaks the correspondence between these two terms, it tends to invert their relationship. As I argued in *The Syncretic Society*, in all previous societies it was the development of the productive forces that took the lead, and productive and ownership relations, concretized in class structures, that lagged behind. In contrast, in postrevolutionary society it is the development of the productive forces that lags behind the social structure.[1]

Thus antinomic historical necessity imposed upon the new class structure the mission of determining that factor which should by nature have determined it. Unable to fulfill this role, the class structure paradoxically became the generator of a process of destructuring which reached to the very foundations of society. The natural links between the class structure and the productive forces were broken.

Despite its central importance, this phenomenon has been generally overlooked in the specialized literature, although there are some authors whom it had not escaped. Ferenc Fehér, Agnes Heller, and György Markus note "structural similarities between the different (East European) countries" and "the constancy (or the constant cyclical recurrence) of definite negative structural phenomena which resist entirely the will to change them."[2] We can also cite Hillel Ticktin's reference to "a society with laws contradicting each other," or Donald Filtzer's observation that "in economic development the Soviet Union suffered from a chronic lack of correspondence."[3] In view of its importance, it seems to me that this phenomenon, which is absolutely crucial to the societies up for discussion, merits being not just pointed (as it has been), but also conceptualized. The term that I have proposed is *syncretism* (see *The Syncretic Society*).

By syncretism I understand in this case a state of stabilized disarticulation between the forces of production and the class structure in a particular society. What is specific is not disarticulation, which can also occur in other societies, but its stabilization, a quality belonging exclusively to societies born of anticipatory revolutions. This disarticulation, or break in correspondence, occurs at the deepest and most basic level of a society, but in its manifest form appears as a dysfunctionality in the presumptive mediators of the two terms of the correspondence, i.e., relations of ownership and relations of production. Syncretism will be the very likely result of anticipatory revolutions as long as the world remains under the sway of imperialism. The legitimate anti-imperialism of such revolutions is coupled with a premature anticapitalism that leaves one term of antinomic necessity unsatisfied, and conflicts with the other.

A number of corollaries that follow from the above definition should be useful as guidelines in my analysis:

1. Stabilized syncretism is an exclusive trait of societies born of anticipatory revolution.

2. This exclusivity, and the scope of its consequences, makes syncretism an identifying characteristic of these societies.

3. A sociological study of syncretism is first and foremost the study of its dysfunctional consequences for relations of ownership, relations of production, and class relations.

4. Accordingly, the genesis of Stalinism may be seen as an empirical but plausible attempt to convert the entropic effects of syncretism into the premises of a possible social order.

5. The transformation of postrevolutionary society into a Stalinist social order may be regarded as a historical process that is at root objectively determined, despite the diversity of the factors involved.

Before continuing the analysis along these lines, some additional clarifications may be useful. First, syncretism does not describe a kind of relation but, on the contrary, the absence or blocking of a necessary relation. Second, the terms constitutive of syncretism—namely, the forces of production and class structure—are accordingly not in a *relation of contradiction* with regard to one another; they are in *state of incompatibility*. Incompatibility is thus the specific content of syncretism. Third and last, it follows that a syncretic society is in danger of losing its character as a social system.

In law, where it is broadly used, the term incompatibility usually refers to two or more functions which cannot be conferred upon the same actor; the connotation suggests an internal, mutual exclusion. In the special context of social syncretism, I shall use the term incompatibility to imply the coexistence of two or more terms between which the functional interaction necessary to the whole of which they are a part does not or cannot take place.

Theoretically, a state of incompatibility between social elements may be produced between social elements. The most obvious of these are chance and necessity. Chance may bring about the fortuitous intersection or convergence of terms which are normally separate, or it may for some reason or other cause connections which are normally operative to deteriorate. Or incompatibility may come about by necessity, as at the moment of extreme tension just before denouement, when a conflict is at the verge of breaking the unity that brought it about. In the latter case the conflict precedes and creates the state of incompatibility, whereas in postrevolutionary Russia incompatibility existed without conflict. In this case, incompatibility appeared in anticipation of a possible conflict rather than in a concluding phase.

Thus incompatibility is substantially different from contradiction, conflict, or antagonism, with which it can interact or have no relation at all with equal facility.

Contradiction is a key concept in Hegel and Marx, where it implies the natural unity of its terms, whereas the terms of incompatibility are naturally separate. In the syncretism of postrevolutionary Russia, the two terms were totally disjunctive. Usually contradiction is born of necessity, while incompatibility springs from the possible. Contradiction implies the interaction of its terms and tends toward polarization, while incompatibility implies their indifference and tends toward isolation. Contradiction is a process and hence dynamic, while incompatibility is conjunctural and so homeostatic. The first tends to reproduce itself through development, the second through repetition and recurrence. Likewise, contradiction tends to transform the context out of which it arose, while incompatibility, once stabilized, is more disposed to cause the disaggregation of that context. So too, after surviving the Civil War, the incompatibility between the forces of production and the class structure of postrevolutionary Russia was able to survive the denouement of one social conflict while preventing the structuring of a second.

Imprinted in its genetic code, this state of affairs became the condition of existence of postrevolutionary society. The first problem that this society had to face was not how to surmount its syncretism, but how to subsist or even progress under its burden. Having resisted diverse attempts to smash it, society found itself threatened by an even more devastating evil of which it was the unsuspecting bearer.

The anticipatory abolition of capitalist relations of ownership, relations of production, and class relations in postrevolutionary Russia ensured that the Revolution would endure, but it did not ensure the realization of its initial objective—industrialization. Postrevolutionary society was now faced with another obstacle, namely, the hiatus produced by the absence of these relations (or of alternatives to them). The ordeals it underwent attested to its incapacity to dispense with the relations it had abolished or to establish others in their place. Later this mission was to be assumed by Stalinism.

From the disarticulation between the forces of production and class structure, the analysis now passes to the destabilization of their natural mediators. These mediators had been undermined and were not now rebuilt in a form more suited to the new social context. It is difficult in any case to imagine what qualities a mediator would have to have for it to accommodate equally two such totally irreconcilable elements. The mediator most directly affected was relations of ownership.

Relations of ownership vary with the forces of production, while class relations, and consequently class structures, vary with relations of ownership. But ownership, at the center of a correspondence that no longer existed, was itself no longer subject to the determining influence of the forces of production and had lost its determining influence over class structure. Any progress made by ownership toward an accommodation with one of the two terms only intensified its incompatibility with the other. What resulted was not the collapse of certain forms of ownership only, but of ownership itself as a social and economic institution. By totally abolishing capital, war communism tied ownership to the new class structure, but in the process it severed all links with the forces of production. The means of production expropriated from the capitalists could therefore not be appropriated by the workers. Far from pursuing that end, the revolutionary government felt itself compelled to bring ownership more thoroughly into accord with the state of the forces of production and accordingly embarked upon the New Economic Policy, the consequences of which would be the advent of Stalinism.

Because of their extreme generality, the above observations suffer from oversimplification in a number of respects. For example, a one-sided emphasis on the disarticulation between the productive forces and the class structure ignores their common bond: namely, that the workers and peasants who formed the basis of the new class structure at the same time represented the virtual totality of the human productive forces at society's disposal. Therefore, the same human element which as a class structure was the social vehicle of postcapitalism, was, as a productive force, the bearer of precapitalism. The disarticulation of society was thus internalized by its principal productive classes, who were called upon to fulfill incompatible social roles. Their remarkable productivity as the social force of revolution contrasted with their low productivity as the force directly engaged in production. Thus the general destructuring of society reasserted itself as an antinomy within the producers, whose performance in their two principal social roles was glaring unequal. This antinomy would be superseded by Stalinism, which, rather than balancing the two roles, would practically abolish one of them. Once reduced to the bare function of productive force, the producers were *de facto* dispossessed of any other social role as well. Power could only be monolithic by virtue of its negative counterpart, namely, the single role of the productive classes.

The hypothesis of syncretism has a number of implications. For instance, it raises the question of whether systems theory might perhaps be useful for analyzing a society in the process of losing its characteristics as a social system. The answer, I think, is a qualified yes on condition that the method does not try to bend the object of study to fit its premises. What is essential is to keep in mind is that systems theory can be applied not only to the functioning, but also to the dysfunctionalities, of different systems. Parsons' idea that "systems seem to me to be an indispensable master concept, the meaning of which is directly concerned with its relationship to the concept environment," is useful here.[4] Indeed, the state of a society's productive forces at any particular moment in time is defined by the state of its relations with its natural surroundings at that same moment. Like other systems, a society is made up of structures which reveal the extent of society's control over its environment. Accordingly, syncretism arises when there is a temporal lag between these structures and the level of control exercised by society over its environment. More concretely, class structure reflects a seemingly high level of independence vis-à-vis the natural environment on which society is in reality profoundly dependent, as the state of its productive forces will reveal. If it internalizes its real relations with nature in a distorted manner, a society will lose much of its systemic character. By effecting radical transformations in its class structure, a society lays claim to an autonomy vis-à-vis the environment which is beyond its capacity to acquire.

Occasionally some authors will venture to doubt the systemic nature of Stalinist society. In a debate on the concept of "political revolution," Ernest Mandel once commented: "One could say 'mode of production' but this concept is inapplicable to transitional societies"[5]—a diagnosis which while correct enough raises doubts concerning both its object and its motivation. It is not only the process of production which has lost the characteristics of a system, but the society as a whole—hence the problem of the object to which the diagnosis is applied. In principle it should be difficult, one would think, for a transitional society to possess the same degree of stability inherent in a system, but this is not the case with Stalinism. It is not because it is transitional but because it is syncretic that Stalinism loses its systemic quality. One can say that no transitional society is a system, but this does not imply that any society which is not a system must necessarily be a transitional society.

Parkin offers another example on the same subject: "Weaknesses in system integration are a more distinctive feature of socialist society than of modern capitalism."[6] In my terms this comment suggests that an anticipatory revolution can deprive societies of their capitalist character only by depriving them of their character as a system as well. Thomas Masaryk leaves no doubt: "The so-called Bolshevik system has never been anything but a complete absence of system."[7]

In fact, postrevolutionary Russia offered only very few general possibilities which could be translated into political options by the new power. They were:

1. Eliminating the disarticulation between the productive forces and the class structure by turning back the revolutionary changes which had produced that disarticulation.

2. Safeguarding these transformations and hence preserving the disarticulation at the risk of precipitating a social cataclysm.

3. Forging a social order capable of assimilating the absence of structure, while reducing the effects of destructuring by formalizing the revolutionary conquests that had provisionally been maintaining it.

Torn between forces of production lingering from a precapitalist past and a class structure with no effective implementation in the future, postrevolutionary society was powerless to construct a viable present. To surmount syncretism and its paralyzing effects, it plunged blindly into a state of timeless immobility, the perpetual present of the Stalinist order—intolerant of past and future, the real and the possible, in equal measure. It is was an order whose resistance to change toward the restoration of capitalism became resistance to all change, with one exception: that of its forces of production.

Stalinism was the force within postrevolutionary society urging it beyond the impasse of its syncretic condition. In this respect, Stalinism represented a fourth possibility, that of adapting one of the terms of syncretism to the other. At an abstract level it was a matter of indifference whether this meant adapting the postcapitalist class structure to the precapitalist productive forces or vice versa; but concretely, for purposes of the legitimacy of power, adaptation could take only one direction: that of developing the productive forces with utmost rapidity, while retaining intact the new character of the class structure. Despite its apparent rationality, this possible approach imposed a condition that was very difficult to meet or, if it were met, could well have unforeseeable consequences. Specifically, what was required was a set of mechanisms capable of rendering social structures insensitive to a rapid and radical transformation of the forces of production. A strange alliance had to be forged—and Stalinism would forge it—between the dynamic movement of technological change and the social immobility of the new order. Stalinism attempted to overcome the disarticulation at its origins by carrying it deeper. Its battle against syncretism took place under the mantle of syncretism itself, so to speak. Finally, to safeguard the new class structure, Stalinism divested it of its principal functions and so reduced it to no more than a formal social role. Engendered in the womb of syncretism, Stalinism would be able (in the short term) to stave off the most destructive consequences of syncretism only by perpetuating it.

Before the Revolution, the purpose of industrialization was to cast off the chains of underdevelopment. After the Revolution the task was compounded: to emerge from underdevelopment and to overcome syncretism. Stalinist industrialization would revert to the initial historical necessity, and short-term achievements would enable Stalinism to transform a social upheaval into a social order of new kind, i.e., a structural edifice which would make disarticulation the central pillar of its functionality. Functions which previously had been exercised by mediating mechanisms were transferred wholesale to mechanisms of domination. Structurally, this metamorphosis gave rise to a specialized entity which both fulfilled and symbolized the singular role of universal authority. This entity exercised its domination over society by subjecting it to relations of domination, the primacy of which constituted the substance of Stalinist social restructuring. This was no simple substitution as in Merton's model, in which a function is shifted from one agent to another. In this case, the function itself underwent substantial modification in the process. It came to exercise its mediating role through domination and was both contradictory in its content and vacillating in its action.

To overcome syncretism, Stalinism, rather than undertake to rebuild the natural mediating structures, sapped them of their remaining vitality, thereby facilitating their utter and ultimate subordination to a new artificial mediating agent, which was at once an instrument of domination and isolation. But for these functions to be performed effectively, it was essential that this agent have a double locus: one embedded within the social structure, and the other outside of society. "Agent" in this case of course does not refer to a human subject or subjects, but to a constant social mechanism which is in principle independent of the persons who might happen to represent it at any particular moment. To be functional, therefore, this mechanism must be embedded in a social structure that puts it above all the rest of society, or, conversely—what amounts to the same thing—puts all the rest of society under its sway. The separation which Stalinism effected between the task of industrialization and the class structure was compounded by a new isolating process that structurally separated society from the mechanism upon which its activity depended. The initial disarticulation was therefore not only preserved, it was increased and diversified. Stalinism added its own kinds of syncretism to the syncretism inherited from the Revolution. Stalinism seems to have aimed at attenuating the effects of the original syncretism by diversifying it and then attempting to subject the syncretism it had inherited to the control of those it had added. At its very deepest level, therefore, the phenomenon of syncretism seems to be a factor of continuity that reaches back from the Stalinist social order to postrevolutionary society and, beyond the latter, to the anticipatory revolution.

The structural disintegration caused by anticipatory revolution perceptibly expanded the space accessible to the subjective intervention of authority. Stalinist power, therefore, did not develop through its own forces, but rather fed on natural social relations, sapping them of their vital forces. As the surrounding social edifice crumbled, authoritarian interventions grew in social importance without changing in nature. Though they attained social primacy, relations of authority were not a substitute but a surrogate for natural relations, which they tended to absorb. In practical terms, this meant that the Stalinist remedy for structural disintegration was not strictly speaking to replace certain structures with others, but to replace social structure with social organization as much as possible. To clarify this distinction: whereas structures, which evolve through natural processes, develop manifold relations uniting their particular terms, social organizations are created by human initiative and are constrained to develop through human initiative as well.

References to the structures of Stalinist society, therefore, require some special precautions. Two aspects are particularly important. First, Stalinist social organization, though not a social structure, nonetheless assumes the functions of such. Second, while predominant, Stalinist social organization, based on relations of authority, does not bring the disappearance of other social relations and hence other social structures, but instead distorts them. The Stalinist social order thus rests on a social organization with structural functions. Never carried to completion, this functional transfer displays a vast and variable range of inefficiency. But these limitations notwithstanding, it was this type of organization which enabled Stalinism not only to assimilate the general disarticulation of society, but also to shield (up to a point) the production process from its social consequences. This internal antinomy, manifested as an unending to and fro between limitations and achievements, warrants regarding Stalinism as an organization with the functions of a structure, yet also directly conducive to structural disintegration. Thanks to this transfer of function, the Stalinist social order also bears an extreme resemblance to the archetypal bureaucratic organization, from which it also clearly differs in that it does not exist for a certain group or a certain definite activity, but for an entire nation or commonweal and the whole complex range of its social activity.

Bureaucratic by nature, such an organization need expend no particular effort to remain indifferent to the the state of the productive forces or to their evolution as a result of industrialization. The mediating and isolating function exercised by authority thus becomes operative by virtue of this bureaucratic-type organization which replaces social structures, yet plays a similar role.

This substitution had the effect of making the principal social relations more dependent, if possible, on this organization than on the development of the productive forces, in which they participated only indirectly. Of all these social relations, relations of ownership, being directly linked to the productive forces, were the least susceptible to isolation. The ability of the new social order to initiate anticapitalist industrialization and, on this basis, to achieve the historical durability to which it aspired therefore depended primarily on transformations in relations of ownership.

2. Antinomies

History had posed a new and unique problem for which a new solution was necessary: what kind of relations of ownership would be capable of articulating a postcapitalist class structure with precapitalist productive forces? The problem was never truly understood, and pragmatism prevailed. The result is the only modern social organization in which the locus of ownership has remained a mystery.

Before Stalinism provided an illusory solution to this problem, postrevolutionary society merely careened from one mode of dissipation of ownership to another in a chaotic process triggered by the transformation of the bourgeois revolution into Lenin's socialist revolution—in fact, the anticipatory transformation of the Russian Revolution from antifeudal to anticapitalist. The general attack on feudalism, legitimated by the state of productive forces, was spontaneous and radical, and it was incarnated in an immense social class making up the great majority of the population. Not surprisingly, it resulted straightaway in the abolishment of feudal ownership. But the offensive against the bourgeoisie was of another stripe: premature relative to the state of the productive forces, it was inconsistent and strategic in nature and was embodied in a circumscribed political organization. Its initial result was not the abolishment but simply the deterioration of capitalist ownership. The Revolution proved that it was able to move directly from one strategic objective to another, although only at the price of a substantial loss of its power to transform economic and social structures. Discontinuity in performance within a broader continuity of movement is the first perceptible contradiction opposing a belated antifeudalism to a premature anticapitalism within the revolutionary process.

As far as the peasantry was concerned, the real end of the antifeudal movement was not to destroy the property of the nobility, but to transform it into a limitless sea of small private peasant plots. But as merchant trade developed, these small plots by their very nature manifested an irresistible tendency to become agrarian enterprises of a capitalist type. Intended as a stepping stone toward the abolishment of capitalist ownership, the abolition of feudal ownership was threatening to become its principal obstacle, and so arose the second perceptible contradiction in a revolutionary strategy that had aimed at abolishing feudal property but had rejected its inevitable consequence: namely, the rise of private petty peasant property.

Another circumstance which this strategy did not foresee was the reluctance of the revolutionary government to nationalize capitalist enterprises. By resisting spontaneous tendencies among the workers and pressures within Party leadership, Lenin managed to moderate the pace of nationalization. The documents of the period make it unambiguously clear that this hesitance was not due to any intention of protecting capitalist ownership, but was dictated by an awareness of the limits within which its abolishment was not merely socially possible but also economically profitable or even bearable. This is the third discernible contradiction between the unlimited capacity of revolutionary power to expropriate capitalist property and its extremely limited capacity to appropriate it on a new basis. This contradiction left a deep mark on the nature of postrevolutionary Russia: the anticipatory, anticapitalist revolution could give birth only to an antibourgeois society. It could divest the bourgeoisie of its power, but not of its property.

Stopped dead by the very success of anticipation, the government thereupon concentrated its efforts on obstructing the functioning of the forms of ownership it had not the means to abolish. A withering battle was joined between the government and the very social spontaneity that had originally enabled it to establish itself. The direct consequence was a general destabilization of ownership, leading to the progressive collapse of all economic activity. These effects merely rendered visible another contradiction intrinsic to the new society: namely, a real antimony between the growing destabilization of ownership and its continued necessity.

Most analysts of postrevolutionary Russia tend to touch upon the subject merely cursorily, if at all. Sporadically one or another aspect of the erosion of relations of ownership will be pointed out, but with no attempt to get to the root of the process. Other authors, in an effort to elaborate a theory to explain the historical facts, arrive at conclusions which seem at least debatable.

One very well known example illustrates this nicely: namely, Djilas, who observes: ''The new class obtains its power, privileges, ideology, and customs from one specific form of ownership—collective ownership.''[8] This view in my opinion brings up three valid points for consideration. First, in the society in question, ownership underwent a radical transformation; second, this transformation consisted essentially in a change in the form of ownership and its agent; and third, these modifications did not prevent ownership from remaining a decisive factor in molding other social relations. But as I have said, Djilas unfortunately draws from these postulates a questionable conclusion—that there is a new class of owners.

Another view concludes on the basis of these same changes that the deterioration of relations of ownership implied the deterioration (i.e., disappearance) of their social role as well. "If we want to develop a critical theory of any of these phenomena of state socialist societies," says Szelenyi à propos of this subject, "we have first to fight the myth of ownership and develop a substantive understanding of the economic institutions and mechanisms of this society."[9] Thus the inveterate practice of dismissing the question of ownership receives a provocative, if contestable, theoretical justification. My reservations are based on the probability that, with any given entity, a dysfunctional phenomenon will not necessarily be less influential than its functional version. What is more, under certain conditions it is precisely the dysfunctional element which is decisive in determining the evolution of the entity as a whole. Szelenyi's thesis, therefore, is just as plausible for the opposite case: the most weighty aspect in the reality of degraded ownership and the most fecund for studying it is the process of deterioration itself, its causes, practical reactions to it, the ideological notions it engenders, and the way in which society and the economy ultimately surmount, assimilate, or jointly accommodate to it.

From this perspective, the known historical facts seem to follow a logic which suggests that Stalinism was in essence simply the way in which postrevolutionary society was able to absorb the degradation of relations of ownership brought about by the anticipatory revolution. Rosanna Rosanda was perhaps thinking along similar lines when she said: "The decisive element lies in the domain of ownership, and the Revolution seems to consist of the transition from private to state ownership"—a functional formula for destabilized ownership, in my opinion.

These contemporary ideas aside, what turns our attention to the "domain of ownership" are the events of the period, often played out in an evident enough fashion at the margins of or even within this domain itself.

3. General configuration

The first fact to meet the eye in this respect is the shifting panorama that ownership presented in postrevolutionary and pre-Stalinist society (1917–1929), with its constant and variable factors serving to maintain ownership in a state of instability.

A distinction between the forms of ownership in industry and in agriculture respectively persisted in substance after the Revolution, although a change in the terms of the distinction had occurred. In prerevolutionary Russia these terms were capitalist and feudal property on the one side and small peasant holdings on the other. In postrevolutionary Russia these terms became (with the exception of the years of war communism) state monopoly and, opposing it, the debris of private capitalism and small peasant holdings. More even than before the Revolution, the general momentum of these distinctions was toward contradiction. This contradiction evolved in a way that was sterile for the economy, and in the end it would be eliminated by Stalinism, essentially through the elimination of their source: namely, the distinction between forms of ownership in industry and agriculture.

The limitations the Revolution encountered in its efforts to restructure society were even more severe than the limitations it experienced at its outset. Although the Revolution had succeeded in destroying an underdeveloped bourgeoisie, postrevolutionary society was not able to install an underdeveloped proletariat in the role of ruling class. Whereas the Revolution had in fact established the social and political preconditions for the potential abolishment of capitalist ownership, postrevolutionary society proved incapable of preventing the transformation of anticapitalism into underproductivity. The Revolution created a postcapitalist class structure, but postrevolutionary society was powerless to defend that structure against the undermining effects of its lack of economic legitimacy, except by depriving it of its principal functions. The Revolution transformed the peasant movement against feudalism into a political movement against the bourgeoisie, but postrevolutionary society did not have the resources to transform an antifeudal peasantry into an anticapitalist peasantry. In this ambiguous setting, the general configuration of ownership consisted of three principal forms for most of the period in question: state monopoly, small peasant holdings, and a tolerated residual capitalism.

The disarticulation of the whole was translated to its parts, but in different if not opposed forms, expressed in the direction taken by the spontaneous development of each. Thus capitalist-owned property tended spontaneously to go beyond the limits imposed upon it by government and so to become dominant; small peasant property tended spontaneously to grow into capitalism; and the state monopoly concentrated post-haste on consolidating itself at the expense of the others.

At the beginning of NEP especially, the spontaneous tendencies of capitalist and of peasant ownership were convergent, while the state monopoly moved counter to the other two forms; and as it tended to consolidate itself by sapping the others, the net effect could only be harmful for the economy as a whole. A kind of contest emerged in which the state monopoly seemed only able to gain ground at the expense of a decline in social production. To avoid losing the contest, Stalinism did away with it.

But before that path was taken, the destabilization of ownership became evident in three principal areas: (1) the general organization of ownership (characterized by upheaval); (2) the social locus of ownership (characterized by continuing contention); and (3) the exercise of each of the forms of ownership (characterized by varying degrees of decomposition).

4. Unstable ownership

There is ample literature on war communism and the New Economic Policy (NEP). Without wishing to detract from the real contributions made therein, I think it necessary to point out the limitations as well. As one delves more deeply into these periods, there is a risk of losing sight of the fact that they were also constituent stages in a historical process that ultimately went beyond them. This process was without precedent in the modern era; its defining characteristic was the tumultuous changes in ownership. The fleeting period covered by the Revolution and postrevolutionary society consisted of five stages, each of which was defined by one of five variants of the social organization of ownership: (1) up to October 1917, the predominance of feudal and capitalist ownership; (2) between October 1917 and June 1918, the absorption of the lands of the nobility by small peasant holdings, accompanied by opposition from the revolutionary government to both accelerated nationalization and direct worker appropriation; (3) "war communism," during which the government took advantage of the circumstances (the eruption of the Civil War and the war of intervention) to abolish every form of private ownership and mercantile trade; (4) the end of the Civil War and beginning of NEP, which reestablished not only the market and peasant private ownership, but also, within very strict limits, capitalist ownership; and, finally, the last stage of this cycle, (5) the institution of the Stalinist form of ownership, which has lasted with no essential changes for sixty years, signaling the transition from unstable to stable ownership.

I see no reason why these variants should not be interpreted as states in the revolutionary and postrevolutionary history of ownership, extending, through successive continuities and breaks, from the victory of Bolshevism in 1917 to the victory of Stalinism in 1929. The concept I have proposed, unstable ownership, serves as a leitmotif for this period and should help to underscore two historical facts of capital importance to my discussion. First, postrevolutionary society proved incapable of organizing a system of ownership able to reconcile the anticapitalist direction imposed by the Revolution with the economic imperatives of development and—quite simply—survival. Second, the passage from postrevolutionary society to the Stalinist social order is at the same time the transition from unstable ownership, which was economically disastrous, to a kind of ownership which was stable and, over the short term, economically productive.

Basically, although subjective measures determined the specific form of the various stages of this process, at bottom the process itself was but a reflection of the peculiar nature of postrevolutionary society, i.e., its syncretism. In substance these stages were nothing more than attempts to accommodate the organization of ownership bit by bit to one of the terms of syncretism at the expense of the other. Disregarding the diffident gropings of the initial period, war communism was doubtlessly as amenable to the class structure as it was intolerable for the productive forces. NEP, by making an abrupt about-face, adapted ownership to the real level of the productive forces, while at the same time altering the postcapitalist character of the class structure.

A clarification is called for: the pressures exerted on ownership by the productive forces and the class structure were not only opposite in direction; they were also unequal in force. This inequality was due to the very nature of these categories, and not to the particular circumstances. How ownership is organized socially depends on the state of the productive forces. On the other hand, ownership is the economic content of class structure, which in turn determines how ownership or rights of ownership are distributed. Each time the state set about attempting to reorganize ownership with the intention of mitigating this inequality, it was implicitly pitting itself and the potential it could muster against objective social determinants. The unequal relation of ownership between the productive forces and the class structure was translated into an economic inequality derived from priority being given to one or the other. War communism, which gave priority to the class structure, brought the economy to the verge of collapse; but NEP, which gave relatively free rein to the productive forces, was able within a period of five years (1921-1926) not only to arrest the precipitous disintegration of economic activity, but to quintuple industrial output and restore it to prewar levels in the major economic sectors. Despite these achievements, NEP failed to avoid repeated crises so violent as to shake the foundations of society. It was, in short, unable to neutralize the factors that were keeping ownership in a state of extreme instability. Most basic of these factors was the general destructuring, which provided a setting within which these upheavals could occur. Most immediate was the continuing contention over ownership.

5. Contested ownership

An attentive examination of the twelve years from 1917 to 1929 will show that every historical agent with a potential ownership role was prevented from exercising that role either by other possible alternative agents aspiring to such a role themselves or by agents exercising rights of ownership through other competitive forms. The ultimate effect of this contest, which I shall call the question of "contested ownership," was to weaken the property base of the whole society.

Contention over ownership, which had many varied manifestations, was the one constant factor in the events of this period. Two processes were at work. The first was a dispute which obscured the historical agent of ownership and hence its social locus. The second was a series of upheavals in the social organization of ownership; it was fueled by the first process and reflected its spasmotic nature.

These changes were always the product of direct governmental interventions. While it may be correct to say that upheavals in ownership reflected shifts in Bolshevik economic and social policy, it is also irrelevant. At bottom, at the level of social organization, they expressed the accumulated tensions resulting from the disputes over ownership. The decisions taken by the government merely interpreted and translated the fluidity of the social locus of the ownership into fluid institutional forms.

The dispute over ownership took three main forms: (1) a spontaneous tendency of the productive classes to assume possession of the means of production expropriated from the ruling classes; (2) the endeavor of the state to do the same; and as a result, (3) the state's efforts to prevent or impede the productive classes from appropriating or enjoying the usufruct of the means of production. This list of the principal forms of the dispute is also a list of the principal contenders for the rights of ownership: namely, the working class, the peasantry, and the state. To this trinity, which dominated the process, must be added residual capitalism, revitalized by NEP. The weight these groups carried derived far more from their potential as a social force—especially given the rapid stratification of the countryside—than from the material value of their actual possessions. Capitalism, politically smashed and economically strapped, wielded a crucial weapon in this dispute: it had a monopoly over managerial skills, while on a deeper level it was in tune with the state of the productive forces.

The working class was only briefly a direct contender in the dispute over ownership, but the role it did play was highly significant. The spontaneous movement to take possession of the factories began soon after February 1917 and increased momentum in the weeks after October. In enterprises that had not been nationalized it found itself pitted against the owners, and in those that had been, its opponents were the managers accredited by the new government. Totally spontaneous, the action was directed against capitalist ownership as well as against the anticapitalist state and was equally illegal in both cases. At first glance this action, which drove the first wedge between the working class and the state that purported to represent it, appeared to come from the class. But just the opposite was the case: if in order to take possession of the means of production the proletariat found itself compelled to rebel against the state, which was the embodiment of legality, it was because legality did not recognize the proletariat's right of ownership over the means of production.

Nothing could have been more natural after a victory over the bourgeoisie by a regime that defined itself as the dictatorship of the proletariat than for the proletariat to rise up in protest against being separated from the means of production. While perfectly legitimate at the theoretical level, this action posed two practical problems: first, that of the management of enterprises, and, second, that of establishing the necessary norms for regulating the workers' exercise of their ownership. As for the first, workers elected to managerial positions were soon found to lack the necessary skills. As for the second, no regulations existed at all, with the consequence that each factory committee, rather than the class as a whole, made its own law. As Bettelheim observes: "In the weeks following the October insurrection, the Bolshevik Party attempted to transform the diffuse and anarchic activity of hundreds and thousands of factory committees" because "each of them had a tendency to multiply its prerogatives and to treat its particular factory as an independent unit of production, the collective property of its own workers."[10]

The press of the period abounds with information on this issue, describing some at times surprising situations. Under the management of its own committee, one button factory in Moscow was brought to such a pass that its workers decided to shut it down. Other committees rehired their former managers after having expelled them (A. Lozovskii). The People's Commissar for the Postal System and Telegraph published an "appeal-decree" against groups and committees who "usurped the functions belonging to the central power and to me as People's Commissar" (November 9 [22] 1917). For similar reasons, a decree of November 28 (December 11) 1917 dissolved the Soviet of the Admiralty. Railroad workers obstructed control by the constituted authorities over this vital sector for a long period. One of the most telling stories is that of workers who, after seizing control of their factories, distributed the funds among themselves or sold the inventory—and even the plant—for their own profit (G. Tsyperovich). This last illegal and economically disastrous example shows the difficulties that workers encountered in exercising collective ownership other than through private appropriation.

As one of the three groups contending for ownership, the proletariat, distinguished itself not only by its inconsistency, its flouting of the law, and its economically detrimental behavior, but also by splits within its own organizations. Genuine hostility, sometimes latent but often overt, erupted between the trade unions and the factory committees, ending only after the latter were placed under the authority of the state in the form of workers' control. The conduct on the whole was a graphic demonstration of the tremendous disruptive potential of the fact that the class which had emerged victorious was an underdeveloped class.

It would be naive to see only an incidental link between the workers' haste to appropriate factories and the state's reluctance to nationalize them. Barely 1,000 enterprises were nationalized in the first month after October, and most of these were tied to foreign capital. But if nationalizations were slow, irresolution over integrating workers into a new mode of organization of social production produced sheer confusion.

The first government of the proletarian dictatorship made its appearance at the Second Congress of Soviets with its two famous decrees: one on peace, which concerned the entire population, and one on land, which concerned the peasantry. Neither decree attempted to define the new condition of the class the new government represented. It was not until one week later that *Pravda* published Lenin's draft plan for "Workers' Control," and on November 14 (27) 1917, after some lively polemics and extensive revision, a decree was adopted by the All-Russian Central Executive Committee (elected by the Congress of Soviets) by a slim majority of 24 to 10. In the midst of the debate, the project *rapporteur*, Miliutin, was led to observe that "life overtook us," and, with regard to the factory committees, the trade unions' representative bluntly declared: "It is necessary to make an absolutely clear and categorical reservation that the workers in each enterprise should not get the impression that the enterprise belongs to them."[11] But the adoption of this decree was unable to check this truly mass movement, and as Carr observed, "Life continued to overtake the legislators and the carefully thought-out decree of November 14 (27) 1917 had no practical outcome. The spontaneous inclination of the workers to organize factory committees and to intervene in the management of the factories was inevitably encouraged by a revolution which led the workers to assume that the productive machinery of the country now belonged to them and could be operated by them, at their own discretion and to their own advantage.''[12]

Under the terms of the above decree the factory committees should have coordinated their actions with the trade unions through a new joint central body called the All-Russian Council of Workers' Control. But, according to contemporary accounts, this council never met (or met once at most). The first attempts of the state to absorb the spontaneous class movement thus merely heralded the beginning of a historical process of centralization of ownership that would be brought to its completion under Stalinism.

The victory of the anticipatory revolution, made possible by the weakness of the bourgeoisie, found itself threatened by the weakness of the proletariat, together with the "deliquescence of proletarian power," deplored at the time by Lenin. While the proletarian class fought steadfastly to turn its victory over capitalism into a triumph over production, the proletarian power strained to transcend this stage of "deliquescence" and regain stability. On March 3, 1918, a decree was published establishing both a stable structure for the management of nationalized enterprises and authorized central bodies for their accreditation and control. Given the circumstances, the working class's tendency toward decentralization was causing incalculable damage, and it began to lose momentum.

All the while the peasantry was busy moving in the same general direction, i.e., toward a decentralization of ownership. The movement developed unencumbered, rapidly gathering momentum. By 1919, A. Poliakov tells us, 96.8% of all cultivated land was in the hands of individual peasants, the rest being divided up between cooperatives and state farms. At the same time, two processes of enormous significance were shaking the foundations of the new society. One was a very active redistribution of agrarian property among individual peasants, setting the stage for the rapid stratification of the peasantry; the other, a consequence of the first, was that those who had come out on the short end of this redistribution were forced to sell the last of their possessions and leave for the city in search of work. And so the contest for ownership in the countryside gave rise to an extraordinary internal mobility, manifested as stratification, and a growing external mobility, the manifest form of which was urbanization.

A remarkable aspect of the redistribution of the land was that it thumbed its nose at the law. That is to say, the peasants did not hesitate to buy or sell land which did not nor could not belong to them. Their mass disregard for the law extended implicitly to the state which embodied it and which was unable to ignore them. Before the peasants began to vie with one another for ownership of the land, they were already contending for it indirectly with the state, which would later become more directly involved in this confrontation. Thus the peasants' contention for ownership of the land was characterized by three general courses of action: (1) pursuing to completion the appropriation of the former feudal lands; (2) redistribution of the land among individual peasants, which promoted the emergence and growth of a new rural bourgeoisie; and (3) confrontation with the state and its laws. Intrinsically antibourgeois, the state opposed the development of this bourgeoisie by opposing the process of redistribution which perpetuated it. Of all these relations of the peasants—with the remnants of feudal society, among themselves, and with the state—it was their relations with the state which would dominate individual peasant participation in the contention over agrarian ownership and which lead to the ultimate, well known outcome.

The peasantry's involvement in the contest over ownership differed in a number of respects from that of the proletariat. First, and perhaps most evident, was the fact that, while the proletariat was militantly active in this regard for only a short period, the activity of the peasantry continued unabated over the entire postrevolutionary period. This is perhaps one reason why analysts have shown much more interest in the peasantry than in the working class on this issue.

Second, the two productive classes displayed clearly different attitudes toward the possessions of the expropriated classes. The peasants had a definite, functional, postfeudal alternative to replace now abolished feudal ownership; but the workers, unable to define a functional alternative to capital, tended in practice to transform the abolishment of a particular form of ownership into the utter and total disintegration of effective ownership of the industrial means of production in general.

Finally, empirically, the starting positions of the two productive classes were different. The proletariat aspired to an ownership it had never had, while the peasantry merely wanted to preserve, exercise freely and consolidate an ownership it already possessed in practice. The task of the workers was therefore much more difficult: they would have to effect nothing less than an alteration in the social organization of ownership, while the peasants had merely to expand on the situation that already existed.

The general objective of the two classes was the same: to eliminate the separation between the producers and the means of production. In the pursuit of that objective, they started from different premises, proceeded differently, and achieved unequal interim results—but the final result was the same in the two cases: both classes were eliminated as contenders for ownership (actually the contest itself was canceled) by the transformation the Stalinist social order wrought in the social organization of ownership.

The peasantry had abolished feudal ownership in a general uprising, a truly revolutionary movement with no political overtones, and it was this apolitical, antifeudal movement that made possible the installation of an antibourgeois political power and, through it, the abolition of capitalist ownership. The abolishment of feudal ownership corresponded historically to the state of the productive forces and, to that extent, was indifferent to political relations; practically, this abolishment was the affirmation of its viable alternative: the proliferation of small, private peasant holdings. The converse was true of the abolishment of capitalist ownership (in the form in which it was attempted). It was made possible by the new political relationships, did not correspond to the state of the productive forces, and was followed by the affirmation of no viable class alternative.

The relative successes of the peasantry and the clear failures of the proletariat in the pursuit of their respective objectives were a reflection not so much of the unequal subjective capacities of the two classes, but of the social conditions under which they operated. The nature of the class which it was their aim to expropriate and, implicitly, of the means of production they were intent on seizing, situated the workers in postcapitalist anticipation; their spontaneity merely continued the Revolution's final strategy. In contrast, the peasants, also by the nature of the class that they had expropriated and of the means of production that they had appropriated, found themselves in a postfeudal reality, and hence this side of anticipation.

The differences between the two classes in this general context extended to the ways in which they adapted to the new conditions and to how they assumed their principal social roles, i.e., the role of social force and the role of productive force. The peasantry tended to merge these roles, and the proletariat to disassociate them. The working class had internalized its anticipation, with asymmetric results: the class's revolutionary potential developed at the expense of its productive potential. The workers' behavior toward ownership corresponded to the social form in which anticipation was embodied, i.e., to the class structure, but it disrupted the forces of production and hence the production process itself. In contrast, insofar as the peasants' behavior toward ownership corresponded to the state of the productive forces, it brought about a restratification that risked dislocating the new class structure. Thus, while pursuing a common end, the proletariat and the peasantry participated in the contention over ownership in different ways, and in social syncretism in even opposite ways.

Beyond all these objective differences and oppositions, the most salient characteristic of relations of ownership between the two productive classes was their mutual indifference. Each was immersed in its own problems, and neither exhibited any evident concern in the way the other attempted to resolve the question of ownership. This was not the case with the state: as the workers and peasants pursued their common aim to appropriate their means of production and establish their respective forms of ownership, the state did not remain a passive bystander. It resolutely opposed the designs of both classes, albeit in different ways. The historical message underlying this like response to apparently dissimilar situations was as momentous as it was subtle. Unlike the two classes, the state was unable to accommodate to only one term of syncretism, but instead found itself constrained to adapt, reluctantly, to syncretism as a whole. In opposing the development of small peasant holdings, it aimed to protect the new class structure against the emergence of a new bourgeoisie; in opposing direct worker appropriation of the factories, its design was to safeguard the productive forces and the process of production from collapse.

On a social level, the thrust of its seemingly uniform response went in opposite directions in the two cases: against excessive anticapitalism on the part of the workers in the one, and against the absence of anticapitalism among the peasants in the other. These objectives were imposed by material circumstances long before they were stated explicitly in policy, a policy which itself would prove at core paradoxical: originally formed to reunite the producers with the means of production, the revolutionary government in the end found itself applying the whole of its efforts to maintaining their separation.

Once in power, the Bolshevik Party adopted an agrarian policy that was no more coherent than previous policies. For example, at the Fourth Congress of the former Russian Workers' Party in Stockholm in 1906 (April 23/May 8) Lenin proposed calling for the nationalization of the land in a discussion on the draft program, but was rebuffed by the Mensheviks. Coming on the heels of the 1905 revolution, this proposal did not accord well with the previous position of the Bolsheviks, who had been resolute opponents of the SR agrarian program which likewise called for socialization of the land (1903). Eleven years later, Lenin again defended this political about-face when, as leader of a small Bolshevik delegation to the first All-Russian Congress of Peasant Deputies (Petrograd, May 1917), he declared to a hostile SR majority: "It is impossible to continue farming in the old way. If we continue as of old on our small farms, even as free citizens on free land, we shall still be faced with inevitable ruin."[13]

No statement of similar clarity can be found in the first act of domestic policy the Bolsheviks adopted when they became the party of government, namely, the land decree. The decree went right to the point: it gave legal sanction to the abolition of feudal ownership which the peasants had already made a fait accompli. It stipulated immediate expropriation without indemnity of estates held by the large landowners and the clergy—an area of 150 million hectares—and cancellation of the land debt (the peasants' bank alone held 1.5 billion rubles in private debt, farming bonds, and outstanding mortgages for the acquisition of lands that had belonged to the large landowners, for a total of 700 billion gold rubles).

As regards the ultimate fate of these lands, the first concern of the decree appeared to be to avoid binding formulas. Precise terms such as nationalization, statization, etc., were studiously avoided. The land was proclaimed "national patrimony," a term which confuses more than it clarifies the definition of agrarian ownership. Article 2, which is an attempt to concretize this excessively abstract phrasing, specifies that the land and the holdings of the large landowners were to be "placed at the disposal of the agrarian committees of the cantons and departmental soviets of peasant deputies." This provision was clearly of crucial importance for the ultimate organization of agrarian ownership, yet it was not free of two obvious ambiguities.

First, the decree grants right of use, not right of ownership. Second, the beneficiaries of this right are not persons or groups, but two untested institutions with few roots in the realities of the countryside, which the decree puts in competition with one another by investing both with the same responsibilities. The text defines these responsibilities as maintaining order during the continued confiscations, establishing which lands and other possessions would be subject to confiscation, and keeping these possessions under the "strictest surveillance." The exercise of these prerogatives is clearly distinct from the exercise of ownership. The precision of the provisions concerning the abolishment of feudal ownership stands in stark contrast to the singular imprecision of the provisions regulating its transfer. The uncertainty is further compounded by the fact that the decree proclaims itself provisional, thus deferring responsibility for the final solution of the agrarian problem to a Constituent Assembly which would not have the power to adopt it. Article 5 stipulates that lands belonging to peasant workers and cossack workers shall be exempt from confiscation. Although never identified, these two categories thus were confirmed as owning lands which another article defines as "national patrimony." The same law thus at once both validates and invalidates petty peasant property, an incongruity greatly aggravated by the law's division into two formally distinct parts: the decree itself, comprising five articles, and its appendix, the so-called "model decree," consisting of seven articles.

The first article of the model decree stipulates: "The right to private ownership of the land is abrogated forever. . . . All lands, those of the state, those of the appanage, those of the crown, the monasteries, and the churches. . . , lands that are now private property, those of the *obshchina*, the peasants, and so forth, are hereby expropriated without indemnity and shall become the property of the entire people for the use of all those who work them." Guaranteed in vague terms in the body of the law, small peasant holdings are unambiguously subject to expropriation in its appendix. "While the model decree declares that all lands, those of the noble landlords as well as the lands of the peasants," shall become "the property of the entire nation, the basic law is in general silent on the new form of agrarian ownership," observes Trotsky. "Even the most tolerant jurist would be startled by the fact that nationalization of the land, a new social principle of world historical importance, was established in instructions appended to the basic law."[14]

The model decree was added (as the decree itself specifies) as a "set of general guidelines for the implementation of major agrarian reforms." It was in fact the work of the SRs which circumstances compelled the Bolsheviks to adopt. The agrarian question was at the top of the agenda at the first Congress of Soviets in May 1917, where the SRs held a crushing majority. Two hundred and forty-two peasant delegates submitted as many memoranda containing the wishes of their electorate on how agriculture should be organized. A summing up of these memoranda written by a group of SRs and dubbed the Model Decree was published by *Izvestia* on August 19 of the same year.

After having fought against these demands (which they considered utopian), the Bolsheviks drew up a summary of this summary, which they then appended to the land decree. "Lenin copies our resolutions and publishes them in the form of 'decrees,' claimed the SR leader Chernov, aghast."[15] Lenin replied to SR protests at the second Congress of Soviets: "Does it matter whose work it is? We, as a democratic government, cannot evade the decision of the rank and file of the people, even if we do not agree with it.'' While they were in the opposition the Bolsheviks had enough strength to express this disagreement; in power, they backed down and supported what they had previously disavowed. About-faces of this sort readily occur in the political life of any country. But what was important in the present case was that the about-face concerned not politics but relations of ownership. Trotsky offers an at least plausible explanation of this behavior: ''For the dictatorship of the proletariat, the decree and the appended model decree established the obligation not only to consider attentively the interests of the farm worker but also to tolerate his illusions of being a small landowner.''[16] There are two particularly important points implied by this argument. First, for the Bolsheviks, the appending of the model decree to the decree was not a strategic choice but an act of submission to constraints imposed by history. Second, petty agrarian property, which was a fundamental reality for the peasantry, was, from the perspective of the state, only an illusion. In the ambiguous legal framework set out by the decree it was no longer the peasants who were contending with the large landowners for property, but the new power that was in contention with the peasants not only for the property that had been confiscated, but also for the property which the peasants had already possessed before the Revolution. The state, a product and extension of the anticipatory revolution, was attempting to build a postcapitalist society before having built a postfeudal one. In this first document with a social content, the state's resolve to put an end to feudalism in such a way that it did not become a springboard to capitalism in agriculture stands out clearly.

The Bolsheviks adopted the SRs' agrarian program, observes Gilles Martinet, ''surely with the idea that this was only a transitory phase, and with the firm intention of organizing the struggle of the poor peasants against the rich peasants.''[17] Indeed, the Bolsheviks were effectively quite open in their intentions, as when Lenin acknowledged in his report on the decree to the second Congress of Soviets: ''We will gain the confidence of the peasants only through the decree, which abolishes the property of the large landowners.'' Years later, in exile, Trotsky would corroborate this intention: ''If the redistribution of the lands consolidated the socialist government politically, as an immediate measure it was entirely justified.''[18] Thus the state offered a politically motivated provisional solution to a vital economic and social problem. But the terms of the problem were not the terms of the proposed solution. It was this discrepancy expressed in legal language which gave the decree its ambiguity. The limits of the solution gave a decisive insight into the limitations of the government even as it was consolidating itself, and it was primarily these limitations, and not the ''hasty character of the proceedings,'' as Carr proposes, that caused an ''unresolved contradiction to appear between the main decree on the land and the model decree.''[19]

Just as ownership could not in this society satisfy one of the terms of syncretism without coming into conflict with the other, this ambiguous decree created a situation in which it was impossible to respect certain prescriptions without violating others. In their contention over ownership, therefore, the peasantry and the state cannot be said to have gone beyond the limits of the law for the simple reason that no unambiguous legal limits existed. Legislation that is self-contradictory cannot regulate individual behavior. And so it was not relations of ownership which eluded the law, but vice versa: the law eluded relations of ownership. Along with relations of ownership, the whole society was plunged into a legal void. The state withheld from the peasants the legal ownership of property it had originally encouraged them to appropriate. It was obvious that the peasants should prefer to abandon the law rather than abandon their land. The erosion of the law set off by the land decree would prove to be irremediable. The large landowners had been deprived of ownership of the land without a new owner being assigned to it. What disappeared was not feudal ownership, but ownership itself. H. d'Encausse observes: "The land decree established in the countryside a principle contrary to ownership."[20] Deprived of legal sanction, ownership was replaced by contention over ownership. A succession of laws followed, but the contest between the peasants and the state for agrarian ownership essentially took place outside the law, which was hardly to the peasants' advantage. More and more laws were passed as legal regulation became less effective. In February 1918, only three months after the land decree, the Bolshevik government introduced a new agrarian law entitled "Socialization of the Land." But this law was no more able than any other to improve the situation in on the farms, where the disappearance of true ownership was associated with an intensification of procurements and an increasingly acute shortage of even the most elementary farm equipment.

For the Russian peasantry, the importance of the land decree lay not so much in its legal provisions, which were ambiguous, as in the freedom it permitted them in practice. The Civil War was, therefore, also a political war to gain the trust of the peasantry, and to further that end the White leaders felt obliged to come up with various alternatives to the Bolshevik decree while the war was still going on. For example, the sixth point in Denikin's Seven-Point Program read: "Immediate approach to land reform for the elimination of the land needs of the working population."[21] But declarations of such general nature could not have the desired impact on the peasantry; Denikin therefore appointed a committee presided over by Kolkoltsev to work out a draft bill for a new agrarian law. Its proposal to limit agrarian property holdings to between 800 and 1,350 acres obliged Denikin to form a new committee under Professor Bilimovich to deal with the same problem. According to Chamberlin, the bill drafted by this committee "failed to recognize that the transfer of the landlords' estates to the peasants was an accomplished fact, which could not be undone."[22] On April 8, 1919, Kolchak in turn issued the Declaration on the Land Question, stipulating that "those lands which were formerly tilled entirely or predominantly by the resources of the families of the owners of the land, individual holders, and those who separated from the village community, are to be restored to their legal owners."[23]

More even that Lenin's decree, these tergiversations with their legal overtones remained perfectly alien to the real conditions which the White troops imposed on the peasants on the territory they controlled: under Denikin, for instance, "the demand that the peasant who had seized land should pay a third of the grain harvest to the former owner in the form of rent"[24] was applied.

Caught between these unmistakable tendencies to restore feudal ownership and the extreme incongruities in the Bolshevik decree, the vast majority of peasants preferred the latter, and expressed this choice through their decisive support of the Reds in the Civil War. Thus the land decree unquestionably helped the Bolsheviks obtain a victory on domestic fronts, but it did not help the peasants gain a similar victory in preserving their petty land holdings in their later confrontation with the state which owed its very survival to their support.

The land decree was not merely an isolated episode in the contest for ownership, it was archetypal of the later behavior of the Bolshevik Party. This initial document contains a number of features which later became constants in the agrarian policy of the revolutionary power. The most important of these were:

1. Regulation of the basic economic relation, i.e., ownership, could not be entrusted to the spontaneity of rival tendencies in agriculture. Such regulation was an exclusive and essential prerogative of the state.

2. The state's agrarian policy was not guided by an elaborated strategy but by ungovernable fluctuations in private accumulation and productivity, and by peasant resistance to state pressures, and especially to the procurements.

3. The material negation of peasant ownership took place under the illusion of its being preserved.

4. The state tended to base its agrarian anticapitalism on an essentially capitalist relation, the separation between producers and the means of production.

The changes that occurred in the relations between the state and the peasantry were in a broad sense the expression of revolutionary changes which had transformed an illegal party into a state and serfs into landowners. Originally united in this anticapitalist struggle, the Party and the peasantry were separated anew by the anticipatory victory over capitalism. And so it came to pass that the peasantry, the primary actor in the victory over feudalism, became the prime target of the restrictions imposed on capitalism. The conflict that took shape around ownership was socially hybrid in the sense that it did not oppose two social classes, but rather pitted a political power in the process of establishing itself against a social class in the process of becoming stratified.

In the contest for ownership, the two productive classes found themselves confronting neither the possessing classes nor one another, but a state that, while it was in theory their representative, turned out in this case to be their principal obstacle. The direct involvement of the state in this contest in the end settled the entire dispute by instituting the utterly uncontested relations of ownership specific to Stalinism. The same factor opposed both the productive classes, but in different ways: while it prevented the workers from assuming ownership, it prevented the peasants from exercising it.

With no strategy, the government spontaneously opposed the spontaneous actions of the two classes in the contention over ownership. The central strategic objective of the Bolshevik Party before the Revolution had been to abolish the separation of the producers from the means of production; after the Revolution the Bolshevik government ended up reinstituting that separation on a new basis, in contradiction with its own doctrine and its revolutionary legitimacy. As it became more immersed in this role, the state began to experience an internal disintegration: its leadership split into factions with increasingly irreconcilable ideas. Although these schisms were manifested politically, they were economic and social in substance, and the political manifestations would disappear entirely once the dispute over ownership had ended.

The centralizing tendency of the state was further abetted by a dichotomy in its role in the contention over ownership. On the one hand it confronted other constituted social agents, while on the other it was squared off against constituents of its own apparatus. Examples include the bitter struggle within enterprises over the appointment of management (a prevailing topic in Gorbachev's reform); the tendency for diverse local administrations to evade central control; and competition at the central level among the trade unions, the factory committees, and the state; or, within the state itself, competition among the different departments aspiring to broaden their powers at each other's expense, e.g., among the different ministries (People's Commissariats), between the ministries and various higher councils, between different administration boards, etc. Even state proprietorship was the object of a dispute which Stalinism would bring to a radical and abrupt end.

The contest over ownership had two direct effects of major importance. One concerned the social environment and assumed the visible form of unstable ownership, as discussed earlier on. The other concerned the functional structure of ownership and assumed the invisible form of internal decomposition.

6. The internal decomposition of ownership

a. Incomplete ownership

The nodal point of the general disarticulation of society, ownership in all its forms was itself touched by a process of degradation—or even loss—of certain of its attributes. Disintegrating from within, ownership became less and less able to fulfill the commanding functions indispensable to the production process. None of the forms of ownership that had survived the Revolution or had been born of it were able to regain these attributes on an anticapitalist basis; hence they were unable to become productive to an economically viable degree. Little troubled over its lawless seizure of the land, petty agrarian landowners were nonetheless anxious to reestablish access to appropriation, i.e., total control over the product of their property. The dispute over ownership was more a dispute over its attributes.

In a study of the demarcations between social classes in contemporary capitalism, Wright offers a fruitful suggestion which may help to define the special status of ownership in the Revolution. Thus, "participation in the control of the overall investment and accumulation process" is a situation which he designates as "full economic ownership."[25] The concept also of course implies its complement, which Wright does not use but which might be called "incomplete ownership." The reality seeking expression in these conceptual gropings is the limits of ownership in the industrial era. The managerial phenomenon as analyzed for capitalist corporations will, perhaps, by way of contrast, illuminate the very special conditions of relations of ownership in postrevolutionary Russia. Under capitalism, the dominant form of ownership had merely to adapt to the new managerial phase of its development; in Russia, on the other hand, the problem was to devise a new system of ownership that would be both anticapitalist and economically functional. As Barrington Moore, Jr. says of the French Revolution, incomplete revolution engenders incomplete ownership. That is to say, the different social beneficiaries of revolution have access respectively only to different fragments of ownership.

But this ownership is not only incomplete in its internal structure. It also suffers from profound instability at the level of social organization; hence its tumultuous existence. Finally, its social locus is so ill-defined that it is transformed from an object possessed into an object in perpetual contention. Unstable, ill-defined, and incomplete, the predicament of ownership under the Revolution is too unusual and too rich in its implications to remain conceptually ignored. The concept of incomplete ownership perhaps best sums up the disorders which ownership manifested in this crucial period.

b. Appropriation proscribed

One phenomenon, procurements, will perhaps better than any other illustrate the process of internal decomposition of ownership addressed above. Procurements represented a peculiar type of social relation which obscured the harsh realities of extra-economic constraint under the guise of illusory economic exchange. Since the time of Roman law, ownership has been regarded as a prerogative without limit. The jurists and economists of antiquity defined ownership in terms of three attributes: *usus*—the right to make use of, *fructus*—the right to profit from, and *abusus*—the right to dispose of as absolute master. Most modern legal systems are in the same spirit, e.g., the Napoleonic civil code proclaims: "Ownership is the right to make use of and dispose of things in the most absolute manner" (Article 544). Reflecting on its implantation in society, Durkheim defines ownership in relation to nonownership: "The right of ownership is the right of a given individual to exclude other individual and collective entities from the usage of a given thing"—an approach retained and developed up to the present. Macpherson, for example, defines ownership as ''the right to deny men access to means of life and labor.''[26]

Petty peasant ownership departed considerably from these definitions under the procurements. It retained only one of the three attributes specified in Roman law: namely, that of use, which had been set down in the land decree. As for the two others, *fructus* and *abusus*, the procurements for all practical purposes simply voided them. Under the pressure of procurements, peasant ownership was transformed from an unlimited right into an unlimited obligation, inasmuch as its extent was defined not by the owner, but by an outside factor. In Durkheim's terms, it was therefore no longer the owner who excluded nonowners from access to the product, but on the contrary, a kind of nonownership which excluded ownership. The procurements deprived peasant ownership of a crucial attribute, namely, the attendant right of the owner to dispose freely of its product. Similar if not identical phenomena beset the other forms of ownership as well. It is this generalized loss of an attribute, which was most clearly manifest in the procurements, which I call the internal decomposition or disintegration of ownership.

Just as ownership vacillated between the two extremes of adapting to the productive forces and preserving the class structure, procurement vacillated between confiscation and the market, although with a stronger leaning toward the former. These fluctuations tended to take the opposite tack of the contention over ownership. The peasants, already separated from their principal means of production, i.e., the land, were also separated from their product by the procurements. A touch of feudal agrarian relations is easily discernible in this postrevolutionary innovation. Procurements were the state's precapitalist answer to the peasantry's tendencies toward capitalism.

Whether initiated by the state or by the peasants themselves, the frenetic redistribution of the land had disastrous effects on the harvest. The situation was extensively discussed at the Seventh Party Congress and was the occasion for a decree issued in the summer of 1919 ensuring ''the stability of farm holdings.'' ''Every peasant,'' it continues, ''shall rest assured that his piece of land will remain in his possession.'' Thus caught between the threat of agrarian capitalism and that of a general famine, the government opted for the latter. It backed off from separating the peasants from the land in order more easily to separate them from their product.

The general function of procurements under these circumstances was to make up for the flawed economic articulation—actually a lack of articulation—between agriculture and industry, in effect replacing exchange by constraint. Recourse to economic constraint to regulate economic relations struck at the very foundations of peasant ownership, and indeed any ownership; namely, the inherent attribute of ownership allowing the appropriation of its product and, implicitly, its surplus product. Some authors interpret the notion of appropriation quite broadly. Branko Horvat, for instance, feels that ''production implies appropriation. The end result of production—the product—always belongs to someone.''[27] But in tying appropriation to the process of production and not to ownership, one runs the risk of ignoring or underestimating the essentially exclusionary nature of appropriation. Appropriation is not accessible equally to all who participate in production. On the contrary, it is the principal criterion for discrimination between nonproducing owners and nonowning producers. The exclusion of nonowners by owners is most forcefully manifest in the act of appropriation. Appropriation means that, at the end of each cycle, the product belongs in its totality to those who own the means of production. It is through appropriation that ownership is extended from the means of production to the product. There can be no appropriation without ownership (such is the legal definition of theft), but, as the procurements show, there can be ownership without appropriation, i.e., an ownership divested of its crucial attribute. Ultimately it is because he has appropriated the product that an owner can decide how it is to be redistributed.

In addition to reinvestments and the owner's personal expenditures, part of the surplus product goes to its direct producers who, however, are not owners. Despite being direct participants in the process of production, the producers participate only indirectly in the redistribution of the product created. The owners gain access to the surplus product through the mechanism of appropriation; the producers do so through a mechanism of allocation. The two processes, appropriation and allocation, are of opposite quality, the one being an act of relative freedom based on ownership, and the other, allocation, an act of economic constraint exercised by owners over nonowners. Excluded from appropriation by procurement, small peasant holdings began to acquire a merely symbolic value.

The force which imposed this situation on the peasantry was no longer the power of a retrograde class but a revolutionary power, and its means for controlling the situation were no longer economic but extra-economic. The peasantry responded in kind. It countered the direct coercive measures of the state with a resistance that was itself extra-economic. A number of factors, of which peasant resistance was of course one, caused the state to adopt a now harder, now softer line on the procurements. Whereas in June 1919 it declared that its concern was to stabilize distribution of the land as it was, in December of the same year, with the worsening of the Civil War and the intervention, it was decided at the Seventh Congress of Soviets to extend procurements to include all farm products. Once the counterrevolution was defeated, thanks in large measure to the peasantry, the state introduced NEP. On March 21, a decree was issued announcing the end of procurements, and on March 28 another decree abolished restrictions on the transport of food products. Contrary to what seemed to have been the intention of these initial measures, NEP did not succeed in abolishing procurements; instead the procurements caused the demise of NEP.

The loss of the right to appropriate was suffered in one way or other by all forms of ownership in postrevolutionary Russia. For capitalist ownership, appropriation was forestalled by tax laws and other restrictive measures. For state ownership, neither the state agencies nor the individuals working in them had access to appropriation of the product except through infraction or abuse. Like the capitalist owner, the anticapitalist state could decide over the redistribution of the social product, but unlike the former, it had no access to appropriation, from which it was barred—primarily for reasons of its historical legitimacy.

In Durkheim's terms, exclusion from ownership could only be the work of the nonexcluded; he cogently observes that ownership is defined by the "exclusion it involves rather than the prerogatives it confers."[28] Under a system in which private ownership is dominant, from a Marxist perspective, exclusion will be the negative abolishment of ownership, i.e., the power to dispose of the fruits of ownership, for all nonowners. Under capitalism and feudalism, all dissimilarities aside, the excluded constitute the vast majority of the population.

In postrevolutionary Russia, this majority tended to become a totality. Exclusion from ownership is first and foremost exclusion from appropriation. The procurements merely institutionalized the incapacity of the small peasant landowner to exclude all nonowners from the usufruct of the harvest. Insofar as exclusion is a truly defining attribute of ownership, losing that prerogative placed the economic reality of peasant ownership itself in doubt. It was not the peasant who had excluded the rest of society from control over his product, but the state which had excluded the peasant from the freedom to dispose over it, i.e., to appropriate his harvest. When the state thereupon extended its own exclusion from appropriation of the product to the whole of society, it was only generalizing the negative abolishment of ownership, reducing ownership itself to a vestigial existence. Agnes Heller seems to agree with this view: "This conception which Marx qualified as abolition of ownership was negative in the sense that it proposes to resolve the contradiction . . . not by an attribution of ownership, but by the suppression of all rights of ownership."[29]

Ownership, the supreme embodiment of economic and social inequality, can only disappear when the fundamental cause of this inequality, namely, scarcity, also disappears. Postrevolutionary Russia was leagues removed from this state; the economy devastated, it set about destroying ownership, yet its need for ownership was far from over. Once again social desynchronization was the product of revolutionary anticipation, and a crucial aspect of this desynchronization was that the negative abolishment and positive abolishment of ownership were not simultaneous. Over the course of history, radical transformations in ownership have resulted from actions that were both negative and positive at the same time. The negation of preceding forms and the affirmation of new forms of ownership were part of the same historical process.

The Russian Revolution, taking place under conditions of profound scarcity, achieved the almost simultaneous negation of the two predominant forms of private ownership but was unable to affirm alternatives to take their place. The logical outcome of this unfinished process was the suppression of not just one or several forms of ownership, but of ownership itself. This disjunction was perceptible even within the revolution in the fact that the two dominant forms of ownership, feudal and capitalist, were destroyed in different ways. The abolishment of feudal ownership was complete—that is, both negative and positive—and consisted basically in a transfer. Ownership passed from one social agent to another, while at the same time the form of possession changed with the possessor. Abolition of capitalist ownership was anticipatory, i.e., indifferent to the state of its object, and remained for the most part incomplete—only negative. The object owned was wrested from one social class with no other class able to assume the rights of ownership, and the object of ownership hence became an object of contention. Barred from the right to appropriate, the exercise of ownership began to dissolve, and in the process threatened the object of ownership with disintegration as well. It was no longer a question of the social transfer of ownership, but of the actual destruction of its object. Unable to proceed further than the negative abolishment of capitalist ownership, the state set about undoing the positive abolishment of feudal ownership as well, in the first instance through the procurements.

The limitation of appropriation to its negative form was a manifestation of the limits of anticipation, which had less difficulty overcoming the active resistance of the capitalist class than it did the latent obstacles posed by the productive forces: the immaturity of the working class and the backwardness of the industrial means of production. An object cannot be possessed indifferently in any way: the form that its possession takes will depend upon the state of that object. This relationship in fact is underscored by Marx as it relates to human subjectivity: "private property can only be abolished on condition of the full development of individuals." Postrevolutionary society had not even the remotest possibility of assuring the full development of its members and so tended spontaneously to erode private ownership rather than abolish it abruptly (especially in the country); unable to move beyond this stage, with private ownership only incompletely and negatively abolished, the Revolution internalized the perturbations which the triumph of anticipation provoked in the flow of history.

c. An eviscerated legality

Compared to feudalism, capitalism was able quite substantially to consolidate the legal basis of ownership. It is hardly surprising that a revolution directed against capital should reject a legal order which guarantees the inviolability of capitalist ownership. Again, as with ownership, the anticipatory revolution had had the strength to challenge and even smash the existing legal system, but not to replace it with another. Indeed, ownership and law crumbled together. To the extent that ownership continued to exist, it did so in a gray dimension beyond legality in the strict sense. Having lost one defining attribute, namely, the right to appropriate, ownership was now in danger of losing another, namely, the attribute of legality.

From the very outset, the new legal order evaded legal ratification of the ownership of property already possessed de facto by the peasants. This evasive attitude very soon gave way to an offensive stance, which was further facilitated by the vagueness and ambiguities of the legislation on procurements. With their specific content, the elusiveness of their formulation, and their tolerance of illegal practices by the representatives of the law themselves, these laws abundantly contributed to the undoing of peasant ownership. The same legal order which refused to recognize an ownership the peasants were already de facto exercising invested workers with an ownership to which they had no access in practice. The result was in the one case real possession without the attribute of legality, and in the other, legal ownership with no real existence. But it was not only the law which shunned the realities of ownership; the spontaneous tendencies of workers and peasants to establish their respective forms of ownership likewise ignored the law.

Nor did state ownership escape the effects of this disaccord between ownership and the law. To begin with, state ownership was consecrated in the law before the state was even constituted—so producing the bizarre phenomenon of a state instituting its ownership before creating the structures to dispose over it. Yet at the same time the state frequently ignored its own laws—especially in its relations with peasant ownership—thereby risking becoming the embodiment of illegality. Finally, blind to the growing gap between the proletarian state and the proletarian class, the law continued to present state property as the property of the proletariat. Quite naturally, as ownership and law broke down, the connection between them did so as well, and in such a situation it was also quite natural that forms of ownership which did not enjoy the attribute of legality should display an economic vitality often superior to those forms of ownership with that attribute.

"Civil law . . . is the palladium of ownership,"[30] observed Montesquieu. "There is no natural ownership," says Bentham, "Ownership is uniquely the work of the law."[31]

All revolutions experience difficulties in establishing a new legal order, but what made the Russian Revolution unique was the concentration of these difficulties in relations of ownership. Irrespective of subjective intentions, postrevolutionary legislation, rather than consolidate ownership, tended to contribute to its destabilization.

Legality with regard to ownership was only an illusion in postrevolutionary Russia; the hallmark of the real state of affairs was its illegality. Without being identified specifically, this ambiguity became part of the legal thinking of the period. One widely discussed proposal called for dual legislation: an economic law to regulate state ownership and the "socialist exchange of goods" (including procurements) and a civil law regulating private ownership and merchant trade. The same ambiguity is indirectly reflected in the peculiar concept of unequal law, the intention of which was to compensate economic inequality by the institution of countervailing legal inequalities. The first constitution of the RSFSR adopted on July 10, 1918 by the Fifth Congress of Soviets denied certain civil rights to "those who employ others for the sake of profit, those who live on income not arising from their own labor," "private businessmen," "monks and priests." These legal discriminations would remain in force until 1936.

The inefficacy of the law with regard to relations of ownership extended to other social relations as well. The less effectively the law was able to regulate social behavior, the more frequent became the calls for the use of force. At first glance, the state should have had the advantage: its specific monopoly over economic prerogatives ought to have been reinforced by its general monopoly over the legal use of force. But in reality, the state found itself increasingly inclined to use illegal and arbitrary violence to back up its illegal behavior in the economic domain. Illegal ownership does not mix well with legal violence. Thus while the state retained its monopoly on violence, legality was unable to maintain its restraining force on the exercise of state violence. Aspiring to socialize ownership, postrevolutionary Russia succeeded only in socializing the exercise of force.

The state was much more inclined to adapt the law to its behavior than to act in conformity with its own laws, especially in regard to peasant ownership. Indeed, peasant ownership was spread over such a vast territory that the state was able to gain access to it only by being represented by a multitude of persons whose actions it had no means of controlling. And so centralized, illegal violence was compounded by a decentralized, illegal violence emanating from the state, which necessarily turned into abuse and arbitrary actions.

The peasants were hardly disposed to respect an elusive and vague body of law of which even its own representatives were ignorant. Accordingly, they moved to defend their ownership, and especially what they produced, making use of mass illegal violence to do so. A new term entered the official language of time: "peasant banditry." From the spring of 1918, observes Linhart, the contradiction between city and the country, made antagonistic by famine and the survival needs of the urban population, assumed the most radical form possible: a *military form.* "The war for grain" declared by Lenin "would be renewed under different circumstances in one form or other practically every year up until 1929 and even beyond."[32] The peasant war against feudalism and for the Revolution soon gave way to a war of the revolutionary government against the peasantry, for grain.

Peasant resistance reached a critical turning point in Southeast and Central European Russia, and most especially in the province of Tambov, i.e., the most fertile region. Long before its formal abrogation of procurements (July 1921), the government was forced to reduce the area in which it continued to practice them. During the winter of 1920-21, the People's Commissariat of Supplies suspended procurements in the thirteen regions where peasant uprising had become the most threatening. The degree to which legality had been eroded was reflected in the scale of these confrontations. Even as state violence threatened to destroy peasant ownership, peasant violence threatened to nullify the conquests of the Revolution and plunge society into a famine of unforeseeable duration. The state use of violence against peasant property did little to improve food supplies and succeeded only in provoking the peasantry to take up violent resistance against the state. Events spoke a harsh and unmistakable language, yet the state, beleaguered by the antinomies of its situation, would react in directly opposite ways at two different points in time to achieve basically the same end: in 1921, with the peasantry in open rebellion, it renounced the use of force, and relaxed the pressures on small peasant holdings; later, in 1929, with the peasantry again in turmoil, it resumed state violence and abolished small peasant holdings totally.

To say that ownership lost the attribute of legality is merely to say that the law became ineffectual in the regulation of ownership. The supplanting of the force of law by the direct use of force was merely a symptom of the general process of decomposition of ownership, and while postrevolutionary society was relatively ineffective in its attempts at the use of violence, it did prepare the way for the thorough triumph of state violence over state law under Stalinism.

The two attributes of ownership, legality and the right of appropriation, are brought together in different ways in the two principal forms of ownership. Small peasant landowners lost access to appropriation by being pushed beyond the law, while state ownership, though sanctioned by law, did not confer the power of appropriation. A similar distinction marked another relation of ownership: i.e., between its attributes of legal regulation and of management.

d. Management

With peasant ownership lacking legal guarantees, the peasantry was prevented in practical terms from managing it. State ownership, on the other hand, had these guarantees, and the state tended to become entirely absorbed in the process of management. This tendency was to be of momentous importance for the transition to Stalinism.

In the first months following the October Revolution, Lenin opposed those who called for accelerating nationalizations, arguing that bookkeeping and accounting, the elementary operations of management, were in a deplorable state. The growing number of enterprises on the verge of bankruptcy managed by factory committees or by democratically elected administrations were ample proof that revolutionary spirit was no substitute for competence. The government went from talk to action: stupendous salaries were offered to former specialists, foreign experts, and even former owners if they would consent to work for the new regime.

The discussions and the practical measures undertaken demonstrate that the main hindrance to the transformation of capitalist ownership into public ownership was not the resistance of the bourgeoisie, but the inability of the new power to manage industrial enterprises in a way that did not bring about their collapse. Indeed, difficulties were not confined to the enterprise level; they were also present centrally. For a certain period the government did not have trustworthy bookkeeping figures on enterprises scheduled for expropriation or on their equipment and stocks, or even on enterprises that had already been legally expropriated. The number of firms listed, for example, in the accounts of the Supreme Council for the Economy varied from one month to another. If public ownership of property was so elusive as a material object, it could hardly become effective as a social relation. For it to become real in economic terms, the property owned had first to become manageable. The negative abolition of capitalist ownership extended its negative quality into the domain of management.

At the heart of the problem was the necessity of effecting a discontinuity in the system of ownership while maintaining the continuity of the productive process. But another problem was also involved: the political legitimacy of the revolutionary government. The proletarian state had denied self-management to the workers because of their incompetence, yet it could only offer its own managerial incompetence in its stead.

Lenin steadfastly insisted on the obligation of Bolsheviks to learn how to manage, but Bukharin went further and placed this primacy of management in a theoretical context. Under the new order, the order of the day was no longer, he said, the "transformation of the relations of production, but the perfection of a form of management that will provide maximum competence."[33] Thus the great historical mission of constructing an anticapitalist system of ownership was made contingent on the pedestrian administrative drudgery of management, and it was to this that state ownership was soon reduced. Under capitalism, ownership and management are separate. In postrevolutionary society, however, this distinction became blurred; the relationship between the two ultimately became inverted, and ownership found itself subordinate to management. Stalinism was to transform this peculiarity in radical fashion.

The first anticipatory revolution created the first anticapitalist social framework and with it the material premise of an unresolvable crisis: none of the presumptive natural agents of ownership, i.e., the social classes, were capable of assuming that role. As a consequence, a surrogate agent, the state, replaced them, yet it too was unable to exercise ownership in a way that would permit satisfaction of the people's elementary needs and at the same time permit the productive forces to develop unencumbered.

The principal generator of the historical movement that carried postrevolutionary society into Stalinism was an intolerable economic crisis for which the existing state of affairs could offer no solution; but behind that crisis was a deeper crisis of ownership—the absence of a social class able to assume that function and restore stability on a new level.

7. Negative assessment

It has become an almost obligatory tradition to note that the crisis of war communism gave rise to NEP, the crisis of which in turn gave rise to Stalinism. Although obvious enough at first glance, this observation is fully valid only with reference to the particular circumstances. The immediate circumstances out of which Stalinism emerged were indeed dominated by the crisis of NEP. But the latter merely continued the crisis that had preceded and produced it; and the two crises in turn were merely two different expressions of a deeper crisis which, beyond the vicissitudes of events, was eroding the structures of postrevolutionary society. In its least discernible form this structural crisis resided in the syncretism of the new society; in its most easily decipherable form, in the destabilization of ownership; and in its manifest form, in the formidable economic and political tensions that ravaged society. Though variable in its manifestations, the crisis was uninterrupted, and thus most threatening at the structural level.

The real social force which permitted Stalinism to triumph was not the proletariat, as Stalinism itself boasts, nor the bureaucracy, as the theory of Thermidor tells us, nor a specific political group; the real force was the universal despair and general paralysis caused by a devastating crisis that persisted for fifteen years (including the war). At no time under control, it placed not merely the social order but the very survival of the members of that order at risk. It was therefore not the final symptoms of the crisis, but the accumulated tensions of long years of upheaval which brought to power those most determined to gain control of the crisis. A few facts will give a clearer idea of its extent at different moments in time.

Russian industry was quite backward even before the War relative to European standards. However, by 1920 output was only 26.8 percent of that of 1913 for coal, 41.1 percent for oil, 1 percent for iron, 5.9 percent for sugar, and 5.2 percent for cotton. Total 1920 output in heavy industry had decreased to one-eighth of the 1913 level. As Mandel says, "Industrial output went into vertical fall."[34] In 1913 industrial output per capita was 22 times lower in Russia than in the United States; with a population four times that of France, Russian industrial output was only one-fifth that of France, and to this must be added the absolute preponderance of the extractive industries (coal, oil), which were dominated by foreign capital.

In March 1918 the Fourth All-Russian Congress of Soviets deplored "the chaos, disorganization, and disintegration" that was ravaging the entire economy, and called for "strong and solid organizations, covering inasmuch as possible all production and all distribution of goods." The disintegration evident in 1918 reached cataclysmic proportions by 1920 under the disastrous effects of the Civil War. In these two years the number of workers declined from 3.1 million to 1.1 million, and agricultural output from 4078 puds in 1913 to 1617 puds in 1929. The devastation caused by the Civil War was compounded further by famine and epidemics. The country teemed with refugees, cities were abandoned, and in the capital city of Petrograd alone, which had 2.4 million inhabitants on the eve of the Revolution, only 740,000 remained in 1920. Not only the economy but the whole of society was disintegrating. The population of the 40 provincial capitals was reduced by 33 percent and that of Moscow by 44.5 percent during this period. In 1920 the trade unions estimated that the best-fed workers received between 1,200 and 1,900 calories per day instead of the necessary minimum of 3,000. Another trade union estimate was that in certain enterprises half of the objects manufactured were sold directly by the producers. In industrial enterprises 50 percent absenteeism was deemed normal. Thirty-six million peasants were being decimated by famine.

War communism, inspired by doctrine, could not survive the situation which up to a point had justified it. The inexorable imperatives of economic survival were making themselves heard, but the retreat was not a concession to the Russian capitalist class; it was rather a recognition of the necessity of giving some free rein to capitalist economic relations, a necessity which the anticapitalist state, left to its own resources, could not afford to ignore.

And, in fact, making the best of this necessity, NEP did achieve some positive results without permitting a return to capitalism. By 1926–1927, industrial output had regained its 1913 level (100) and soon after even surpassed it (103.9). But some of the measures permitting this growth did not contribute to a consolidation of the economy on a more general plane. For example, oil production increased, but iron and steel production did not, thereby further accentuating the gap between the extracting industries and the manufacturing industries. Financial measures were to a large extent inflationary.[35] The number of workers reached prewar levels by 1925–1926, and grew by another 700,000 by 1928–1929.[36] But the number of unemployed increased at the same pace as the number of workers, and according to official statistics which "considerably underestimated the number of unemployed,"[37] there were more than 1 million in 1925–26, more than 1.3 million in 1927–28, and 1.7 million on April 1, 1929. Thus in absolute numbers, the unemployment rate approached 50 percent of the industrial labor force.[38] And the flip side of this moderate growth in production was a staggering expansion in the nonproductive apparatus: in 1927 2,766,136 wage laborers and salaried employees in industry were matched by 2,076,977 functionaries in various administrations. While workers' real wages declined, administrative expenditures rose to 2 billion rubles (as estimated by Stalin and Rykov in 1926).

Although the introduction of the gold ruble in 1924 was able temporarily to check inflation, by 1926 inflation was back and money in circulation increased from 1.157 billion rubles on July 1 of that year, to 2.213 billion rubles on July 1, 1929. The issuing of bank notes began to replace the production of use values at a steadily accelerating pace.

But beyond these successes and failures, what must be regarded as particularly significant in any assessment of NEP was the activity of the capitalist sector. For example, Mandel tells us that "in 1923, 91.4 percent of commercial firms were private firms and accounted for 83.4 percent of all commercial transactions. Almost 150,000 small private industrial enterprises, employing more than 12 percent of the total industrial labor force, accounted for 20 percent of industrial output in 1925–26."[39]

A deeply paradoxical situation had arisen. Within a period of a few years the bourgeoisie—ignoring for the time being its rural component—had undergone an astonishing metamorphosis. Traditionally scorned for its lack of vitality, impotent in the face of Western imperialism, a failure at industrialization, invested by the February Revolution with a power it was able neither to exercise nor to keep, politically broken, militarily defeated in the Civil War, and socially destroyed by war communism (only later to be resuscitated in the interests and under the strict control of those who had originally abolished it) fragmented, vestigial, hated, despised, and openly harassed—the Russian capitalist class experienced a wondrous rebirth. Under NEP it demonstrated a vitality, ingenuity, and above all economic aptitude that placed it in a class apart from the state monopoly, despite the fact that the latter had the power, theory, and the country's intellectual elite at its disposal, and moreover enjoyed the support of the masses for most of the time as well. Not only were capitalist entrepreneurs more successful than the managers of the large nationalized factories, worker labor was more productive in private enterprises than in those owned by the state. But at bottom these successes were due less to the prowess of individual capitalists than to capitalist relations of ownership, and hence implicitly the relative inferiority of the state sector was due less to its managers than to the type of ownership it was their task to establish and manage, despite objectively hostile conditions. The success of a short-lived capitalist reality contrasted sharply with the founderings of tenacious socialist aspirations—negative testimony that the crisis of NEP was in fact a crisis of prematurely established anticapitalist structures.

An analysis of great historical transformations must look beyond the manifest levels of direct political action if it is to go beyond a superficial examination. Broué deplores those spectators of the great turning points of history who "condemn themselves to understand nothing about the depth of these economic transformations and their long-term social consequences, both independent of official policies."[40]

Confining the analysis to political events is no more warranted than aspiring to understand them from the transcendental vantage point of what might have been. Specifically, a one-sided emphasis on the role of the mistakes of NEP in the transition to Stalinism implicitly attributes virtues to possible alternatives that could never be tested. As regards effects of historical scope, what distinguishes two opposing policies is not necessarily the fallibility of one and the infallibility of the other. In criticizing the mistakes of a policy that was actually implemented, there is the risk of disregarding the probable mistakes of those who aspired without success to implement another policy in its place. Further, two opposing policies do not necessarily produce mistakes that are opposite in kind. Fundamental errors may be common to both. In our efforts to understand history, we must consider the errors of which we have knowledge rather than those we do not know or can at best only imagine.

This takes us back, then, to my general approach which, by studying the conditions under which Stalinism first appeared, proposes to discover analogies with the conditions under which Stalinism was later established in other countries. These analogies are not to be found in particular policies nor in the errors attendant upon them, but rather at the level of structural transformations. Generally at this level we find an anticipatory revolution (or, for example, its military equivalent), followed by the more or less deliberate and conscious attempt to impose an anticapitalist structure onto a society still in the precapitalist stage of development, with its destructuring the result.

Functional perturbations and the process of destructuring played a crucial role in the appearance of the vast difficulties which weighed on Revolutionary Russia and are generally attributed exclusively to political errors. That these errors occurred and that they had weighty consequences is a plausible enough assertion, but attributing to them this exclusive role fails to account for the very nature of postrevolutionary society—an unpredictable, poorly understood, and uncontrollable generator of crises almost without end. Legitimated by the laws of the imperialist system but not by the internal laws of development of the countries in question, this kind of revolution diverts the historical process, creating problems which human policies have not yet been able to resolve. The mistakes in question may therefore represent not only lapses of policy but also the insufficiently defined terms of a problem which mankind was capable of creating but not of resolving. In the conclusion of her unsparing criticism of Bolshevism Rosa Luxemburg wrote: "In Russia the problem could only be posed. It is in this sense that the future belongs everywhere to Bolshevism."[41]

This insoluble situation did not make the emergence of Stalinism inevitable, but it did ensure the impossibility of an adequate alternative emerging in its place. To be sure, among the factors directly conducive to the triumph of Stalinism in Russia were also the mistakes of NEP and its implementation. But mistakes and excesses notwithstanding, the underlying consideration in the rise of Stalinism in Russia in 1919–1930 and later in other countries under quite different political conditions was its prima facie plausibility as a means for immediately transforming the destructuring caused by anticipatory revolution into accelerated anti-imperialist, noncapitalist industrialization.

It is worth remembering that the anticipatory revolutions that have taken place in underdeveloped countries in the 20th century have derived their impetus from the necessity of industrialization which the world imperialist system has blocked or obscured. By eliminating a home-grown capitalist class better able to manage underdevelopment than industrialization, an anticipatory revolution actually eliminates the natural agent of industrialization. The supreme failure of NEP consisted in its inability to shepherd the relative recovery of industrial production along the path of industrialization. The principal historical function of the shift of course to Stalinism was to effect the transition to industrialization.

To attain this, Stalin invented a surrogate agent of industrialization whose creation and ultimate stabilization were achieved through lasting transformations in the structure of society and the structure of ownership.

Histories of Stalinism often devote more attention to the means employed to achieve these transformations than to their substance. But in this respect Stalinism merely carried to completion—with a special resolve and brutality—a work which the Bolshevik government had diffidently pursued from the very moment it was constituted. At the Second Congress of Soviets, Lenin's government had avoided even touching upon the key question of worker appropriation of the factories and had obstructed the peasants' appropriation or continued possession of the land. Stalinism merely institutionalized the rigorous separation between the producers and the means of production—a mode of organization of production fundamentally opposed to socialism.

What enabled Stalinism to succeed where its predecessors had failed was the global nature of its action, its abandonment of all scruples in the face of doctrinal legitimacy. The global nature of these actions was conditioned by their object— nothing short of the whole of the nation's material fortune and by the social groups affected—the two productive classes, but also other social entities contending for control over property: first and foremost the state and the bureaucracy. The producers were separated from the means of production as well as from any control over the productive process, the conditions of their own participation in it included.

Thus was fashioned a society stripped of every vestige of real ownership of the means of production and of the least measure of control over economic and social activity. Stalinism signaled the passage from constraints exercised from within existing structures to the transformation by constraint of these structures or, more exactly, from actions within a destructured environment to actions aimed at specifically restructuring it. With that as a basis the alternative to a restoration of capitalism was not social ownership but, on the contrary, the most thorough social expropriation in modern times and accordingly the formation of the most global monopoly.

To be able to serve effectively as a surrogate for the natural agent of industrialization, this global monopoly needed to replace the destructuring left by anticipatory revolution with a surrogate structure that would ensure the requisite conditions for the exercise of its role. This generalized expropriation marked the triumph of the underdevelopment of the productive forces over the new class structure implanted by the Revolution.

Three sources of generally divergent social energy came together here to generate and sustain this spontaneous historical movement. One of these was the necessity of primitive accumulation. The second belonged essentially to another era, but was made concomitant by anticipation: the resistance of the noncapitalist social framework set in place by the Revolution. Finally, the third, in total disaccord with the two others, was the trend inherent in the development of monopolies, i.e., centralization. "Only centralization and concentration would create conditions propitious to the development and relative stabilization of the monopolies," Mandel comments.[42] Generalized expropriation, which resulted in an unprecedented centralization of all social ownership, was subject to the general laws of development of monopolies, albeit under the particular conditions of precapitalist anticapitalism and primitive accumulation, carried out in the absence of capital but essentially employing its methods.

Finally, another peculiarity of generalized expropriation was its specific object: diverse forms—or, more accurately, vestiges of forms—of ownership and control over production and the social product, at the time still exercised by the working class, the peasantry, and the state (and implicitly its apparatus). Consequently, what the new centralized Stalinist monopoly excluded from ownership and control was not merely one or another social class, but the whole of society.

III. A STRUCTURE EMERGES

1. Generalized expropriation

a. The working class

Unlike the peasants and the state, by the late 1920s the working class as such had no property, even in vestigial form. It had almost nothing left to lose, other than mere memories of the social control it had exercised in a generally ineffectual manner through its trade or political organizations. What generalized expropriation meant for it, therefore, was the total emasculation of these organizations. The trade unions, the Party, the production conferences—a new version of the former workers' control—would very soon be forced to perform roles contrary to the one which had legitimated their formation in the first place: instead of struggling for the liberation of the working class and defending its interests, these organizations henceforth became the direct instruments of its subjugation. The social identity of the working class, already altered in its content by circumstances to which I shall return later on, was now perverted in its expression by this functional transformation of its organizations. "In state socialist societies . . . the worker is deprived not only of the products of his labor, but also of his social identity," notes Szelenyi.[43]

Despite the harsh living conditions of the Russian proletariat, the trade unions had introduced a number of far-reaching changes in its working conditions, some of which, given the tradition, were truly revolutionary, e.g., the law establishing the eight-hour work day, the adoption of the labor code, etc. The 1927 platform of the left opposition states: "The trade unions have been given the possibility not only of embracing large masses of the population who under other social conditions would have eluded them, but also of exerting influence directly, without intermediaries, on the day-to-day policies of the workers' state."[44]

The evolution of the trade unions displayed over the course of these years the same profound ambiguities as that of the society as a whole. After vetoing workers' appropriation of the factories, the Bolshevik leadership harshly criticized the trade unions on several occasions, although in reality the criticism was directed at the proletariat. After having carried off the victory in the great historical battles of the Revolution, the war of intervention, and the Civil War, the Bolsheviks now found themselves utterly perplexed by a totally unforeseen obstacle admitting no facile solution: however inexplicable and inadmissible it may have appeared, the undeniable fact was that the working class worked much less productively under an anticapitalist regime than it had under its former capitalist employers. By the end of war communism especially, it had become clear enough that the crisis that was laying waste to the economy had its roots not only among the peasantry, but also among the proletariat as well, and this directly affected the trade unions.

In March 1920 the Ninth Party Congress called on the Bolsheviks to "struggle systematically, concertedly, resolutely, and vigorously against job desertion by publishing blacklists, by forming punitive labor platoons, and finally by interning deserters in concentration camps." Thus what was to become the future gulag was originally invented to repress not a class enemy or political adversaries of the new regime, but the very class whose hegemony that regime should have embodied; its prime purpose was to combat the class's refusal to work, which by that time had become a mass phenomenon. In June 1920 Lenin attempted to explain this absolutely intolerable situation: "Capitalism left us with its legacy of totally ignorant and besotted workers who do not understand that it is possible to work in any other way than under the cudgel of capital." Lenin's somewhat violent metaphor aside, the deeper meaning of this caustic statement of the facts leaves no doubt: on the objective plane, i.e., from the perspective of the working class seen as a productive force, whereas capitalist relations of production had stimulated worker productivity, their premature abolition had ruined it.

This revelation contradicted the very premises of the Leninist strategy of anticipatory revolution. In this respect that strategy had failed, and in its place there now came attempts, as urgent as they were fruitless, to understand and to allay this crisis. The documents of the period abound with reports on measures taken in an effort to control the frenetic turbulence of the industrial work force; the astronomical number of hours spent by workers discussing how to organize production instead of engaging in it; mass absenteeism; acts of indiscipline, including the anarchic dismissal of leaders appointed by authorized bodies or the stripping of workshops on the basis of collective democratic decisions. The government responded with countermeasures such as introducing workbooks, requiring the unemployed to accept any job offered them, and instituting disciplinary courts.

The most aggressive reaction to this situation came from Trotsky. In 1919 he prepared a draft bill for the Central Committee recommending the employment of wartime methods on the economic front, which implicitly amounted to placing the economy under the command of the Commissariat of War. The turmoil of the Civil War had scarcely subsided when Trotsky declared: "Our economic situation is a hundred times worse than our military situation ever was."[45] His ultra-radical proposals on the "militarization of labor" and "subordination of the trade unions'' may perhaps have been plausibly argued under the given circumstances; but unfortunately they assumed the qualities of the proletariat's natural state under its own dictatorship when exposed to Motokey's penchant for excessive theorizing. The draft project, which was confidential and meant only for the Party leadership, was made public, for reasons not completely clear, by *Pravda* on December 17 (Bukharin was editor-in-chief at the time). The Bolshevik faction in the trade-union leadership rejected the project by a large majority. In February 1920 Trotsky made a half-hearted *mea culpa* but then returned to his original theses. Put in charge of restoring transport, he turned from projects to action. Brou remarks, ''Although he got the trains running once again—a true miracle—he also provoked the irrevocable hostility of the railroad workers' union. The Committee for the Organization of Transport which he created to supplant the trade-union leadership became the *bête noire* of trade-union officials, Bolsheviks included, who denounced it as a dictatorial and bureaucratic body.''[46] On November 8, Tomskii petitioned the Central Committee to prohibit Trotsky or anyone else from dismissing elected leaders. Lenin and the Central Committee majority, more sensitive to this breach of workers' democracy than to economic disaster, withdrew their support for Trotsky. Despite its placating references to ''healthy forms of militarization of labor,'' the resolution adopted on the matter excoriated the ''degeneration of centralization and militarized labor into bureaucracy, haughtiness, petty officialism, and meddling interference in the trade unions.'' A commission was set up under the chairmanship of Zinoviev to study relations between the Party and the trade unions. Following Trotsky's refusal to participate in this committee, the discussion became public. And so at the brink of economic ruin, on the eve of the painful shift to NEP, thousands and thousands were engrossed for months on end in a vast popular debate over the choice between workers' democracy and workers' productivity—a definition of the problem which testifies to the incapacity of the society to unite the two. Of the seven initial contending platforms, only three were left at the end: Trotsky's, which had gained the rather unexpected support of Bukharin; the platform of the workers' opposition which was situated at the opposite extreme; and Lenin's, which recommended Party control over the trade unions provided it did not become a relation of tutelage.

At the Party Congress, the workers' opposition gained only 18 votes, the Trotsky–Bukharin platform 50, and Lenin's group 336. Afterwards, Lenin commented: ''This luxury was in fact inadmissible, and we certainly committed a grave error in permitting such a debate.'' Thus came to an inconclusive end one of the most democratic debates on the fate of democracy as a condition of the working class and of its organizations in a society born of anticipatory revolution.

The role Trotsky played in this debate very likely contributed considerably to his defeat in the debate over the internal situation of the Party, in which he called for a ''new course.'' He sent a letter to the Central Committee on October 8, 1923, stating that since the 12th Congress the ''bureaucratization of the Party apparatus has reached unprecedented proportions." A week later came the famous "Declaration of the 46" (signed by Piatakov, Preobrazhensky, Osinskii, Antonov-Ovseenko, Smirnov, and Kossior, among others) which took more or less the same line, implicitly ratifying Trotsky as leader of the opposition. If there is one point in this polemic—in which personal attacks abounded—on which there was agreement, it was surely the decision to convoke a Party conference to deal with the problem. The opposition made a special effort to gather support among the working-class members of the Party, but obtained meager results. Its best performance was in Moscow, but even there it obtained a majority in only 67 out of a total of 346 factory cells. The debates were concluded three days before Lenin's death, and the 13th Congress adopted a resolution which censured Trotsky, who had abstained from participating.

"The incapacity of the opposition establish grass-roots support among the proletariat," concluded Carr," was a symptom of the weakness not only of the opposition itself, but also of the proletariat."[47] The defeat was a decisive one politically for Trotsky, and it was by no means unrelated to his inclement attitude toward the real weaknesses of the workers during the preceding debate. His abrupt metamorphosis from the champion of the bureaucratization of the trade unions into a just-as-resolute champion of the debureaucratization of the Party hardly strengthened his credibility in the eyes of the proletariat. General judgments aside, his declining influence in the Party must be attributed at least in part to the severity, extreme by any standard, of his reaction to the weakness of the class he purported to serve, stripping it of all its freedoms, even the freedom to work and the freedom to organize.

But the principal significance of the 1923 trade-union debate lay elsewhere: the principal Bolshevik leaders were in almost unanimous agreement that the trade unions should not be given any effective autonomy. Interestingly enough, Bukharin organized a conference on the topic "Proletarian Revolution and Culture" in Petrograd in early 1923. Whereas the Western bourgeoisie had triumphed over a class to which it was culturally superior, fortune was not so generous to the proletariat, which remained culturally inferior to the bourgeoisie despite its victory over it. Bukharin seemed to fear the forces carrying the working class toward bureaucratization of the whole of postrevolutionary society more than a decline in production. The danger was augmented, he thought, by mass promotions of uneducated proletarian workers to posts invested with a high degree of social, economic, or political responsibility for which they were culturally not yet adequately equipped. There was a huge discrepancy between the power that had been put in their hands and their abilities, and this did not auger well for the stability and viability of postrevolutionary society. What is important is not whether Bukharin's apprehensions were warranted or not, but the fact that, long before it became a reality under Stalin, the need for subjugating the proletariat—and hence the trade unions—to a power which should have been their own had been impressed in one way or other on the minds of the Bolshevik leaders who were the most gifted, but at the same time politically the furthest apart in their views.

The toppling of the powerful trade-union chairman, Tomskii, was left to Stalin to complete, but it had been prepared by Stalin's most intransigent adversaries. The 1927 platform of the left opposition deplored the course taken by the unions toward bureaucratization. It quoted a July 23, 1927 article in *Pravda*, which commented that the vast majority of the delegates at trade-union congresses no longer held down factory jobs. Less than 15 percent of the members of the executive bodies of a dozen industrial trade unions was comprised of workers working in factories. The platform noted that "the working class and the trade unions have never been further from the management of socialist industry than at this moment."[48] It went on to say that the right wing of the Party and the state included a "group made up of high-level trade-union functionaries who have prevailed over the best-paid wage laborers and salaried employees. . . , as personified by Tomskii."

What is important is not to what extent this description strictly speaking is correct, but that even judged by quite divergent political criteria the situation of the trade unions and the position of their principal leaders were both profoundly unsatisfactory. There were no substantial differences between the left opposition and the group around Stalin in their critical assessment of trade-union activity or in their assessment of Tomskii. Where they did differ was in the solutions they advocated. If the left opposition had won the debate, it would have replaced Tomskii with one of its own militants; Stalinism, victorious, did in fact replace Tomskii by Shvernik. But the essential change lay not in the reshuffling of personnel, but in the change of content. Unlike the left opposition, for Stalinism it was not a question of correcting the policy pursued by the trade-union leadership, but of prohibiting it from making any autonomous policy at all. Henceforth, trade-union policy was to be made elsewhere, and not by the trade unions. The total subjugation of the trade unions, the culmination of a long but sterile controversy punctuated by shifting positions and wavering aims, was a decisive component of the condition reserved for the working class by the emergent social order. Despite having opened its doors to the workers, the Party was no longer really able to be the political organization of the class it had deprived of its own professional organization. The same fate was in store for the vestiges of the ''Workers' Inspectorate''—especially the ''production councils,'' abandoned by both factory management and workers alike, albeit for different reasons.

With no organizations of its own, the proletariat was unable to fulfill its role as dominant class or even to defend its elementary interests. In 1926 salaries began to decrease after having risen until 1925 under NEP. Any later improvements concerned first and foremost workers in Moscow and Leningrad. The 1.6 million farm workers received on average no more than 63 percent of their prewar wages and were paid irregularly for work the duration of which remained in practical terms undefined. Frequent inequalities in wages affected broad categories of women and youth.

The picture was not very encouraging, but it was made more somber still by the persistence and even worsening of unemployment. On April 1, 1927, the number of officially registered unemployed was 1,656,000 (which was quite a bit lower than the actual number). Only 20 percent of the unionized unemployed received assistance from the trade unions. The factory committees were gradually eased totally out of the picture, and the weapon of the strike was henceforth considered an act of hostility toward socialism. According to the trade-union newspaper (*Trud*, July 4, 1927), "The collective contract is becoming a mere administrative arrangement" as a result of "the diminution in legal guarantees." Indeed, the administration countered the workers penchant for obstructing the production process under the pretext of democratizing it with ever harsher measures in an effort to re-establish a minimum of labor discipline. "The situation within the enterprises," stated the above article, "is growing worse. The administration is stepping up its efforts to carry its unlimited power into the factories. Hiring and firing in effect depend solely on the administration. It is no rare thing to see relations just like those existing before the war developing again between foremen and workers."[49] But the platform, more a plea than an analysis, attributes to foremen a function which was largely beyond their competence and of which they were merely the most direct vehicles. For what characterized the relations being reinstituted was not their temporal aspect, i.e., their being like those existing before the war, but their social nature.

It was not the ill will of the foremen (or the administration) which was forcing this menacing return to the past but the fact that, cut off from the means of production, the proletariat could not be induced to produce effectively except by capitalist production relations. Antinomic necessity again moved into the breach, calling for the reestablishment of capitalist-type relations, yet without the restoration of capitalism. After having set in motion tendencies toward the militarization of labor and forced the introduction of the Taylor system, antinomic necessity was now paving the way for the emergence of Stalinism through the expropriation of the proletariat of its organizations, thereby facilitating its total exclusion from every other social activity but labor. The outcome was that the establishment of Stalinism did not represent the restoration of capitalism; it was merely the most resolute attempt to adapt capitalist work relations to a noncapitalist social framework. The adaptation was necessarily reciprocal, and what above all defined Stalinism was not so much the manner in which it went about adapting capitalist work relations to the noncapitalist framework, but the immoderation of this adaptation. Instead of permitting the gradual resorption of capitalist work relations by the noncapitalist framework, the end result of this immoderation was to make the latter dependent on the former for its continued existence.

Of course the key measure by which Stalinism proposed to obtain this double objective was generalized expropriation. Directed against workers and producers in general, it reestablished work relations of the capitalist type; directed against capitalism, it preserved the noncapitalist social framework, but in a way which extended capitalist relations beyond the limits of the enterprise and into its broader social context. Thus capitalist work relations tended to become capitalist relations of production. At the origin of this tendency was a congenital, determining, and for a time insuperable handicap of the new society: the immaturity of the class appointed by history to dominate it.

As a class the proletariat had helped to smash capitalism; but once victorious it demonstrated itself incapable of rising above capitalism as a social relation and hence unable to work without the constraints of capitalist relations of production after it had contributed to making them socially untenable.

This limit on its victory was also a limit on its development, and it was this rather than the future development of the proletariat which Stalinism transformed into a functional and hence indispensable condition of the new social order. To the constraints imposed by capitalist relations of production Stalinism opposed another type of constraint, but a constraint which showed fewer and fewer advantages as time went on, insofar as coercion was the only way that the economic effects of generalized expropriation could be maintained.

The lesson brought out by this disconcerting experience was that, though the chains of the proletariat may have been forged by capital, it was not the existence of capital which prevented that class from being free but its own incapacity to be socially productive without the coercive powers embodied by capital. Total abolishment of capital did not yet permit the abolition of constraints on the working class. The alternative form of coercion instituted by Stalinism allowed anticapitalist industrialization, but the price paid was its own perpetuation.

This price, in fact, was already inscribed in the contradictory nature of Stalinist industrialization which, though anticapitalist, did not become proletarian. The proletariat was too weak as the productive agent of industrial labor to become instantaneously the agent of either industrial property or industrialization. On the contrary, it was to remain both the executor and the object of that industrialization for an entire epoch.

Once it had been divested of its organizations and rendered powerless to take any decision concerning the conditions of its productive activity, the working class changed its social role (a change, moreover, which would affect in one way or another all the factors involved in generalized expropriation). The proletariat's change of roles served only to legitimate and give substance to a new social role, that of a global and absolute monopoly over property and power. The profound desynchronization that existed among the principal social roles of the working class made the Stalinist monopoly possible, and it in turn brought about a radical restructuring of these roles. The Russian proletariat had been called upon to fulfill three preponderant social roles, although of course the weight it carried in each was heavily dependent on circumstances. They were: its role or mission as a revolutionary force; its role as the agent of management and ownership;

and its role as a productive force.

The historical discontinuity of the Revolution was reflected in the discontinuity of the manner in which the proletariat fulfilled each of these roles and, most especially, in its action as a revolutionary force during and after the Revolution. In dealing with this subject, Stalinist ideology ensnared itself in an ambiguity that has remained to this day. Basically, Stalinism has never been able to identify the social force which led the Revolution. Was it the Bolshevik Party or was it the working class? Stalinism says both. Even if it did not lead the Revolution, the proletariat was certainly one of the most resolute revolutionary forces, especially in certain of its detachments and at certain moments. But while the pursuit of victory had fired the revolutionary energies of the proletariat, they seem to have abruptly burned out once victory was achieved. Revolutionary militancy disappeared as soon as it attained its objective. Although certain elements of the class may have retained their revolutionary fervor undiminished, for the class as a whole this discontinuity was clear. From having been a driving social force of revolution the proletariat became a source of social inertia and even regression in its aftermath.

To explain the abrupt fading of this role it must be seen in connection with the other roles exercised by the proletariat during the revolutionary period.

The proletariat's aspirations to assume the functions of management and ownership were first openly manifested by the mass formation of factory committees soon after February 1917. It proceeded to assume the broadest political prerogatives, as well as the task of monitoring owner management of industrial enterprises. During this first period its role as direct agent in the management of the economy was merely tributary to its role as a revolutionary political force. But there was a flagrant inequality in the performance of these roles. The proletariat's contribution to the victory of the Revolution far outweighed any improvements it may have achieved in the management of capitalist enterprises (which, in fact, were never actually in its hands).

The spontaneous tendency of the working class to assume control over private enterprises is not specific to the Russian Revolution of 1917. It had also occurred in other more or less similar historical circumstances. Supek observes that "seizing control of factories took place in Russia in 1905 and 1917, in Germany and Italy in 1920, and in Hungary and Poland in 1956."[50] In fact, it has been manifested on an even larger scale. Though stigmatized by the respective Communist parties as "anarcho-syndicalism," it occurred near the end or after World War II in all the countries of Eastern Europe. But in none of these cases did the working class become the manager of the economy or even of individual enterprises, with the exception of in Yugoslavia. Long-term results aside, it must be noted that the Yugoslavian version of self-management was not the product of spontaneous working-class action, but of official central decisions which were precipitated (according to Djilas) by the conflict with the USSR in 1948.

In Russia, this movement of the proletariat changed in content with the October victory. On the one hand, the proletariat passed from keeping check on capitalist owners to their outright expropriation, and on the other it opposed the state's efforts to take possession of nationalized enterprises. Thus, in a logical progression, the target of the spontaneous movement of the proletariat was no longer the functions of management but those of ownership. The more vital the role it found thrust upon it, the more evident became the working class's lack of preparation.

The growing discrepancy between its ends and the means available to it for achieving them ultimately put the working class in opposition not only to the capitalists, but also to the state, which was committed to represent it even as it prevented it from adopting this role. A distance was opening up between party and class, owed in part to this contradiction, and there was evident disagreement within the party leadership on how to deal with the disquieting prospects of this separation. The workers' opposition group supported the right of the proletariat to assume this role on doctrinaire grounds. Lenin's reply, shrugging doctrine aside, consisted of some disconcerting empirical observations. "There are little more than fifteen hundred workers in all of Russia who are capable of managing enterprises," he said. "The central government has need of these workers to reinforce the dictatorship of the proletariat."

By creating the necessity of a role beyond its capacity to fulfill, the proletariat implicitly created the necessity of its own replacement in this role. Its persistent attempts to adopt this role thrust it into conflict with its own objective limits. In short, these attempts possessed a political legitimacy that was untranslatable on the economic plane. The proletariat indeed had the necessary political credentials for assuming the tasks of management, but it lacked the requisite economic skills. Its replacement in this role therefore was inevitable. Stalinism's answer to this necessity was to transform replacement into subordination. A specialized body was formed, consisting mainly of individuals recruited from the class it replaced, to assume the functions of management in the place of the proletariat.

But the principal obstacle preventing the proletariat from assuming the functions of management and ownership was the collapse of its own productivity. The catastrophic manner in which it fulfilled its fundamental role, that of a productive force, effectively barred access to new social roles. According to Marx, "Of all the instruments of production, the greatest productive force of all is the revolutionary class itself." But far from bringing a spectacular improvement in production, the Russian proletariat's anticipatory victory over capitalism caused its further development as a force of production to come to an abrupt halt, and even regress.

The syncretism of postrevolutionary society was directly reflected in the quandary experienced by the working class as a productive force. Concretely, the general disarticulation between the productive forces and the class structure became for the working class a disarticulation between its possible roles and its one necessary role. Before Stalinism ruthlessly reduced it to the latter, the proletariat had been forced to do battle in two contradictory and disarticulated environments. As a revolutionary class it had been thrust into a class structure of a postcapitalist type where it was called upon to defend and maintain a position of dominance. As a productive force it was immersed in a labor process whose internal relations and technological means were situated on the borderline between precapitalism and capitalism. Contrary to Lenin's forecast and to the momentum of its own revolutionary impetus, the proletariat was unable to adapt its presumptive role in the first environment to the realities of the second. Thus it endeavored to modify its role within an inauspicious environment that it perpetuated or even worsened by its unproductive labor. The incongruity of the class was created by the new conditions of its existence and existed before it had even begun to affect its actions.

This historical experience indirectly confirms the spirit of the *Grundrisse* by proving its converse false. One may argue that a class of exploited producers is unable to achieve the effective negation of its condition until the productivity of its own labor has rendered both exploitation and the class division of society into producers and nonproducers socially superfluous. Of course this objective premise can become socially operative only if the class which stands to benefit from it is also subjectively militant. Today these two premises have become disjunctive on a world scale. As a rule, the working class in the advanced capitalist countries has tended to develop its productive capacities more rapidly than its subjective militancy. In contrast, in countries which have been or are candidates for anticipatory revolutions, the terms of this inequality are usually initially inverted, and the productive capacity of the working class remains far behind its subjective militancy. Stalinism was the attempt to eliminate this imbalance, but its result was little to be desired: subjective militancy was stifled while the productivity of the labor force developed much less rapidly than did the technological means provided by industrialization.

In reality none of the three roles of the proletariat was manifested autonomously. They were interconnected, and the connections varied depending on the conditions. For limited periods, the fervor and energies generated by anticipation had in fact a stimulating effect first on the proletariat's role as revolutionary force and then, later, on its role in exercising the functions of management and ownership. But the overall effect of anticipation on the working class as a productive force was regressive. Anticipation appears to have introduced a schism in the working class between its potential existence as subject and as object. On evidence, this schism initially favored subjectivity; but the turnings of history soon effected a lasting about-face, and its objectivity was the price paid for anticipation.

In reality, the connections among the three roles of the working class represented just so many variations on their general disarticulation. This disarticulation was in fact historical desynchronization, a perturbation in the flow of history of the same general order as anticipatory revolution.

The same disjunction which had made the working class a formidable driving force of revolution transformed it, owing to the decline in productivity, into a brake on progress and even a regressive force in postrevolutionary society. In the end the working class would threaten the very foundations of the new society which had been born to make possible its dominion.

The disarticulation between the proletariat's role as a productive force and its potential managerial role had unique features of its own. The disenchantment experienced by the working class from its inability to fulfill the managerial role into which it had been thrust by its revolutionary prowess merely aggravated its deficiencies as a productive force. The interaction between the two roles was exclusively negative, but it was direct. Desynchronization assumed the manifest form of contradiction. At another time in another country, history was to demonstrate in its cruel way that even when bidden, the proletariat is unable to manage its factories with the requisite competence before it has attained a commensurately high level of development as a productive force. That is the lesson of Yugoslavia.

These roles depend essentially on subjective premises, namely, that of revolutionary force and that of management and were unable to influence substantially the role of productive force, which is rooted in objective conditions.

To some degree or other the working class can be replaced in its subjective roles, but it remains absolutely irreplaceable in the role which defines the objective essence of its social identity.

Stalinism was sensitive to these distinctions between the contents of these roles. The working class had ceased to be a revolutionary force in a society which no longer had need of that function, and accordingly Stalinism stripped it of its independent organizations. In the exercise of managerial functions it was replaced by the bureaucracy; and as a productive force it was reduced to subordination vis-à-vis both the bureaucracy and the monopoly. Thus in the midst of a disarticulated society, the working class was torn by a false dilemma. Whether it generalized its control over the factories or abandoned it, the end result would perforce be the same: the loss of both the roles in which it was the manifest subject/doer. But as the working class began to lose its role as a revolutionary force, the revolution itself lost its class legitimacy, and it is this crisis of legitimacy which distinguishes postrevolutionary society from Stalinism. Whereas the former endeavored to understand and to surmount this crisis, Stalinism accepted it and drew the necessary conclusions. Confronted with the impossibility of renouncing proletarian legitimacy, the Bolshevik leaders strained against the facts to demonstrate the possibility of preserving this legitimacy. A comment of Bukharin's on this subject may serve as an illustration: ''A culturally oppressed class cannot develop as to prepare itself for the organization of all society. It can be ready to prepare itself for the destruction of the old world. It must 'remake its nature' and ripen . . . only in the period of its dictatorship.''[51] This great Revolution which had counted externally on its spread to the developed countries of the

West and internally on the historic mission of the proletariat was forced to acknowledge that both had failed. One may well imagine the intense drama of this realization, only glimpsed in Bukharin's theoretical writings. Bukharin merely suggests that the proletariat cannot acquire the capacity to manage society except by exercising its dictatorship over it but makes no attempt to explain how it can exercise its dictatorship without having the capacity to manage society. One can understand how such confusions were able to take root in the circumstances of the time; it is much more difficult to understand why they have survived to our day.

Rendered clearer by historical distance, these circumstances reveal significant parallels. In October as in February, the Russian Revolution attempted to transfer power to a class incapable of exercising it. In February this class was the bourgeoisie, in October the proletariat. For the one as well as the other, the lack of the requisite political skills and experience was coupled with an organic incapacity to fulfill its fundamental economic function as circumstances required. The bourgeoisie had been unable to initiate industrialization and, on this basis, to achieve the ascendancy of capitalist relations of production. The proletariat had been unable to acquire under capitalist exploitation a level of productivity which would have enabled it to appropriate the means of its labor in the interest of the whole of society and, on that basis, to manage and administer the whole of the economy and society. Beneath these parallels lies a profound historical commonality. Opposed by their interests, these two classes were united in their underdevelopment. But whereas the immaturity of the bourgeoisie had been nurtured over a long period by the imperialist system, the immaturity of the working class was rudely dredged up into the light of day by the victory of the anticipatory revolution.

Some subtle connections between the Revolution and postrevolutionary society may also be perceived in these parallels. This aspect of the defeat of the two principal social classes makes more transparent the secondary role each played in the Revolution, especially in its final act. A revolution not dominated by class conflict gives birth to a society in which class relations are also not predominant. And as so often in history, the social vacuum created by the failings of the existing classes invites their replacement by a particularly powerful state. Thus, "Stalinism was not the cause of the proletariat's immaturity; the converse was true: it was the immaturity of the proletariat that produced Stalinist society. What Stalinism did do was forcefully to perpetuate this immaturity, despite the fact that the class had matured objectively as a productive force. It is impossible to arrive at an understanding of the class nature of Stalinism if the role played by the proletariat in the revolution is not itself adequately understood."[52]

Stalinism does not merely structure the hierarchy of the roles of the working class; it simply eliminates some of them. It prohibits those roles in which the proletariat as subject/doer is most manifest, leaving it solely with its object role, that of a productive force. Of course in the particular example of the Russian Revolution, the process was more nuanced. For instance, the proletariat had in practice already abandoned its role as revolutionary force before Stalinism prohibited it—or, better said, it was the role that abandoned the proletariat under the pressure of circumstances and its own productive fatigue. The loss of the other role, that of managing, was less peaceable: the working class and its organizations continued tenaciously to covet it despite debilitating setbacks, until Stalinism destroyed not only access to it, but also any hope of ever gaining it. But Stalinism merely hastened and brought to a head a process that had begun long before and was already far advanced. The separation of the proletariat from these two roles, whether directly instigated or already in progress and simply assimilated, was an indispensable condition for the constitution and functioning of the global Stalinist monopoly. Even as it continued its ideological refrains on the dictatorship of the proletariat, Stalinism transformed the presumptive dominant class into a class under its own strict domination. Under the pressure of Stalinism, the proletariat underwent a second transformation. From the inertia into which it had fallen after ceasing to be a revolutionary force, obedience emerged to become its enduring condition.

This condition of servitude proved to be more than a transitory constraint on the working class. It became its defining trait and hence an invariable quantity in the structure of the new Stalinist order. It therefore did not disappear as the class improved its ailing productivity, which is what had initially provoked and therefore justified it. It was this stabilization of the proletariat in a condition of servitude which transformed Stalinism from an expedient, plausible within certain limits, into an intolerable social order. For the stability of an enslaved proletariat meant the stability of the enslaving monopoly. Such was the ultimate result of the generalized expropriation directed against the working class.

b. The peasantry

All versions of Stalinism create essentially the same conditions for the working class. The peasantry is a different case, yet Stalinist expropriation of the peasantry has been studied far more than that of the working class. The consequence or perhaps the cause of this has been an inordinate concentration on what from an international perspective is only one of many variables in this social order, at the expense of grievously neglecting one of its crucial constants. Second, the expropriation of the Russian peasants is artificially treated as a topic in itself, divorced from the broader context of generalized expropriation of which it was but one component. Finally, it is usually referred to as "collectivization," a word which in fact belongs to the intangible treasure of terms manipulated by Stalinist ideology. The consequence is, to use Michel Löwy's expression, "interpretations of Stalinism [which use] concepts inherited from Stalinism itself."[53] How common are the acerbic criticisms of the violent expropriation of the peasantry that then refer to it as collectivization, suggesting their voluntary adherence. Thus by force of habit, scholarship, whose ostensible purpose is to disclose, avails itself of an ideological terminology that pursues but one undivided end—dissimulation. (To anticipate a bit, the study of Stalinism can only gain from a more critical attitude in the use of another term as well, coming from the same source and referring to the same event, namely, "revolution from above," to which I will come back later on.)

It is in its application to the peasantry that generalized expropriation most unambiguously revealed its integral role in the process of primitive accumulation. But, as with other historical episodes, Stalinist expropriation of the peasantry bore a set of traits which invest with a certain originality. First, its agent was not a social class but a political power; its action aimed not at restraining petty private agrarian property, but at abolishing it; and its principal effect was not the resurgence of capitalist property, but the seizure of the means of agricultural production by the same monopoly that had already taken possession of the means of industrial production. Given these factors, Stalinist expropriation of the peasantry was simply the illegal transfer, based on extra-economic constraint, of the whole of agrarian property from the hands of private peasants to the hands of the global monopoly.

Considering these singularities it is evident that, relative to that of the proletariat, the expropriation of the peasantry displayed more imagination and inventiveness, which later had their impact on the new social order reserved for both of these classes. It is perhaps this inventiveness which gave on Stalinist expropriation of the peasantry the excessive fragility it has shown in the irregular and erratic manner in which it has been reproduced in other countries. China, for instance, under Mao, set about establishing agricultural communes with a zeal that would only be exceeded later under Deng, when they were abandoned and private peasant holdings restored; under Gierek, Poland imposed a kolkhoz-type organization on agriculture which would later be dismantled under Gomulka in 1956; Hungary, while maintaining agricultural cooperatives, made them much less subordinate to the central monopoly than in the classic model. Finally, even in countries like the USSR, which has never abandoned this form of agricultural organization, its fragility is manifested in the flexible dimensions of the individual plots conceded to the peasants and the changeability of kolkhoz rules.

Considering these variations in time and place, two remarks are in order. First, what is inherent to Stalinism is the absolute domination of the global monopoly over agriculture, not the particular form of this domination. Second, unlike industry, Stalinist agricultural organization has never led to a spectacular growth in productivity. The chronically poor performance of the original kolkhoz model in the Soviet Union did not make for its enthusiastic acceptance in other countries, hence the variations. However, all these different schemes have one common trait: not one of them was imposed by the peasantry on the monopoly. Rather, their institution, as well as their abandonment, was always imposed on or conceded to the peasants by the monopoly. The net effect of this unilaterality has been that not one of these variations has eliminated the domination of the global monopoly over agriculture which has consequently remained fundamentally underproductive. Even Hungarian and Bulgarian agriculture, both distinctly superior to agriculture in the other Stalinist countries, have never proved competitive by American or even French standards.

Regardless of how one may choose to explain it subjectively, it is an objective and undeniable fact that the reorganization of agriculture, industry, and the Party all took place within roughly the same period at the end of the 1920s. This concomitance was more than just a coincidence in time: the three transformations were interdependent. They belonged to the same process of generalized expropriation and institution of the global monopoly.

Suffice it to mention the 15th Party Congress held in December 1927, which decided simultaneously to embark upon the first five-year plan, the expropriation of the peasants, and the forging of a monolithic power. The conjunction of all these transformations paved the way for the structural mutations which ultimately converged to form the monopoly. The expulsion of Trotsky and Zinoviev from the Party and of Kamenev from the Central Committee, as well as Bukharin's return to the line of a "stepped up offensive against the kulaks," were not only formally related to the expropriation of the peasants. As Bettelheim observes, "The 15th Congress was likewise in favor of a policy of *collectivization*, though stressing that it had to be carried out *with prudence, by persuasion, and without force*. Still, there were a number of nuances in the way that Bukharin, Rykov (at that time president of the Sovnarkom), and Kalinin, on the one hand, and Stalin, on the other, posed the question of collectivization. For the former, collectivization was only *one of the elements in a policy* for resolving the problems of agriculture. For Stalin, "There was *no other solution* than collectivization" to the problems of Soviet agriculture."[54] Bettelheim seems to be accepting the concepts of the historical actors along with their terminology. In reality, "collectivization" was not only the creation of an agrarian policy, it was also the creator of a new structure of political power and, in general, a new social structure. The decision of the 15th Congress on this issue after ten years of sterile controversy signals less the triumph of a specific agrarian policy than the beginnings of a "monolithization" of political power in the face of the problems that had rent it from the first moments of its birth. To the unacknowledged centralization of agrarian ownership in the hands of the monopoly was added the loudly proclaimed and roundly praised centralization of political power in the same hands.

All, from the protagonists of the time to the contemporary scholar, seem to agree that the problem that had dominated the scene immediately prior to the expropriation of the peasantry and which had precipitated it was the procurements crisis. But the tensions created by the procurements merely made transparent tensions already existing in relations between the government and the peasantry. Instead of concentrating on the reconciliation of these two actors, Stalinism would proceed to their radical transformation, and so to the radical restructuring of relations between them. An approach which places primary focus on the procurements crisis runs a great risk of ascribing to circumstances themselves a process of which they were only the expression—a risk, that is, of seeing only a conjunctural crisis where what was actually present was a perpetual structural crisis in the new society.

In stressing that the procurements crisis was only the outward expression of a deeper crisis, I am far from suggesting that there was no such crisis, or that it was not grave. On the contrary, it was grave enough to place the whole of society in mortal danger. On January 1, 1928, the procurement plan was only 39.3 percent fulfilled, compared with 63.7 percent one year previously. Despite "extraordinary measures," 1928 procurements were only three-quarters of the 1927 level, and in the first three months of 1929 they were only half the figure for the same period in 1928.

It became more and more evident as time went on that the peasants simply did not accept this illusory form of commerce which the state was endeavoring to perpetuate. But the unpopularity of the procurements was aggravated by other aspects of the state's agrarian policy as well. First of these was its price policy—the famous price scissors, which placed prices for farm products relative to industrial products at a disadvantage. To compound the problem further, market prices for farm products were three to four times higher than the prices offered by procurement officers. Finally, as part of this same unfortunate policy, industry did not even partially meet the need for farm equipment: in 1927, the best period, the total number of tools used in farming was less than a third the number in use before the war, but industry's response to this acute shortage was to supply peasants with a quantity of tools valued at less than 1 percent (0.8 percent to be exact) of the national income. With such a shortage, it was only natural that the simplest and hence most indispensable tools should be resold by middlemen at black market prices. The ultimate result was that these tools could be bought only by those who had the means to do so, i.e., the rich peasants, who would then rent them out to the poor peasantry on extremely oppressive terms. Although originally intended to prevent the means of production from accumulating in the hands of the rich peasants, the policy of maintaining a scarcity of farm equipment had the opposite effect. It made the rich peasants richer and the poor peasants poorer. In the end agricultural production as a whole suffered, rather than merely the rich producers against whom the policy was originally directed.

This is a particularly revealing illustration of the tendency for this society's inherent resistance to capitalism to be manifested as a resistance to production. In 1925, in one of his most brilliant formulations, Bukharin ridiculed the consequences of this paralyzing confusion: "The well-to-do stratum of the peasantry and the middle peasant who wants to become well-to-do *are afraid to accumulate nowadays*. . . . Higher technology becomes conspiratorial."[55] Through its deliberate policy of cultivating a shortage of the agricultural means of production, i.e., farm equipment, the state left the potential economic sources of accumulation without the technological means to do so. It was Bukharin's view that public accumulation must be primed not by stifling but by controlling private accumulation. He defined the alternatives clearly: steadily growing agricultural production, permitting the controlled development of capitalist elements, or the effective throttling of these elements, bringing about the uncontrollable collapse of agricultural production.

But a more extreme path was also clear: to prevent entirely the development of capitalist elements at the sacrifice of production itself. This was the official policy, and over and above its fluctuations it was propelled by its inner logic to convert its competition with capitalism into coercion of the peasantry and ultimately to turn both into an obstruction of production. The procurements and the fictitious prices they implicitly created separated the peasants from their product, while the deliberately maintained scarcity of tools separated them in practice from their means of production before that separation had been established by law. Under the combined force of these pressures, petty peasant property was reduced to an illusion, and with its disappearance, agricultural production disappeared as well. By the late 1920s the decline in farm output could no longer be blamed on the war: it was the fruit of the new relations between the government and the peasantry. Stalinism's expropriation merely carried this situation to its completion and gave legal expression to the total separation of the peasants from their means of production. These modifications would over time improve the agricultural equipment situation, but they would be unable to lessen the profound impact of the bizarre social phenomenon of a peasantry that had lost interest in producing.

Agricultural output had been brought to a state of collapse in the early 1920s by the effects of war and again later by the relations outlined above, but between these two points it had undergone fluctuations and even showed some improvement. Although growth was irregular and in the end could not be sustained, it began in 1921, reaching a peak of 76.4 million tons in 1926–1927 which, however, was still below the 1909–1913 average of 82.6 million tons. After this a precipitous decline set in, and by 1927–1928 the harvest was not only below the 1926–27 level, but also below 1925–26. At its lowest point in 1925–26, the deficit between agricultural output and population growth was about the same (7 percent) relative to 1913. The population continued to grow in the years that followed, but the harvest resumed its decline. Thus postrevolutionary society found itself faced with a famine that threatened the cities as well as the countryside. Society had been driven to the brink of disaster by the vital sector in which underdevelopment was gravest owing not only to the legacy of the past, but also to the policy of the present.

That policy had already begun to turn accumulation into famine even before industrialization had truly gotten under way. In distress, agriculture becomes an insurmountable barrier rather than the principal sustaining factor of industrial effort. Raw materials were in short supply, food and provisions for the workers were often scarce, and the indispensable and inaccessible technology could not be imported from abroad. Before the war grain exports had been about 10 million tons per year, whereas in the peak year after the Revolution, 1926–1927, they reached the modest level of only 2.1 million tons. The next year, 1928, grain trade registered a deficit, with exports of 89,000 tons, as compared to imports of 250,000 tons. The balance of trade, still positive in 1926–1927, showed an alarming deficit of 153.1 million in 1928.

Official documents of the period attributed the twin collapse of procurements and production to the "kulak offensive." It was hardly surprising that well-to-do peasants should have no particular liking for a state that was despoiling them of their product and preventing them from accumulating. Nonetheless, according to Strumilin's data, this group made up only 3.1 percent of the total rural population compared with 29.4 percent poor peasants and 67.5 percent middle peasants. Thus, even despite the considerable superiority of their economic weight over their demographic weight, it seems very unlikely that the kulaks were accountable for the entire decline in supplies and production. Moreover, in practice the delimitation of these categories was more than fluid. The more likely explanation therefore is that the procurements affected not a mere negligible minority of the peasantry, but indeed the great majority of them, and that it was therefore this great majority, either in whole or in part, which attempted to counteract the coercive measures of the state by imposing constraints of its own. The "extraordinary measures" were roundly deplored in advance by their initiator and indeed affected directly or indirectly every social category of the rural population. Although stratification of the peasantry had long since become a social fact, the peasants were reunited by the same pressures from above and, in the end, by their resistance to it.

The economic forms of this resistance have already been described. But it also assumed an extreme political form: uprisings. In another context, Barrington Moore makes the following relevant general observation: "What infuriates peasants (and not just peasants) is a new and sudden imposition or demand that strikes many people at once and that is a break with accepted rules and customs."[56] More specifically, Medvedev comments that without hope of success and without the support of the middle peasantry, "the majority of the kulaks would have been incapable of the decision to institute a counterrevolutionary terror. Unfortunately, in numerous provinces and regions the kulaks were neither isolated nor neutralized."[57] Bettelheim rejects the slogan of the "offensive against the kulaks" and observes merely that "in 1929 the peasants [undifferentiated, P. C.] observed that the system of 'extraordinary measures' was becoming more and more onerous and that they had begun to be applied uninterruptedly. . . . Disturbances even broke out in certain regions." The unreliability of the sources permits only a very rough estimate of the scope of these disturbances. Kozlova, quoted by Cohen, mentions in *Moskovskie Kommunisty* more than 2,000 officially recorded peasant demonstrations, some of them violent, in the province of Moscow alone.[58]

The most important consideration for Shapiro is not the magnitude of peasant disturbances but their extensive and intensive dynamic, and above all their prospects. ''To a party for which its own monopoly of power had by now become an obsession, the danger that here was the beginning of a national peasant movement which might grow strong enough to threaten it may have seemed real enough.'' In his view this danger perhaps even explains the victory of the Stalinists and the Party leadership. ''There was however another reason, apart from fear of disciplinary reprisals, which may have rallied the Party at this date against its right-wing critics. There was open war in the villages, and the desperate peasants did not hesitate to kill any communists.''[59]

There are two important implications to all this. First, the government's action in 1929, specifically the expropriation of the peasantry, was also a reaction to the unrest among the peasantry itself. This retaliatory quality merits more attention than has usually been given to it. Second, the critical aspect of peasant disturbances was not their extent at any particular moment but rather their invariable tendency to be massive and intense whenever they erupted. No sooner did peasant resistance begin to spread than it became peasant violence. The state should in principle have been able to diffuse peasant violence by easing the conditions which sparked it in the first place. But it chose instead to crush it by violence of its own, which it then again later used against the peasants as its principal instrument of expropriation.

Of course insofar it is a crucial component in the primitive accumulation of capital, expropriation of the peasantry is always violent. But in the case of Stalinist expropriation, the inordinate use of violence stemmed from a number of specific factors. First, the agent of expropriation was a constituted but beleaguered power whose one fundamental privilege was its monopoly over the legal use of force. Second, the presumptive target of expropriation was not a segment of peasant property, but rather all the property of a peasantry in open revolt against this power. Moreover, Russia had a centuries-long tradition of peasant uprisings, and now to this were added the two most recent demonstrations whose terrifying potential invested them with a historical dimension: in 1917 the generalized revolt of the peasants destroyed feudalism and with it feudal ownership; and, in the early 1920s, peasant uprisings hastened the decision of the Bolshevik government to abandon war communism and introduce NEP.

On each of these occasions the peasant revolts achieved their end. On this third occasion, however, their end was to reinvest their mutilated ownership with an economic reality, and restore the full attributes of ownership, which would enable the small landowner to dispose in perfect autonomy over his means of production and his product. Consequently the 1920s ended as they had begun: with the same scenario and the same social actors, the peasantry and the state, contending over the same object, agrarian ownership, within the same relational framework with the same principal function, i.e., to separate small agrarian producers from their product, punctuated by the same tendency to transform economic relations into violent confrontation. At the end of the road was Stalinism, which sprang up to break this cycle and constitute itself as a lasting new order.

In both cases the state reacted hastily to the peasant revolts to prevent their spread. But whereas in the first case it yielded to peasant grievances, in the second the peasants were obliged to bow to the demands of the state, which met the violence of the peasant uprisings with mass repression. Beyond political options and personal psychologies, the explanation of the massiveness of repression in Stalinist expropriation of the peasantry lies in the catastrophic concomitance of the famine, the "extraordinary measures," and the peasant uprisings. The latter threatened to plunge the country into a new civil war, directed this time not against the possessing classes, with the peasantry providing crucial assistance, but against the peasantry by a state which, having lost its class base, was breaking down.

The disruptive factors in the two cases were also different. On the earlier occasion, it was the famine rather than the peasant uprisings as such which induced changes in—or at least attempts to change—the structures of postrevolutionary society. The regime did not seem to react with the same alacrity to the threat to its own survival as it did to the danger threatening the population. Assuming this to be a normal priority, which seems reasonable enough, and considering the effects of appropriation—which did little to improve food supplies—it may be presumed that for Stalinism the immediate and principal end of this measure was not to halt the famine but to crush the peasant uprisings—so thoroughly that they could never recur—and insofar as this was indeed the primary end, mass repression of the peasantry was the logical primary means.

In no other case did mass expropriation depend so thoroughly on mass repression as it did in that of the peasantry. After due prevarication, official ideology dubbed this episode a "revolution from above." The persistence of this term seems more significant than the fact that it was chosen in the first place. Its tenacity makes its choice less likely a product of chance than of a conscious weighing of the advantages to be derived from such a term—and for the official ideology such advantages are weightier than any negative connotations the term may have.

These advantages would have mainly to do with the legitimacy of the new social order. The apologetic intent of the term "revolution from above" is to make acceptable if not desirable the stark reality of a supreme authority above society, with the implication that society has only to gain from unconditional submission to it. If that is so then there would be nothing more natural than to delegate crucial initiatives to this entity, which alone possessed the requisite strength and competence not only to decide what individual and group behavior was most appropriate, but also to effect the most thorough and radical transformations in social structures. If this is so, it is necessary to reject the bucolic image the term "revolution from above" attempts to project, and instead endeavor to bring clarity to the fundamental reality it conceals—a reality which consists in making repression from above the principal mechanism for the restructuring of society. Therefore, despite the vested interest of the official ideology in this expression, there are definite limits to its validity.

A first objection is of a general order. All Stalinist societies are subject to absolute control from above by virtue of the global monopoly enjoyed by the state. To concede a revolutionary potential to this control is tantamount to giving implicit recognition to the revolutionary credentials of the monopoly exercising it, and secondarily to the potential socialist nature of its undertakings. A second objection is theoretical. It has become all but commonplace to recognize the decisive role played by mass repression in the expropriation of the peasantry and then derivatively to define, or accept the definition of, this historical episode as a "revolution from above." Clearly the theoretical problem is that of the compatibility between mass repression and revolution. The third and last objection is also theoretical: it can be argued that the expression "revolution from above" is a contradiction in terms.

These three objections can in essence be reduced to a simple syllogism of sorts: (1) any social revolution brings about crucial changes in the basic structures of a society; (2) not every change in the basic structures of a society is necessarily caused by social revolution; and (3) the emergence of Stalinism in general and the expropriation of the peasantry in particular are crucial changes in the basic structure of postrevolutionary Russia which were not the work of social revolution but of centralized repression. Thus there are two paths toward structural change, of which the principal difference is their agent: the agent of revolution is the masses acting against a constituted power, that of repression is a constituted power acting against the masses.

The term "revolution from above" has perhaps been so readily accepted because it was not in fact the invention of Stalinist ideology, but was borrowed by the latter from the classic literature of Marxism. Following Marx, who described the works of Louis Napoleon Bonaparte's reign as a "revolution from above," Engels used the term in his critique of the Erfurt program to describe the political feats of Bismarck. In its ideological usage, however, the term neither refers to the same type of phenomenon nor implies the same value judgment. In the classic literature it was an allegorical expression designating a preponderantly political transformation of which Marx and Engels were clearly critical. Stalinist ideology, on the other hand, takes the term literally, endeavoring to raise it to the status of a theoretical, totally apologetic concept designating a social transformation. Moreover, none of the periods referred to by the classics witnessed anything even approaching the mass repression that accompanied Stalinist expropriation of the peasantry. We can of course not be certain that Marx and Engels might not have used the same metaphor even had such repression taken place, but one thing is sure: that unlike Stalinist ideologists, they did not use the term to dissemble real repression under the guise of its very opposite.

On the other hand, insofar as it uses the term, Stalinist ideology implicitly admits a minimal resemblance between the genesis of Stalinism and the phenomena to which the classics referred: a resemblance resting on the explicit assumption that these societies are divided into an 'above,' from which all social change must necessarily emanate, and a 'below,' whose function is solely to follow the fiats handed down. And so Stalinist ideology apparently accepts at a symbolic level what it denies at a descriptive level, namely, a real division of the Stalinist order into a global monopoly jealously guarding all social initiative and a society reduced to the role of the executor of this initiative. The presence of this monopoly is too pervasive for the ideology meant to conceal it to avoid indirectly avowing its existence, and therein perhaps lies the sole heuristic value of the term "revolution from above": in this particular case it indicates not the absence but the defeat of the revolution the peasantry was in the process of unleashing from below. In the event, it is not easy to determine whether the "revolution from above" was a revolution or in fact a counterrevolution.

Thus for Tucker, "the Stalinist revolution from above, whatever the contingencies involved in its inception and pattern, was an integral phase of the Russian Revolutionary process as a whole" and, consequently, "Stalinism, despite conservative, reactionary, or counterrevolutionary elements in its makeup, was a revolutionary phenomenon in essence."[60] E. H. Carr seems to incline toward a very similar view,[61] and Deutscher refers to this process as the "second revolution." In contrast, Lewin feels that "in the 1930s, after the deep political revolution of 1917, came the stage of an industrial revolution—and there the legitimate use of the term 'revolution' ended."[62]

But while the classic texts may have inspired the choice of words, it was the brief history of postrevolutionary society that created the preconditions for the action. First, there were the attempts to achieve some of the ends of revolution from above by fomenting revolution from below; then came the effective embarkation upon a revolution from above and, finally, the hasty and recurrent backtrackings to avoid a revolution from below by making concessions from above.

The Bolshevik leadership initially placed great hopes in the committees of poor peasants. The key idea, going back to even before the Revolution, had always been that the Bolshevik Party must ride with objective processes, applying its guiding hand, rather than replacing them. Faithful to the spirit of this principle, relevant decisions should only have accelerated the objective process that was leading ineluctably from the stratification of the peasantry to a social conflict within it. But the actual process was infinitely slower than the Bolsheviks had hoped. And so where history tarried, the Party moved, and rather than the spontaneous creation by the poor peasants of their own committees which the government then hastened to legalize, a government decree was issued on June 11, 1918, creating the committees of poor peasants out of thin air and defining their prerogatives.

In gambling on the anticapitalism of the poor peasants, the Bolsheviks were simply yielding to the constraints created by the victory of their own anticipatory revolution. But the poor peasants seem to have been rather slow to take advantage of this legal structure; in any event, five months later, on November 8, 1918, Lenin declared before the delegates of the committee of poor peasants in the Moscow region: "We have decided to divide the countryside." Thus where legal incentives proved insufficient, political resolve intervened. The resistance of the countryside to internal processes of stratification left but one alternative: stratification was imposed upon it by external decision, i.e., decision from above. Indeed the June decree may be interpreted as an initiative from above undertaken to foment a "revolution from below" which its presumptive social agent had been late in initiating. The slowness below prompted certain changes in perspective above. To think that the division of that vast universe which was the Russian countryside could be the object of a political decision and to announce it publicly are certainly signs enough of abrupt changes in outlook among the leadership. These changes were heralded in by the first "revolution from above," war communism, the second example to which I have referred.

In 1918 as in 1929, generalized expropriation was initiated by the central government, not the popular masses. In this broad sense war communism represented a "revolution from above" and thus as such was the historical precedent for what was to follow eleven years later. A feature common to these two historical interludes was that force played a crucial role in both, suggesting that every revolution from above is based on a particularly broad exercise of force. In 1929, it took the form of repression of the peasant masses by the central government; in 1918 it was in the form of a civil war of the former possessing classes against both the central power and the masses constituting the broad base of the population.

Every revolution involves the use of violence, but not every use of violence is a revolution. If this distinction is not kept clear, revolution and repression, two diametrically opposed social phenomena, are easily confounded. To avoid such confusion, it is essential to establish the agent, the object, and the end of violence. In 1917, the principal agent of violence was directly or indirectly the productive classes of society; the object of violence was the possessing classes and the constituted power, which in fact represented their interests; the end was to divest these classes of their property and their power to the benefit of the productive classes. Nothing even roughly equivalent was the case in 1929, when the agent of violence was a power that had already become centralized; the object was the productive classes, and the end was their total and utter expropriation to the benefit of a global monopoly over power and property. The true character of this latter episode, Lewin tells us, is illustrated by the "emergency measures, the key to which is Article 107 of the Penal Code."[63]

Drafted in 1926 by the Central Executive Committee, this article was directed explicitly against rises in prices, and so against speculation on the market. But, when applied to the essentially nonmercantile relation of procurement, the article became no more than a legal cover for repressive acts against the peasantry. As power became more centralized, it was less able to execute these acts itself, and hence sought support for this undertaking in two areas. The first was the bureau-cracy, which was directly subordinate to it; the second the urban population, and especially the working class, which was the most affected by the food shortages.

There was a duality in the bureaucracy's role in this action which later became a defining characteristic of its general place in the nascent social order. In the repression of the peasantry, and in every other of its activities down to the present, it has been the executor of initiatives which at the practical level it had no hand in determining. Yet despite this exclusion, it has had to bear the whole responsibility for its actions.

Stalin's article "The Year of the Great Turning Point," published in *Pravda*, November 7, 1929, gave the signal that initiated the excesses which he later deplored in another article entitled "The Dizziness of Success," in *Pravda*, March 2, 1930. In thus dissociating itself from its own initiative, the central power placed its apparatus in an extremely delicate situation. A text published in Moscow in 1964 illustrates this predicament through the example of the "dele-gates of collectivization" from the Sosnovskii region, in the Tver district. In mid-February they received the order to complete "collectivization" within five days and to appear before the Regional Committee on February 20 at nine in the morning to present their report on the execution of the order. The order stipulat-ed: "There is no justification for not completing the assigned tasks. Those who have not carried out their mission will be brought to justice within twenty-four hours." During this same period, more than half of the chairmen of village Soviets in certain regions were dismissed. Each of the two articles was followed by mass dismissals of state and party officials, except that after the first they were accused of "right-wing deviationism" and after the second, of "left-wing devia-tionism." Medvedev tells us that there were mass purges of local officials during the spring of 1930 in numerous oblasts, and in a number of raions "left-wing deviationists" were brought to trial.[64] This split character of the apparatus, designed to ensure both the real efficiency and the illusory infallibility of the monopoly, was revealed in its full light by the drama of the events surrounding the expropriation of the peasantry. This character would remain as an inalienable trait of the new social order. As servile and submissive to power as it was tyrannical toward the population, Stalinist bureaucracy challenges by the duplicity of its social position those theories which ascribe to it a leading role in society.

The government also appealed to workers' detachments in the dekulakization campaign, but they were less important for their effective contribution—they were apparently relatively few in number judging from the documents of the period—than for their actual social significance. After all, workers certainly had an intense interest in improving the food supply to the cities, and the fact that such workers' detachments existed and were active would, it was presumably hoped, give centralized repression the appearance of a mass campaign. But the net effect turned out to be quite different. It caused the peasantry to lose, together with the last vestiges of its property, every illusion it might still have harbored concerning its alliance with the proletariat. The rupture between the two productive classes at this crossroads of history created a new source of indirect but substantial power wholly under the control of the monopoly. Claims of official ideology to the contrary, the involvement of one expropriated productive class in the expropriation of the other merely accentuated the centralization of power. More and more, the state became the sole regulator and real beneficiary of the social use of force, independently of its direct executors in the particular case. As it overstepped class relations, centralization of ownership became inseparable from centralization of force.

The centralized use of force would fulfill three principal functions: it would permit the monopoly to entrench itself; it would ensure its perpetuation by forestalling every attempt at weakening its domination; and it would give the monopoly the best and most effective instrument for extra-economic control of all economic and social activity. Though projected over the long term, these functions were made possible by the pursuit of an immediate end, that of quelling peasant violence through the state's use of its own centralized violence. Government tactics in 1929 seemed to take their inspiration from the measures employed by Lenin in 1918. In both cases, power capitalized on an extremely adverse situation to effect changes in the social structure that were adjudged by doctrine to be legitimate. But whereas in the first case these changes vanished into thin air along with the situation that had permitted them, in the second the structural changes would long outlive the original situation. The changes wrought by Stalinism in the social structure through the use of repression were able to persist only through the continued potential or actual use of repressive methods. The social reorganization of the Soviet countryside which has lasted to the present day has perpetuated the effects of the repression that accompanied the historical process leading from the smashing of peasant uprisings to ultimate expropriation.

The historical process which gave birth to Stalinism thus took the roles assigned by repression and set them in stable structures specific to the new social order. If that order was repressive in its nature, it was not because it effectively perpetuated mass repression, but because it perpetuated the possibility of repression. As the last three decades have shown, this social order is very well able to survive without recourse to mass repression—on condition, however, that the possibility of such recourse is permanently inscribed in the predominant social relationships. Once the repressive process had been crystalized into a lasting and stable social structure, the relations begotten by repression could be perpetuated without necessarily perpetuating repression itself. It is precisely this circumstance which gives the term ''revolution from above'' its invidious character: by attempting to give generic repression the appearance of its opposite, it conceals the true antecedents which have permitted contemporary Stalinism to enjoy the fruits of mass repression without being necessarily obliged to exercise it. The constitution of a global monopoly was, it seems, the crucial event that made possible the passage from repressive action to repressive structure.

It is of course always better for the population if the state refrains from the use of mass repression. But the absence of repression does not necessarily mean progress toward democracy. It may in fact very likely mean a decline in popular resistance to relations of coercion and subordination. A wide range of means, from brutal repression to consensus based on resignation, have been used over the course of history to reproduce these relations, although the relations themselves have been tediously unvarying. The relations that subordinated the productive classes to the global monopoly came to dominate relations between these classes themselves—indeed relations among all of the social groups—until, understandably, they alone prevailed.

The expropriation of the peasantry had specific importance for rural life, quite apart from its more general implications. In a sense it was but the culmination of the long war of attrition which had relentlessly sapped the viability of petty peasant property until it definitively succumbed to the blows of Stalinist repression.

The collective farms that were the lasting result of peasant expropriation served a plurality of ends from the government standpoint. First in importance among these was of course the goal of embarking agriculture upon an anticapitalist path; second, that of reconciling agrarian anticapitalism with agrarian productivity (an end never achieved to this day), and third, that of making this anticapitalist and productive agriculture the economic mainstay of anticapitalist industrialization. The mere listing of these ends makes clear that the one that was least realized was (and would remain indefinitely so) that of achieving a compatibility between anticapitalism and productivity in agriculture. The state succeeded in assuring the stability but not the productivity of the new agriculture. These ends proved to be contradictory, not because they were attempted at the same time, but because one worked to the detriment of the other. The new, economically renegade agriculture paid for its stability with unproductiveness, and the root cause of that unproductiveness lay in the noneconomic foundations on which its stability was based.

The restrictions imposed initially upon petty peasant property had made it both unstable and unproductive. Its abolition brought stability to agrarian ownership but the unproductiveness remained. At a very abstract level, it could be argued that there was an element of progress after all in this transition from a mode of organization that combined unproductiveness with instability to another which combined unproductiveness and stability. Instability in whatever form impedes development if it persists—which is not to say that the converse is true, that stability is a sufficient condition for development. To illustrate the point, agricultural output reached its lowest point in 1933, while the average levels registered during NEP would not be permanently exceeded until after 1948 for cereal grains, and after 1953 for fodder.

It may be argued that, over the long term, Stalinism did not overcome the productivity crisis in agriculture but rather assimilated it. The form it gave to agrarian ownership in the final analysis merely adapted the structure of society to the everlasting imminence of crisis. Stalinism carried the relations which engendered the crisis to their ultimate limits and in doing so absorbed and broadened its principal source. With agrarian ownership totally under its sway, the monopoly proceeded to transform the periodic crisis of agriculture, with its famines, into a chronic and crisis. After the disasters of the first years, the famines, however, would never be repeated. Hence the chronic crisis that has plagued Stalinist agriculture does not reside in the perpetuation of famines, but in the perpetuation of scarcity. And its distinctive feature is the persistence of scarcity even as the means of production in agriculture experienced a relative development. In other words, the output of Stalinist agriculture has grown much more slowly than its technical equipment, and considering how the latter has developed it is difficult to say if actual productivity in Soviet agriculture is superior or inferior to its level in 1929. The level of technical equipment is certainly an important, if not the only, factor in determining economic growth. But in the case of Stalinist agriculture its evident inefficacy evinces a disjunction within the forces of production. For one reason or another, labor employed the technical means placed at its disposal rather unproductively. Actually, the visible shortcomings in the work force were merely the expression of a deeper phenomenon, the incompatibility between the character of the new means of production introduced into agriculture and the character of the social relations which regulated this activity. The mechanized equipment working the land throughout the Soviet countryside was invented elsewhere and employed with better results there as well; in fact it was a creation of capitalism, whereas the social relations based on extra-economic constraint that governed the activity of Stalinist agriculture had a hybrid character, with precapitalist relations predominating. In its attempt to implant forces of production of a capitalist type in a predominantly precapitalist social context, Stalinism merely reconstituted in modified form the syncretism that had given it birth.

Just as it had dissimulated the means it had used to establish the new social relations in the countryside, Stalinism sought to dissimulate the nature of these relations themselves by, for instance, leaving them initially undefined; even the "Statutes for an Agricultural Artel" in force up to 1969 were not adopted until 1935.

The collective farm is a point of intersection, so to speak, between the actual continuity and the formal continuity represented by the legal prescriptions and the ideological projection of this organizational form of agrarian ownership (which sees it as a faithful implementation of the theses of Marx and Engels, not to speak of Lenin). The formal continuity is thus but the reflection in sham legal and doctrinal terms of the very real continuity of those measures which had made the abolition of petty peasant property almost the natural epilogue to the mutilation it had suffered previously. What is more, a series of fundamental similarities persisted between the status of private ownership at the time it was abolished and the newly established so-called cooperative ownership. As was the case with private peasant property, the collective farm does not own its land, has no access to the means of production, and cannot dispose of its product, but is obliged to cede it to the state in quantities and at prices that are regulated not by market relations, but by extra-economic constraint. Neither, of course, could count on any legal guarantee. This being so, kolkhoz property, like petty peasant property, is more a legal fiction than an economic reality. Although there were of course substantial differences which must not be underestimated (I shall come back to these later), within the limits of these similarities the transformation of private peasant property into "kolkhoz property" may be considered as a passage from one legal fiction to another.

It can be argued that it is the breadth of these similarities which largely explains the flexibility of the Stalinist model in its application to agriculture. Several countries with Stalinist regimes have not adopted the kolkhoz organization of agriculture or, having done so, have abandoned it again or modified it considerably. With the partial exception of Hungary, the links between industry and agriculture are not based on economic exchange. Formal ownership may be predominantly private or cooperative, but the decisive regulator of these links remains extra-economic constraint exercised by the same type of global monopoly in each case. Within these limits, small, private peasant property and cooperative property are the possible agrarian variables in a social order whose essence is invariable.

This basic continuity provides, of course, the background to these variations. But, as the foundation of generalized expropriation, the passage from private ownership to the kolkhozes also had important elements of discontinuity which are revelatory of the distinctions between the two Stalinist forms of agrarian organization. These distinctions demonstrate that the essential factor in defining the Stalinist social order and its organization of agriculture is not the form of its legal dissimulation but what in fact it endeavors to dissimulate. As legal fictions, private ownership and cooperative ownership conceal the same economic reality: namely, the dissimulated appropriation of all agrarian property by the global monopoly.

The absorption of kolkhoz property by the monopoly was total, embracing both its material substance, i.e., the land and industrial farm equipment, and its functional attributes. It may be recalled that to lessen the paradox of an agrarian ownership legally deprived of the principal means of agricultural production, Khrushchev attempted to transfer the machinery and tractor stations to the kolkhozes—a decision which contributed materially to his fall. At issue was more than a mere practical question; indeed the material and formal separation between this form of agrarian ownership and its means of production constituted the economic base of the total subordination of the kolkhozes by the monopoly. By eroding this base, Khrushchev created the potential for the kolkhozes to acquire greater autonomy, which would of course have weakened the position of the monopoly. This is why the post-Khrushchev leadership lost no time in restoring the old order of things as soon as it came to power. Thus a crude attempt to improve productivity at the price of the monopoly's relinquishing a part, be it ever so small, of its total power abruptly ended with the resolute return to the traditional and time-honored usage of sacrificing the productivity of labor for the sake of continued omnipotence.

Whereas the monopoly's control over the material form of kolkhoz ownership, i.e., the land and the industrial equipment used to work it, was explicit and legally validated, with regard to the attributes of that ownership, the monopoly routinely acted in abusive and despotic disregard of legal prescriptions. Formally, the general assembly of the kolkhoz members is legally empowered to decide on all matters concerning kolkhoz activity. In fact, the general assembly is under dual subordination: it is subordinate both to the central state plan and to the local bureaucratic bodies which appoint the members of the kolkhoz administration. Thus, in strictly functional terms, the general assembly is the equivalent of the Supreme Soviet, that is, it is a ratifying institution. It is unable to decide any major question which according to its statutes should fall within its authority— whether with respect to production, the use of the product, or the remuneration of the members of the cooperative. As Marie Lavigne observes, "The Soviet experience shows that the readiness of the authorities to carry out plans at any price provoked the peasants to reactions that were extremely damaging for the further growth of agriculture."[66] Thus the situation of the general assembly was one in which the status of law was typical of the status to which law is generally reduced in Stalinist society. Another institution, the plan, moved in to take its place, operating with the force of natural law to render practically nugatory all the prerogatives with which the general assembly had been formally invested by agrarian legislation.

But the pressures of the plan, though intense, are at least defined. More debilitating by far are the arbitrary and undefined pressures of the local authorities and the individuals representing them. A vast and intricate tangle of overlapping and conflicting interests, both real and illusory, convergent and contradictory, turned the kolkhozes into an inexhaustible source of abuse, waste, peculation, and corruption. Gorbachev's ambitious campaign against these symptoms stops short of their causes. These illicit activities are so extensive as to gravely restrict the monopoly's effective control over agriculture. Measures taken to strengthen this control have traditionally tended to focus on the symptoms while consolidating their deeper causes. A particularly revealing indicator of the extent to which the monopoly controls the kolkhozes is how their numbers have fared over the course of time. Between 1940 and 1968 (the year new agrarian laws went into effect in the USSR) the number of kolkhozes declined from 236,900 to 36,200; that is to say, within an interval of less than thirty years, almost 85 percent of the kolkhozes simply vanished. This tendency toward concentration can hardly be explained by some contagious, self-destructive frenzy of the kolkhozes themselves. The explanation is a much simpler one. For whatever reason, the monopoly willed it. In short, not only does it have the power to decide over the activity and the product of the kolkhoz, but their very existence is dependent ultimately on its grace.

Not only do they not enjoy the rights of ownership over the land they work, the kolkhozes can neither manage nor administer their own activities. These are the cardinal realities of the institution of the kolkhoz; they are in fact a forceful demonstration that the universal institution of the kolkhoz form of ownership was merely the particular guise in which the universal expropriation of the peasantry was consummated in extremis. Private peasant property did not become the collective property of the whole of the peasantry, but in fact the possession of the self-same global monopoly that had already all industrial means of production and all power in its hands.

Condemned to this uncertain and divided existence, the kolkhozes bore a double burden: they were called upon to stand in not only for monopolist ownership as such, but also for the form of this ownership that would be most able to sustain the industrialization effort. Agriculture, through the kolkhozes, was supposed to become the principal source of accumulation and cheap labor on the one hand, while on the other was to be prevented from manifesting its needs as a natural market for industrial products. It hardly need remarking that, thanks to the kolkhozes, the relationship between agriculture and industry was not one of economic cooperation but extra-economic subordination.

The disappearance of private peasant property by no means did away with the necessity of providing industry with agrarian products on terms more favorable to the latter. Quite to the contrary, it was to better satisfy this need that peasant property was replaced by kolkhoz property. The kolkhozes, in becoming the general instrument to that end, changed only the context of this unequal relation but not the principal mechanism for assuring its efficacy. Regardless of the names given it by various official sources, in substance the mechanism of procurements remained the preponderant instrument in the practical regulation of relations between a rapidly growing industry and kolkhoz agriculture. But it was also true that the new social context afforded by the kolkhozes created conditions which enabled the procurement mechanism to function much more effectively.

Under NEP, the state had to confront the resistance of a peasant invested (or at least so he considered himself) with two roles: that of proprietor and that of producer of a product over which the procurements prevented him from freely disposing. The loss of the first of these put the peasant in the unviable position of creating a product over the use of which he no longer had any say. So long as he had retained title to his private holding the peasant had spontaneously opposed the excesses of the procurements. The heads of the kolkhozes, on the other hand, were the appointed representatives of the state on which their position consequently depended. They therefore had a vested interest in ensuring the fulfillment of the procurement plan, whether excessive or not. Instead of creating an external confrontation with millions of peasants, the procurements became an internal question of the state presuming cooperation among its different agents. The principal advantage of the kolkhozes, therefore, was that their institution shielded the peasant from the procurement operations, the object of which was, as always, the product of his labor. Procurements still remained the paramount and vital relation between agriculture and industry but ceased to be a directly social relation and became essentially a bureaucratic one. As such the procurements are a particularly revealing example of the transformation of an economic relation of exchange into an extra-economic relation of coercion. The bureaucratization of social relations is a metamorphosis which engulfs the whole of social life in Stalinist societies, giving them the "monolithism" that is their specific hallmark.

With the establishment of the kolkhozes, a specious peace returned to the countryside. The procurements, formerly the source of interminable and direct confrontation between the central power and the majority of the population, marked by a plethora of explosive conflicts, were henceforth transformed into a specific, practical administrative routine. Grain harvests were effectively processed in reverse order. Formerly, the grain had passed directly into the hands of those who harvested it, the peasants, and it had been the task of the administration to wrest it from them. Deliveries to the state depended to a high degree on the peasants. But under the kolkhoz regime it went directly to the administration, which would then decide on the amount to be conceded to the peasants; henceforth peasant consumption depended entirely on deliveries to the state. The function of power vis-à-vis the peasants was no longer that of contending over grain but of allocating it. This marked a crucial turn, for it was by extending this function of allocation to the entire economy that the new power would succeed in rendering its domination absolute. "Disposition over the surplus," comment Fehér, Heller, and Markus, "always realizes some definite form of its appropriation. If no specific social group can be located with a formally acknowledged right to the latter, then the question of ownership is a question of the character of these activities of distribution of surplus and ultimately a question of the social determinants of this distribution."[66] Generalized expropriation became centralized allocation, and the allocating monopoly became the veritable regulator of all economic activity.

This allocating function, a function whose execution is quintessentially subjective and covers the whole of society, is the one identifying trait of the Stalinist monopoly which distinguishes it from every other type of monopoly. The breadth and depth of its application is utterly pervasive, so much so that the most diverse social categories are persuaded that their docile submission to centralized extra-economic constraint is in their own interests. At the same time, because of its extreme degree of centralization and the subjectivism this fosters, both the allocating function and the monopoly exercising it have a natural tendency to become personified. The penchant toward passive compliance that characterizes the regular functioning of Stalinist societies can be largely explained by this inherent subjectivism of the allocating monopoly.

And so, in the case of Russia, an interlude punctuated by the most brutal exercise of centralized repression against the masses enabled the monopoly to put an end to the diffuse repression that had always accompanied the procurements in an agricultural system based on small private plots. Its disruptive impact was absorbed by the new social context, and the mechanism of procurements was transformed from a generator of social conflicts into a pillar of a social order in which centralized extra-economic constraint was not merely imposed, but was also made acceptable. Under NEP, the procurements were required to separate the peasantry from its product while it maintained some possession of its means of production; under the kolkhoz regime, separating the peasantry from its product and separating it from its means of production were but complementary aspects of a single process. In the end the most momentous effect of this change consisted of the radical reduction of the sheer social energy that had to be expended for the mechanism of procurements to function. Once the peasants were separated from their means of production through the establishment of the kolkhozes, the acquisition of their product was ensured a priori insofar as it was built into the kolkhoz structure. It was henceforth no longer necessary after each harvest to repeat a process which invariably required the extensive use of repression that provoked, just as invariably, extensive resistance. The mass repression that had made possible the expropriation of the peasantry and their forcible concentration into the kolkhozes could now be dispensed with. Indeed the role played by repression in the procurements was to a large degree taken over by the new rural social structure. But the easing of repression hardly signified a step in the direction of democracy, or even merely of peasant consensus; quite to the contrary, it signified hardly more than the forelorn acceptance of the results of oppression.

The passage from repression, which incites resistance, to oppression, which encourages connivance, obviously brings relief and even considerable positive benefits to the population. At the same time, however, it contributes substantially to the stabilization of the new social order and to the de-dramatization of daily life in general in Stalinist societies. Now grossly disguised as accepted oppression, the repressive nature of the society henceforth has a much broader purpose than the formal deprivation of freedom. Its primary aim is no less than freedom's socially assimilated, utter deterioration, i.e., the repressive organization of the formal state of freedom.

To change the principal social relations in this regard, generalized expropriation had also to effect lasting changes in the principal social bearers of these relations. Thus, abruptly, after having been undergoing a process of unrestrained stratification, the peasantry acquired a homogeneity never hitherto achieved. But because of the ways and conditions in which it was achieved, rather than strengthen the social identity of the class, this homogenization merely rendered it even more undefined. This retrogression is owed in part to the fact that the fundamental social relations maintained by the kolkhoz peasantry were relations of subordination to the monopoly, and as such they did not differ essentially from those linking that monopoly to the other productive class. Because of the universal nature of expropriation, the impact of homogenization was not felt by each productive class individually, but undifferentiatedly by the totality of these classes. Thus the overarching concept of "productive classes" might be profitably used to provide some important analytical insights.

But the deterioration of the social identity of the peasantry was related to another contextual phenomenon as well, namely, social mobility, which reached unprecedented levels. In losing the vestiges of its ownership, the peasantry lost the principal economic source of its social energy. And it also lost a sizable portion of its human energies in the masses who chose to migrate to the cities, in their majority the peasantry's hardiest members. The fact that the mass in-pouring of peasants into industry had similar effects on the social identity of the working class is beside the point. For, as the social identity of the monopoly assumed more and more distinct contours, to the point of its ultimately becoming personified in a single individual, the social identity of the two directly productive classes tended to lose definition to the point of frequent interpenetration—a phenomenon noted by sociologists and admitted even by official ideology. If one then adds the systematic destruction of its own organizations, one completes the picture of the most important factors behind the striking docility manifested in Stalinist societies by the proletariat and, to an even greater degree, by the peasantry. First in Russia after the completion of expropriation, next in Hungary after the victory over Nazi Germany in 1956, then in Czechoslovakia in 1968, and most recently in Poland in 1970 and 1980, history has provided abundant proof of the particular talent of the Stalinist social order to render the peasantry politically inert and to keep it in that state regardless of circumstances.

c. The state monopoly

No one who has dealt with the problem has any doubt that the advent of Stalinism entailed the transformation of bother agriculture and the power structure. There are specialized disciplines which study each of these transformations, but studies of their interconnection are infinitely more rare. If I have dwelt on the transformation of the state monopoly into a global monopoly above the state it is because this transformation was integral to the process of generalized expropriation, and I have therefore thought it essential to center my analysis on the connection between the two. In describing this connection, it is not very useful to begin with political relations and then illustrate their evolution with examples of an economic and social nature. What is essential, rather, are the economic and social transformations which the monopoly was able immediately to effect without, however, being able to control their consequences. One of these uncontrollable consequences was the transformation of power itself as an integral component in the general changes that swept through the whole of society. From this perspective the great conflicts that took place within the Party leadership, the material embodiment of power, are of secondary importance relative to the transition from one institutionalized form of control to another, each representing a specific type of monopoly.

This analytical strategy is clearly inspired by my general hypothesis that the transformation of relations of ownership is one of the determining factors in the historical process leading from postrevolutionary society to the Stalinist social order. A corollary to this general hypothesis is a special hypothesis according to which the specific form which Stalinism gives to ownership is that of a monopoly held by power, distinct not only from monopolies of the capitalist type, but also from the state monopoly which had preceded it.

The term "monopoly" is frequently and variously used in the literature on Stalinism. The diversity of the conflicting interpretations given to the term, which is touted as a defining trait of Stalinism, is indicative of the confusion concerning this subject.

"The government both administers and distributes national property," Djilas wrote in *The New Class*. "The new class or its executive organ—the Party oligarchy—both acts as the owner and is the owner. The most reactionary and bourgeois government can hardly dream of such a monopoly in the economy."[67] But while emphasizing the existence of the monopoly, Djilas gives no clear indication of who exercises it, nor over what it is exercised. It must be presumed from the assertion that it only administers and, specifically, distributes national property that it does not possess it. As for the social vehicle of the monopoly, this statement suggests a multitude of possibilities: it could be the "new class" in its totality; its executive organ—an institution common to various types of organizations, but not to social classes; the government; or, implied but not said, unspecified groups and persons who probably benefit from such distribution of national property.

It is quite possible that some of these incongruities are not alien to Djilas's special experience with the situation in his country, whose economic and social singularities are incontestable. Ernest Mandel offers an example that is reflective of the Marxist critique of the phenomenon: "The root of the evil, the historical meaning of the bureaucratic dictatorship, is the totality of the postcapitalist mechanisms and institutions that maintain the monopoly over administration and management in all spheres of social life and the monopoly over general labor in the hands of a privileged minority."[68] This description dwells less on the specific traits of a Stalinist-type monopoly than on certain aspects which it has in common with other similar institutions. For example, there is no monopoly which is not controlled by a minority, specifically, a privileged minority. But what is essential is the social localization of this minority—if it can be called a minority—in Stalinist societies and, accordingly, the description of the specific traits which distinguish it from every other minority enjoying otherwise more or less comparable privileges. According to this concept, the attributes of Stalinist monopoly do not include the function of ownership but are limited to administration—a common characteristic of every modern state—and to management, but a management without owners. On the other hand, the phrase "monopoly over general labor" seems to indicate, despite its excessive laconism, an extremely fertile direction of analysis insofar as it focuses on relations which would appear to be fundamental between the monopoly and the aggregate labor force. Another suggestion worthy of exploration is one which, with regard to mechanisms and institutions, locates the monopoly in a specific social environment defined, in my opinion inexactly, as postcapitalist (the confusion between noncapitalism and postcapitalism is probably more politically than theoretically motivated).

I will cite a last example, in the end only a phrase, but a phrase which has the advantage of containing two highly pertinent imprecisions, namely, Bahro's term "the monopolism of the Soviet state."[69] Interestingly, each of the three major words in this phrase carries a weight of its own. First, the choice of the word "monopolism" suggests that the importance of the monopoly is sufficient to define this type of social organization in its totality. Second, in accordance with a tradition that has come down to us from Weber intact, the monopoly is attributed to the state, although this ignores a crucial characteristic of the historical passage from postrevolutionary society to Stalinism. Finally, the adjective "Soviet" has the uninspiring function of reducing a phenomenon whose international dimension has endured for forty years to its original national limits. Beyond diversities, all arising to some degree or another through doctrinal considerations, all countries with a Stalinist social organization maintain and uphold structures rigorously dominated by global monopoly; the differences amount basically to variations in the functioning of these common structures. Although a study of the ways and means whereby this type of monopoly was constituted for the first time in history is of unquestionable importance, it would be an unwarranted omission to ignore its capacity to survive and proliferate in countries and under historical circumstances that are sometimes quite distinct.

But an awareness of the existence and importance of the monopoly in the social organization of postrevolutionary Russia is not exclusive to scholars looking back over the past and attempting to comprehend it. The principal political actors of the time also had a keen appreciation of the phenomenon, above and beyond all their divergences: "It would be nonsensical on our part to renounce the utilization of our monopolistic position," declared Bukharin.[70] Long afterward, and in much more explicit words, Stalin affirmed the same in the *Economic Problems of Socialism in the USSR* (1952): "The rational organization of the productive forces, economic planning, and so forth, are not questions of political economy, but of the economic policy of the authorities." While obscuring the real identity of the monopoly, Stalin acknowledges its inherent nature as well as its absolute sovereignty as the sole and exclusive regulator of all economic activity. On this vital point (as well as on quite a number of others) he did not hesitate to borrow the ideas of those whom he had eliminated.

It may be supposed that during the period of generalized expropriation the Bolshevik leadership was divided on the best way to make use of the existing monopoly, while agreeing on the incontestable necessity of preserving it. The establishment of Stalinism may then be seen in this respect as a successful attempt to maintain and consolidate the existing monopoly. But consolidation under the tutelage of Stalinism meant supremacy, and the attainment of supremacy entailed radical transformations in the monopoly itself, as well as in the society over which it was to exercise its absolute domination. A cardinal aspect of this process was the transformation of the state monopoly into a monopoly above the state. Indeed, this aspect is key to an understanding of Stalinism.

If, as I have argued, spontaneity rather than conscious strategy presided over the historical process that gave rise to the Stalinist social order, the first task must surely be to identify the principal factors which helped steer this spontaneous movement in the notorious direction it took. Whatever these factors were, it may be argued that they all derived from one basic circumstance: the state's inability to make effective use of the monopoly to prevent the crises from repeating themselves indefinitely and to embark society resolutely upon a path toward rapid industrialization. In fact, the procurement crises were just so many crises of the state which commanded them.

Insofar as the state holds a monopoly in the economic sphere, its activities in this domain will necessarily influence other spheres of social life as well. It will not be independent of them. Marxist criticism of Stalinism has often turned on Marx's comment on the Second Empire in France: "It was not until Bonaparte II that the state seemed to become completely independent."

Continuing in more general terms the argument which preceded this conclusion, students of Stalinism consider that its advent heralded the state's attainment of total independence vis-à-vis society. But despite their undeniable points in common, these two states, i.e., the state in France under Napoleon III and the state in postrevolutionary Russia under Lenin, are marked by deep differences. In Russia, the exercise of the monopoly over the economy tended to become the state's one decisive function while, in the France of the Second Empire, this function did not even exist. In France, momentary equilibrium in the confrontations between the possessing classes lent the state a certain autonomy as the only agency in any way capable of embodying their potential points of agreement under the ideological guise of the general interest. But this autonomy was political and was limited to political relations; economically, its function seems to have been that of preserving the status quo as much as possible.

In Russia, on the other hand, in no sense could the state be said to have represented the interests of the possessing classes, however confused its relations with the productive classes may have been. There is not the least trace of equilibrium discernible from whatever angle one may approach the question; rather, general disequilibrium prevailed. For neither the state nor the classes that had survived was the status quo the end desired in matters economic. Each had its sights set on change, a change, moreover, which each of the vital actors sought to turn to its own advantage. Finally, the state was far from confining itself to political relations. Rather, it was directly and profoundly, perhaps even primarily, involved in the economic sphere. Consequently it was not, nor did it even claim to be, an autonomous arbitrator, but was openly a direct contender with the social classes for ownership, and hence for a dominant economic position.

As in France or Germany in the 19th century, the return of the state to center stage in postrevolutionary Russia was a necessary consequence of the profound crisis that affected all social classes and their fundamental relationships. But there the similarity ends. Under the weight of the monopoly, the replacement of the classes by the state in Russia spilled over from politics into the economy. The crisis of the social classes—their inability to defend and pursue their own economic interests—was a reflection of an even deeper crisis affecting the very structure of society. Under such conditions the state, which had moved into a position of preeminence to put an end to the crisis, became its perpetuator. The monopoly was born from the circumstance that a state in the process of formation was obliged to assume proprietary functions at a time when the institution of ownership was in the process of becoming destabilized. The failures of ownership were compounded by the failures of the state, which did not increase the monopoly's chances of becoming economically functional. The monopoly, aspiring unsuccessfully to exclusivity, vacillated between attempting to consolidate itself and attempting to pass on its own failings to the various forms of ownership with which it was obliged temporarily to coexist. So did the state attempt to transfer the constraints which history had imposed upon it to the society as a whole.

The diverse factors which prevented the new postrevolutionary state from exercising its unifying function, thereby aggravating its general social inefficacy, may be traced to three basic sources: the historical circumstances, the specific nature of its social environment, and its position in the latter.

More specifically, the historical circumstances were the aftereffects of social upheaval, which make it extremely difficult for any society to recover the minimal cohesion necessary to move from social cohabitation to the establishment of a new and stable social order. In Russia, this difficulty was further aggravated by the anticipatory nature of the Revolution. The state's incapacity to fulfill its unifying role ran the entire gamut of social relations: relations between the productive classes and the former ruling classes; the state's own relations with the latter; and, finally, its relations with the productive classes. In the last case, instead of representing these classes, it tended, as a consequence of anticipation, to substitute itself for them. In a first show of this tendency, instead of supporting the attempts of the working class to appropriate the industrial means of production, the state placed them under its own monopoly.

The specific social environment which impeded the state in its unifying function was anticipation's most profound effect: this was syncretism, with the ensuing impossibility of unifying politically or economically a society whose fundamental structures were in a state of such profound disarticulation.

Finally, the specific position of the state in this environment was defined by the fact that the socially anticapitalist character of this environment was crucially dependent on this structural syncretism. The state's dual monopoly over public power and the industrial means of production provided the cement it needed to maintain a certain stability in this fluid environment, something which the productive classes, lacking such resources, would not have been able to do. The state's property was the positive reason for its opposition to the appropriation of the respective means of production by the two productive classes. The negative grounds for its opposition of course were the evident incapacity of the proletariat to assume the functions of ownership and of the peasantry to exercise these functions within the anticapitalist social framework established by the Revolution. The result was that, in defending or expanding its monopoly, the state in effect did more to protect this anticapitalist framework than it did to integrate the productive classes into it. Instead of unifying what were in Poulantzas's words "the private actors, immersed in economic antagonisms,"[71] the postrevolutionary state tended to become the principal instigator of these antagonisms with regard to petty peasant property. In this way, the basic antagonism itself changed in content inasmuch as it no longer pitted groups of private agents against one another, but the public power against all private agents in their totality.

A state monopoly seems in general to be economically ineffectual. Contemporary repeated vacillation between nationalizations and denationalizations in countries such as France or England is enough to show that these failings are proper to every modern state and not just to postrevolutionary Russia. It is a reasonable assumption that this ineffectuality of state ownership, which transcends different political structures and stages of economic development, has certain general causes. One of these presumably is that, at the level they have in general reached in our era, the productive forces are no longer stimulated by the transfer of the functions of ownership from the domain of class relations to power relations. Insofar as this is so, the extent of state ownership in postrevolutionary Russia and the relative underdevelopment of the productive forces probably further aggravated the problem.

But, unlike that of contemporary England and France, the state in postrevolutionary Russia transferred the functions of ownership to a domain beyond class relations. In the process, it altered its social identity, its intentions and beliefs notwithstanding; it ceased being a class state. Its very special historical role thus gave rise to quite specific consequences over and above the general operative factors. Among these consequences are certainly two basic contradictions: the first between its ownership of the industrial means of production and its class legitimacy; the second between relations of ownership based on state ownership in industry and the class nature of the social relations that were still dominant. Both economically ineffectual and politically illegitimate, this form of ownership put to the test both the power that held the monopoly and the monopoly itself.

The catastrophic situation in agriculture was doubtlessly among the circumstances which led to the transformation of the state monopoly into a monopoly beyond the state. Agriculture was still privately owned and did not yet come under the state monopoly; hence its crisis should not have been a crisis of the latter. But the real situation was far from clear cut. The crisis in agriculture was, above all else, a profound crisis in relations between the peasantry and the state. At its origins was the state's attempt through the procurements to institute a *de facto* monopoly over the product of a property that did not belong to it.

The basic idea of NEP was to win the peasantry over to the path of anticapitalism by means of economic competition rather than extra-economic constraint. The the procurement crisis put an end to this idea. In its zeal to root out (real or imaginary) capitalist elements, the state ultimately succumbed in its policies to what in fact were capitalist-type relations. Incapable of controlling these relations, the state simply obstructed their functioning, yet without succeeding in establishing alternative, workable relations in their place. The state's opposition to capitalism put it in opposition to the social relations naturally required for the development of the productive forces in an agricultural context that was still feudal in all but the word. Politically crushed, economically disfigured, and socially disenfranchised, capitalism yet endured on the strength of this natural need, reinforced by the inconsistency of the state's agrarian policy. The state, in short, had lost the contest, and to avoid the consequences of this loss, Stalinism chose not only to cancel the contest but also to get rid of the contenders.

The difficulties inherent in state ownership of any kind were multiplied in the case of the Stalinist monopoly by the historically unprecedented breadth and range of its possessions and prerogatives. It had practically the totality of the industrial sector in its grip: the means of production, the resources and raw materials, the exclusive right to hire, absolute control over prices (including the "price" of procurements and wages), and monopoly over the issue of currency, the banks, and foreign trade.

A simple but crucial question arises: To what extent did this extension of the monopoly's powers parallel the consolidation of the state whose function it was to exercise them? Having just emerged from the Civil War and the War of Intervention, surrounded by international hostility, rent internally by discord and conflict among its agencies and representatives at all levels, the Russian state of the time was characterized neither by its cohesiveness nor its solidity. Continual reshufflings and reorganizations seemed to weaken rather than strengthen it, in contrast to what was occurring with the monopoly it had created. Thus the practical day-to-day routines called into question the capacity of a weak state to exercise a strong monopoly. Two solutions seemed the most likely to surmount this discrepancy: either to buttress the fortifications of the monopoly by fortifying the state or to separate the two. But the Stalinist monopoly was not founded on a consolidated and fortified state, but rather on the relative weakness of the latter. By placing the monopoly in a sphere beyond the state, Stalinism totally transformed its social role. The decisive aspect of this transformation was the removal of all functions of leadership from the state, the effect of which was to reduce it to the status of an ineffectual executive body. Economic expropriation and political subordination went hand in hand, and state monopoly and state power were reduced largely to appearances. The monopoly remained in the grip of power, but the power that held it was no longer the same.

If I have dwelt on these flaws in the state monopoly of postrevolutionary society, it has been neither to impugn its achievements nor to suggest that its transformation into a Stalinist monopoly beyond the state was immanent to it. My purpose has been merely to emphasize the reality of this transformation and to describe the circumstances which made it not only possible but also, to a point, even plausible. The objection that other policies might have led to other developments of course cannot be refuted; nor, however, can it be proven. My concern is not to mention possible alternatives, but to attempt to explain real history. The movement from description to explanation in history is the movement from the chain of perceptible political events to the invisible workings of the latent structures of which these events are but a reflection. A theoretically and methodologically inevitable hypothesis is that what was distinctive about this process in the particular case derived from the contradiction between a genetically destructured society and the natural tendency of every monopoly to consolidate its structures.

In addition to the specific factors of this process there were of course nonspecific factors also operating in postrevolutionary Russia. Describing the specific situation in the United States of another period, Edwin Mansfield remarks: "Some critics of monopoly power and big business are concerned with the centralization of power in the hands of a relatively few firms. . . . Within particular industries, there is considerable concentration of ownership and production."[72] To study this trend, American economists have even developed a special indicator: "the market concentration ratio," which measures the share of the four largest companies in sales and production on a particular market. According to official statistics, this ratio varies between 93 percent in the automobile industry to 4 percent in the printing industry. These examples merely point up the well established fact that the tendency toward centralization and concentration is a general law of development of monopolies. What was special about the context in which this law operated in postrevolutionary society was that the monopoly did not dominate the market for any particular product, but in fact had all the branches of industry under its control. This was an unparalleled degree of centralization of monopolist ownership, and it went far beyond that of the state encharged with exercising that monopoly. Diverse economic organs of the state controlled diverse branches, but no central body controlled them effectively in their totality. Insofar as it provided a solution to this discrepancy, the victory of Stalinism over the state may be regarded as a victory of the general law of monopolies, which dictates their centralization, over the relative diffuseness of ownership within the state. The tendency toward centralization of control over monopolist property was therefore also reinforced by the lack of control over the monopoly's spontaneous tendencies toward centralization. The above hypothesis may then be formulated more clearly: the transformation of the state monopoly into a monopoly beyond the state, which was decisive for the transformation of postrevolutionary society into the Stalinist social order, did not take place in accordance with the laws of the transition to socialism as the official ideology would have it, but rather in conformity with the general laws of monopolist ownership. As it centralized at the level it did, power adapted to the form of property over which it had control, and in that sense it was property in this particular form which controlled power. Similarly, the victory of Stalinism was the victory of the spontaneity inherent in monopolist ownership over the spontaneity of every other form of ownership and over every strategic intent.

The state monopoly pretended to be no more than it was in reality; but the suprastate monopoly, once it was formed, continued to operate as if it were in the hands of the state and so assumed a false identity. Like the analogous transformation of the revolutionary party into a bureaucratic organization, the transformation of the state monopoly into a monopoly with its seat beyond the state, a "suprastate monopoly" so to speak, is one of those moments of profound discontinuity which Stalinism conceals under the cloak of formal continuity, although the dissimulation was rendered much more transparent in the case of the bureaucratization of the Party by the persistent criticisms voiced within its ranks. The distinction between the state monopoly and the Stalinist suprastate monopoly, therefore, calls for careful explanation. First, the historical processes which led to the constitution of the two types of monopoly were different. The state monopoly began with the anticapitalist organization of ownership as its basic premise; it was the misadventures and limitations of its subsequent evolution which set the conditions for the suprastate monopoly which would later replace it.

The emergence of the first was gradual: it existed still only in embryonic form after the Revolution; during the Civil War it underwent boundless but ineffectual growth, while in the competitive environment of NEP it refined considerably its specialized functions, but lost a substantial portion of its cohesiveness. In contrast, the emergence of the Stalinist monopoly was precipitate: it tended to embrace the whole almost as soon as it was instituted. The state monopoly was born at the outbreak of a civil war and consolidated itself in victory. The Stalinist monopoly was born to prevent civil war through centralized repression. In the first case, the state won the civil war thanks to the crucial support of the peasantry. A broad dependency on the peasantry was the necessary consequence, and this dependency was extremely influential in the decision to adopt NEP. In the second case, civil war was averted by crushing the peasantry and reducing it to utter dependency, and this dependency, subsequently imposed on the whole of society, would become the vital and hence constant social relation in the new order. Accelerated by the Civil War, the expansion of the state monopoly took place within the context of an absolutely devastated economy. The constitution of the suprastate monopoly, preceded by NEP, took place in a crisis economy which nonetheless had passed through a stage of reconstruction in several industrial branches. What this meant was that during the course of its existence the state monopoly had accumulated sufficient resources to facilitate the later industrializing achievements of the Stalinist monopoly. Yet it had also amassed sufficient failings to legitimate the latter's stabilization.

The immediate circumstances surrounding the transformation of one monopoly into the other was defined by two intersecting processes: (1) generalized expropriation with practically exhaustive centralization of ownership as its corollary, and (2) the growing subordination of the whole of society, including the state, with as its corollary the emergence of a dominant seat of authority exempt from all social control. The state monopoly contributed amply to both processes, and in doing so contributed to its own downfall as well.

Several theoretical questions intrude: the question of the withering away of the state posed by Marx and periodically revived by official Stalinist ideology; the question of the subordination of society to the state or "state socialism," which has had a seemingly boundless fascination for some critics of Stalinism; and finally, the question of the specialized functions of the state in this social order, a question of interest to all parties. Some clarification of these questions is in order.

What assures Gorbachev his preeminence today is not his supreme function in a state which knows no supremacy, but his supreme function beyond the state. It is this function which, while dispensing with formal definition, renders he who fills it—and who has no state function—the one and only authority, recognized as such by the most powerful nations of the world. Arkady Shevchenko, as informed as anyone on the subject, has this to say: "It may be difficult for people used to pluralistic systems to grasp that the Supreme Soviet (the parliament), 'the highest body of state authority' according to the Constitution of the USSR, and the Council of Ministers, supposedly 'the highest executive and administrative body,' are absolutely and permanently controlled by the Politburo.''[73]

It has long been a kind of erroneous commonplace that Stalinist countries are controlled by a strong state, when in fact the situation of the state is marked by a very high degree of ambiguity. Its severity with regard to its citizens, enhanced by the hardly more than ornamental role of legal regulations, is matched only by its total submission to the suprastate authority upon which it is totally dependent and against which it is literally utterly defenseless. Its true condition is that of an oppressed oppressor, and the picture portrayed by the theorists of "statism" is wrong in that it shows only its oppressor nature while ignoring its oppressed nature. In consonance with the functional requirements of the Stalinist social order, the state must be both weak enough to submit unconditionally to the absolute domination of the source of real authority and strong enough to impose that authority's command on the rest of society. The relations of subordination which the suprastate monopoly imposes on the productive classes for the effective exercise of its domination are mediated by the state. Thus, unlike these classes, the state does not only submit to these relations, it is also their principal transmitter. Although perceived by the population as the one and only power, the state is in actuality only an instrument of power and its outward guise. An eloquent illustration of this unique condition is the fact that Yagoda, Yezhov, and Beria, the three grand masters of the Stalinist mass repressions, which they orchestrated from their positions in the state, themselves met their ends at the hands of the executioner.

Hannah Arendt also refers to the "coexistence of an ostensible and a real government" specifying that "Stalin had to revive his shadow government which in the early thirties had lost all its functions and was half forgotten."[74] By tradition, power and state tend to intermingle. But although the reality of Stalinist society belies this merger, not only is it imputed to Stalinism, it is even made into its defining characteristic by the various subcategories of "statism." To truly understand these societies, the "instrumental" role to which the state is reduced must be adequately appreciated. The concept of a suprastate power may be helpful in this respect. Putting aside Krushchev's slogan of "the state of all the people," it might appear that by reducing the state to a subaltern position both economically and politically, Stalinism was in fact promoting its "withering away." But in reality, the role of the state, though eclipsed, did not become less global nor less indispensable. Far from "withering away," as the classic texts had imagined it, the state extended its sway into every domain of social life. As the suprastate monopoly extended its control from police surveillance into the realm of economic planning and ideological purity in the arts, the state, as the principal instrument of this control, expanded to the point of becoming all but ubiquitous. As the executor of a power it did not hold, and encharged with the management of a property it did not own, the state lost its social primacy but gained thereby immensely in instrumental importance and in its role as an oppressive force. Rather than withering away, the state changed its role from the exercise of a partial and imperfect monopoly to that of the principal instrument of a global monopoly. In being relieved of the direct functions of monopoly control, the state also lost the principal source of its weakness: in subordinating itself to the global monopoly it was constrained to become all the stronger as an instrument in the hands of the true seat of power. Strong yet weak, its essence virtually defined by this contradiction, the Stalinist state compensated for its diminished status in the vertical hierarchy of power by the practically limitless horizontal extension of its sway over the whole of social life.

This brings us to the third theoretical problem. The mutation in the role of the state was only one aspect of the general reassignment of roles which ultimately went to make up the new social order. From the very beginning, the function of ownership could become real for the revolutionary power only through its adequate exercise of the function of management. Accordingly, throughout its entire existence, the state monopoly also regularly intermingled these two functions in its activities; in other words, its function as owner was reduced to that of managing. Now, as the evolution of capitalist monopolies show, the tendency toward centralization necessarily entails the tendency toward a separation between ownership and management. Following this same tendency, Stalinism merely reproduced this movement in its own way, namely, by transforming the state monopoly into a monopoly with a seat beyond the state. Relieved of the functions of ownership, the state's functions as manager were henceforth all the more rigorously defined. The functional distinction between ownership and management had its counterpart in a structural distinction between the state and the suprastate monopoly. This, indeed, came to define the predominant structure of the Stalinist social order (it is essential to be clear that the the same functional specialization could be fulfilled by another, different structure). What is characteristic of the Stalinist social order is that the centralized monopoly does not entrust the specific tasks of management to the producers, but to an apparatus designed to make managerial activities into a profession. In the event, the functional disjunction between ownership and management entails a redistribution of social roles which affects not only the supreme suprastate authority and the state, but also the producers, while the state, excluded from ownership but encharged with its management, reigns over the producers, who are excluded from both.

The general laws of development of monopolies—a tendency toward centralization, separation between ownership and management, and transformation of management into a professional activity—thus seem also to have presided over the transformation of the state monopoly of postrevolutionary Russia into a monopoly beyond the state. This points up an antinomy in Stalinist societies, the anticapitalism of which is based on the broad assimilation of the monopolist model. Stalinism opposed the perils of classical capitalist development by embarking upon a course of development characteristic of the most advanced capitalism. Yet, despite these similarities, the Stalinist brand of monopolist control did not become a form *sui generis* of capitalism. Among the factors which have so far prevented such a metamorphosis, four stand out as particularly important. First, the suprastate monopoly embraces not just one branch or group of branches of the economy, but the whole of it. Second, despite this global nature, the monopoly does not have full control over the attributes of ownership—particularly that of appropriation—and to that extent its ownership remains incomplete. Third, at the time of its constitution, the monopoly established its roots in the sphere of power, rather than in the sphere of the economy. Finally, the seat of power constantly cites its anticapitalism as the source of its legitimacy. Accordingly, all these things considered, the Stalinist suprastate monopoly may be defined as a noncapitalist monopoly.

In light of the above, a more detailed description of the principal distinctions between a suprastate monopoly of the Stalinist type and the state monopoly of which it is both the successor and negation may be useful. The schema below situates the relevant differences at three levels: structure, relations with the surrounding society, and function.

Structures

The State Monopoly	The Suprastate Monopoly
Limited centralization of ownership and power, with a consequent tendency for them to become dispersed and even for inter-institutional disputes to arise over them.	Extreme centralization of ownership and power, giving rise to a strong tendency toward their personification.
The power controlling this monopoly is marked by deep discord and dissention, with the consequent ever-present risk of internal disintegration.	The power holding this monopoly is distinguished by its monolithism; it prohibits not only disagreement, but also the mere discussion of decisions taken at the summit of power. Decisions thus effectively become orders.
Having lost the monopoly over ownership, the state loses all remaining autonomous power as well: it goes from being the center of power to being its instrument. The reassignment of ownership necessarily entails the redistribution of power—the only source of its legitimacy.	Stalinism took ownership away from the state power, not to entrust it to society, but to confer it exclusively on a different power, one beyond the state. As Naville observed, "it was necessary for power to certify a specific mode of ownership."[75] In this sense, power does not create ownership, it expresses it.
The state thus loses its monopoly over the legal exercise of violence and instead becomes its executor and legalizer; the monopoly on violence passes to the suprastate authority.	In the hands of the suprastate authority, the monopoly on legal violence is transformed into a monopoly on legalized violence. Beyond the state, the new monopoly is beyond the law.
For the postrevolutionary state seeking a way toward the transition to socialism, the monopoly over ownership thrust upon it by the immaturity of the proletariat represented its principal limitation.	For the supreme entity in the Stalinist social order, having abandoned all historical perspective other than the perpetuation of its own supremacy, the global monopoly over ownership and power represents its most vital function.
Forced to be economically competitive, the state monopoly became an integral part of society, with which it shared some of the prerogatives of ownership.	Having excluded the whole of society from the functions of ownership, the global monopoly thereby also implicitly excludes all possibility of economic and political competition. Its separation from the state is inherent in its separation from society; above society, it is necessarily also above the state. This double isolation is the most important and most specific feature of its relations with the society around it, as well as of the very structure of that society.

Relations with the Surrounding Society

The state monopoly is in a position of contention with class ownership. The principal structure of its anticapitalist social surroundings is always erected directly or indirectly around class relations.

Coexisting with class structure, the state monopoly throws the natural ties between social classes and ownership into general disarray. But the class structure continues to reflect the social distribution of ownership, albeit in a deeply strained and distorted manner.

The suprastate monopoly is based on the elimination of class ownership. Its social surroundings are non-capitalist. Its principal structures are erected outside and independent of class relations.

Without abolishing the class structure, the suprastate monopoly nonetheless abolishes the natural ties between social classes and ownership. It is no longer the class structure but a surrogate structure replacing it which provides the principal social reflection of relations of ownership.

Function

Under this heading it is useful to distinguish between the general functions exercised by the two monopolies relative to society and the internal mechanism of their functioning.

General functions

The objective of the state monopoly is to strengthen its own ownership by impairing the exercise of the various forms of private ownership around it. One of its principal functions is to render the other forms of ownership dysfunctional.

The state monopoly uses its position of predominance to control the whole of economic activity.

The principal mechanism on which it relies in this function is the systematic deformation of relations of exchange.

The systematic deformation of relations of exchange is a basic function which the state monopoly has in common with every other monopoly.

The suprastate monopoly excludes the whole of society from the exercise of ownership in all its forms. Its principal function in this regard is to stabilize the effects of generalized expropriation.

The suprastate monopoly uses its monopoly to become the true regulator of all economic activity.

The principal mechanism on which it relies in this function is the practical reduction of relations of exchange to the role of providing economic expression to centralized extra-economic allocation.

The substitution in practice of exchange relations by centralized extra-economic allocation or concession constitutes the supreme and specific function of the suprastate monopoly and is inaccessible to every other type of monopoly.

Through these means, the state monopoly is able to achieve a certain recovery in industrial production, but over the long term agricultural production declines steadily. Thus the function of the state monopoly is one of recovery in industry, but of contraction in agriculture.

In the pursuit of these functions, the state monopoly confers a growing role on bureaucratic-type relations, which encroach more and more on other social relations.

Through these means, the suprastate monopoly hastens industrialization; shortly thereafter, agrarian production collapses. The suprastate monopoly thus fulfills an industrializing function, which is its great historical achievement. In agriculture, its function has been a paralyzing one, the consequences of which have never been completely surmounted.

In the pursuit of these functions, the suprastate monopoly gives the decisive role to bureaucratic-type relations, which extend throughout the whole of society and thus become the predominant social relations.

Mechanisms

The state makes broad use of its specific extra-economic powers in the exercise of its monopoly. The relative internal diffusion of its ownership is coupled with a tendency toward the diffusion of its powers as well.

Established in the context of destabilized ownership, state ownership as well is incomplete.

The suprastate monopoly makes use of its absolute power and and the weakness of the state in the exercise of its monopoly. Supercentralization of its ownership is coupled with a supercentralization of its powers.

Born of the generalized expropriation of the various forms of incomplete ownership, the suprastate monopoly further enhances the incomplete nature of its ownership.

Though the forms it assumes may vary widely, the link between ownership and power is omnipresent in every monopoly. Ownership and power are the two fundamental sources of social inequality. They complement one another: those who profit from them are thereby assured of access to control over those who do not have them. Under Stalinism, this connection between ownership and power is distinguished by their inordinate centralization and their total unification. Reduced to a vestigial existence in its own right, ownership is infused with a new, if partial, functionality through its absorption by power. But in all societies of this type, power remains excessive even in its most benign forms. This is a consequence of its direct involvement in the exercise of an ownership which is itself excessive, owing to its extensiveness and its exclusivity.

Disaggregation is a plausible term to describe the powerlessness of ownership to fulfill certain of its specific functions. The same interdiction on appropriation which the state monopoly imposed on private peasant property to prevent its transformation into capitalist property it also imposed on its own functionaries to prevent the transformation of state property into private property. Later, this self-interdiction on appropriation would pass from the state monopoly to the suprastate monopoly, as an indispensable premise of their legitimacy. In this respect, both monopolies were fundamentally alike in possessing only incomplete ownership. But while the state monopoly was prescribed by law, the suprastate monopoly was formed and functioned outside of all legal prescriptions. Preempted by a power beyond the state, in legal terms ownership nevertheless remained in the hands of the state from which it had de facto been removed. The law contributed amply to the confusion between the state monopoly and the suprastate monopoly through its silence on this transfer of the functions of ownership from the one to the other, which permitted the suprastate monopoly to disguise itself in the institutions of the state and so make use of them to give a legal appearance to its real illegality.

A similar distinction is evident in the way each of the two monopolies structured the link between ownership and management. Under the state monopoly they were united to the point of being indistinguishable; under the suprastate monopoly they were separate. The social mechanics of planning in Stalinist societies is an instructive illustration of this separation.

Before acquiring the familiar and final form of a government document or, more precisely, a special law, the plan follows an invariable trajectory, the key point of which is the adoption of its principal indicators (i.e., the balance between the savings fund and the spending fund, investment priorities, the principal growth rates, etc.) by the supreme authority seated above the state. ''These substantive social-economic objectives are essentially determined—within the limits of material possibility—by the arbitrary decisions of the political pinnacle itself, that is, the narrowly understood party leadership. It is here that the ultimate decisions about the distribution of the total national surplus are taken, and though other groups may have influence, none is able to change the content of these decisions.''[76] Next, based on these indicators, now beyond discussion, a draft plan is drawn up by the planning committee (or the equivalent government department). The draft is then studied by the ministries and the major production units of the tasks assigned. This stage is in fact a battle in which each participant endeavors to conceal its own real possibilities for development and to communicate to the others the principal difficulties involved in the realization of the draft. After this battle, the planning committee makes final emendations in the draft plan, whose general framework, fixed at the beginning, remains unchanged. The final draft is then reexamined and adopted with or without modifications by the supreme entity, and this decision is ratified first by a special plenum of the Central Committee, then by the government, and finally by the parliament, whose vote confers the force of law on the supreme will of the supreme authority. This document, destined to regulate the whole of social activity for a specified period of time, is now the official state-plan law. The reality is that it is created outside the law and outside the state.

Beyond legal appearances, the real relations enabling this social mechanism to function are ritual in substance. They are relations of authority which reproduce the subordination of the state to the true holder of the monopoly—the supreme entity. Translated into legal terms, these ritual relations in fact reduce the law and the state to the role of instruments of this supreme entity, which is beyond them both. Though it preserves its illusory ownership, in reality the state has been reduced to the effective economic role of manager. The expropriation of the state, the separation between ownership and management (with the latter function being entrusted specifically to the state), and the emergence of the monopoly thus constituted a whole: that whole is the Stalinist social order.

But the state preserved two of the attributes of ownership: legality, which conferred upon it a ratifying role, and management, which gave it an instrumental role. What permitted the new extrastate monopoly to disengage these two attributes from its ownership was the vast difference between the power entailed by ownership compared with the power these two attributes conferred upon the state; hence the flagrant inequality between the supreme entity, which held the monopoly on ownership, and the state, whose subordination to the former was absolute. It might seem that the state, having lost the monopoly over ownership as a result of these transformations, nonetheless has retained a monopoly over management. But this perception is only partially correct. In fact, the powers of the state in matters of management are defined by the supreme entity which, moreover, maintains the strictest surveillance over this managerial activity. It would be more correct to say that the expropriated state became an irreplaceable instrument which as the social embodiment of management and legality ensured the global monopoly the exercise of ownership and power beyond all social control. The suprastate monopoly, therefore, was both more incomplete and more absolute than the state monopoly from which it had issued.

The two monopolies differed principally on two levels: the economic, where differences between their attributes were located, and the social level, where ownership was transferred from one monopoly to the other. These distinctions intersected at a third level, that of power, driven by the property in its sway along the same path toward supercentralization and the suprastate.

The immediate economic effect of generalized expropriation was the constitution of a global monopoly beyond state and society. Its indirect historical effect was the birth of a new, unparalleled mode of production that was defined by this specific organization of ownership and that itself defined the Stalinist social order. All other considerations aside, in terms only of the material aim of the 1917 Revolution—to eliminate industrial backwardness—the replacement of the state monopoly by the suprastate monopoly and of class ownership by extrasocietal ownership had demonstrated both its effectiveness and its limitations.

IV. ESTABLISHMENT OF THE GLOBAL MONOPOLY

1. Genetic code

Until now the discussion has centered on the historical process leading to the constitution of the global monopoly. It is now time to examine its functioning. Emphasis will therefore no longer be on the conditions that made its constitution possible, but the way in which the totality of these conditions, constituting its genetic code so to speak, are reflected in its functioning. The global monopoly arose out of the universal expropriation of universally destabilized property. Yet it is evident that even as it appropriated the diverse forms of the latter, the global monopoly also succeeded in making its own property stable. Less evident is how it was able to achieve this, as well as the ways and forms in which this prime condition of its genesis left its mark on the monopoly.

As has been said, the destabilization of ownership was shown above all by its incomplete character. The global monopoly introduced a substantial change in this condition: its ownership ceased to be destabilized but remained incomplete, or, more precisely, it was both less destabilized and more incomplete than the forms of ownership that preceded it. Its achievement, in short, was to stabilize a form of incomplete ownership.

The decisive factor in the stabilization of ownership was the fact that it did not take place in society, but beyond and above it. Whereas the forms of ownership left to postrevolutionary society were incomplete, Stalinist society lacked even this. For society at large, incomplete ownership had been replaced by an ownership vacuum. For ownership the price of stability was to become asocial. In total contradiction to doctrine, Stalinism, far from extending the functions of ownership to society at large, established the most radical separation between the two. A further price of stability was thus the permanent abandonment of every chance of advancing from the negation of capitalism to a possible transition to socialism.

Under Stalinism, the stabilization of incomplete ownership meant among other things that, unlike what postrevolutionary society had known, ownership was no longer contested and no longer unstable. Its instability gave way to immobility, and contested ownership gave way to a situation in which the least suspicion of contention was considered the gravest of crimes.

Though distinct, Stalinist ownership nevertheless retained one feature in common with the forms of ownership which had preceded it: their incompleteness. But what was unique about Stalinist ownership, even in this similarity, was that not only did it not recover its lost attributes; it cast off others and grounded its legitimacy in its determination to render the incomplete character of its ownership irreversible.

Each of the attributes of ownership which the global monopoly had shed suffered a separate fate in the new social context. Appropriation, which the monopoly in principle forbade itself, was also prohibited for society at large. Coercive, centralized allocation replaced competitive appropriation. Legality was abandoned by the monopoly and broadly conceded to the producers and the state, i.e., legally, ownership of all the means of production was bestowed on the workers and the peasants, who shared it with the state. Finally, the attribute of management was not abandoned by the monopoly, but simply entrusted under strict control to the state in particular and, in general, to the bureaucracy, which was both a part of and beyond the state. Management was inaccessible to the producers.

Once these attributes were relinquished, the global monopoly was able to exercise the functions of ownership more effectively within the given framework. But the attributes themselves proceeded to lose their economic significance and hence their functionality once they were separated from the other functions of ownership. The attribute of appropriation continued to subsist, but it was misused. Separated from ownership and henceforth bestowed on all categories of nonowners, the law wholly lost its economic functionality and became a mere symbol. As for management, the separation affected the producers much more unambiguously than it did the monopoly, which has always interfered in management. This lack of clarity in the separation of the attribute of management from the functions of ownership had been intended as a protective measure, but its effect has been perceptibly to reduce the economic functionality of management.

Thus Stalinism replaced the effective socialization of ownership by a kind of socialization of its attributes. The centralization of incomplete ownership, divested of certain of its attributes, was accompanied by the formal redistribution of these attributes within society. Barred from ownership, society was left with merely so many fragments, by and large economically ineffectual. Stalinism's answer to the diversification of the forms of ownership was to break a single form of ownership down into its constituent elements.

Outside the global monopoly, ownership henceforth existed only in fragmentary form. Centralized allocation ranged from the distribution of goods, positions, and privileges to the distribution of these fragments of ownership. But feeble though their economic functionality may have been, the distribution of the attributes of ownership also entailed a corresponding distribution of roles within the hierarchy. This latter distribution in fact played a crucial role in the hierarchization of society, both through its agent, the authority of which was now absolute, and through the varying formalism of the attributes distributed.

Within the special context of Stalinist society, the incomplete nature of ownership assumed an extraordinary complexity. For each attribute it had shed, the monopoly developed a set of compensating relations with either the society as a whole or with one or another of its components.

Thus, up to a point, the generalized interdiction on appropriation placed the monopoly in an objective relation of equality with the rest of society, since, according to existing regulations, there was no social class or other entity authorized to take possession of the surplus product. On the other hand, the relations compensating for the impossibility of it becoming legal were marked by a symmetric inequality. It transformed its own forced illegality into the inefficacy of law in general as a guarantor of ownership for the rest of society. In the relations thus formed, the monopoly exercised its ownership despite the absence of legal guarantees, while providing no real prerogative to those who had them.

Each of the attributes the monopoly had shed helped to limit and to stabilize monopolist ownership and hence to define the general nature of this social order. Whereas the interdiction on appropriation enabled the monopoly to prevent a reversion to capitalism, its separation from legality situated it ultimately beyond socialism.

On a more general level, the generalized ban on appropriation and the sterilization of legal guarantees may be interpreted as two different expressions of a general rule, and perhaps a specific law, of the Stalinist order: no functional attribute which remained inaccessible to the monopoly could ever be made accessible to any other social entity. A corollary is that any measure that risks putting the global monopoly in a position of inferiority is dysfunctional for this social order.

The effect of this rule stands out much more clearly with regard to the attributes of appropriation and legality than to that of management. At first glance, it might seem that in this case another social factor did indeed have access to the attribute of management, whereas the monopoly did not. But the fact is that the social factor in question did not gain access to the functions of management by its own means, but because the monopoly itself had entrusted them to it. Also, in making this transfer, the monopoly did not have free choice, but was constrained by its own development. Its separation from management marked the removal of the last impediment to its extreme centralization.

2. Separation between ownership and legality

In his 1857 *Introduction* Marx observed that Hegel "correctly begins the philosophy of law with ownership; it is the most simple legal relation of the subject."[77] The Stalinist monopoly, itself instituted with the aid of repression and perpetuated through the use of extra-economic constraint, divested ownership of its legal quality. As a corollary to the generalized separation effected between the producers and the means of production, the extra-legal monopoly generalized the separation between ownership and law. The same inefficacy of the law that permitted the monopoly to exercise illegal ownership prohibited the producers from reaping the benefits of the property which by law was theirs. There is no significant difference among Stalinist societies on this point, which reflects a defining trait of the structure specific to this social order. In each of them without exception the national wealth is in the hands of a supercentralized monopoly, and in none is this ownership recognized as such and therefore implicitly guaranteed by law. These societies have in effect transcended not the relation of ownership, but only its legal regulation.

Thus was born the only economy in the modern era founded on placing the fundamental social relation outside the law. The dissolution of this, the simplest legal relation, threatened all other relations with the same fate. By evading recognition of effective ownership, the law risked becoming ineffective itself. This is roughly what Alfred Meyer seems to be suggesting when he comments: "The Communist Party does not have legal title to the USSR and does not claim it. Ownership, however, may be defined not only in legal, but also in sociological terms."[7]

Some students of contemporary capitalism (Poulantzas, Wright, etc.) make use of the categories of "economic ownership" and "legal ownership," and it is always tempting to look for points of convergence. Unfortunately, forced analogies are often the result. For premature anticapitalist societies, however, this distinction may indeed usefully be made on the condition that sight is not lost of the fact that the realities to which it refers are quite different in each case. Under capitalism, economic ownership consists of control of the surplus product and investments, while legal ownership consists of possession of a title representing a marketable value. Legal ownership is thus not extra-economic; the legal title merely gives manifest form to the economic substance. But in Stalinist societies legal ownership has no economic substance. The law confers on workers an ownership from which economically they are totally and permanently excluded. On the other hand, peasant ownership, even vestigial, retains an economic substance that for the most part carries no legal recognition. Contrary to capitalism, Stalinism separates the two categories; legal ownership is basically outside the economy, and economic ownership is outside the law.

The global monopoly's extra-legal condition permanently conferred on it a number of crucial advantages with regard to its general functionality and especially to the legitimacy of the social order. By circumventing legal certification, the global monopoly avoids subverting its own political legitimacy. For, from the standpoint of the historical and doctrinal traditions it calls its own, the reality of the monopoly was and is illegitimate. Its illegality therefore serves to attenuate the consequences of the clash between the reality it had originally created and the ideal upon which its legitimacy rests. It remains legally invalid in order to maintain its social invisibility. Capable of changing neither its reality nor the ideals of its inheritance, the global monopoly has made illegality the prime stronghold of its dissimulated social existence. Its second defense is the transfer of the attribute of legality to the producers and to the state. It has conceded to the state a legally simulated ownership so as to conceal the illegality of the ownership it effectively holds.

Freedom of action is a second advantage the Stalinist monopoly derives from its illegality. All law assigns both rights and restrictions. But in assuming an ownership which no law recognizes, the monopoly has thereby also avoided any limitations the law might impose upon it. The ambiguity to which law has been reduced under the monopoly's absolute domination is a further fruit of the latter's illegal status. The practical consequence has been to abolish universal equality before the law. The law's ineffectiveness in regulating the monopoly on owner-ship is matched by its omnipotence with regard to the society at large. Only in its articulation with a society formally subject to the prescripts of the law can the monopoly's illegal ownership assure its social supremacy. Perhaps the most telling illustration of this legal ambiguity is the fact that the exigencies which illegal ownership forces upon society are conveyed in the form of a legal con-straint: namely, the plan. Instituted in disregard of the law, the plan is essential to the functioning of the global monopoly; hence the monopoly's ambiguous posi-tion with regard to the law. In effect, it subverts the law by its mere existence and endeavors to render the law as rigorous as possible in its actions. It employs contempt of the law to defend its legitimacy, yet its efficacy depends on the law's respect, which it outwardly professes. But neither law nor efficacy nor legitimacy is strengthened by this general incoherence. "The Soviet privileged grouping," comments Braverman on what is here referred to as the global monopoly, "is in the unique and anomalous position, among all the privileged groupings of history, that it must teach the nonlegitimacy of its own privileges and power over socie-ty."[79] This double antinomy, between legality and legitimacy on the one hand and legality and illegality on the other, is at the very foundation of the Stalinist monopoly over ownership.

This strange and new phenomenon, all-embracing yet legal ownership, could paradoxically boast a certain historical continuity, the sources of which were principally two. One went back to the society that had preceded the Stalinist social order; the other had its origins in the historical process of its constitution. The first has been discussed amply in the preceding chapters, and only two points of detail need be added. First, postrevolutionary society was unable to avoid trans-forming the evisceration of small peasant property into an evisceration of the law. In a sense, therefore, the erosion of the law was integral to Stalinism. Second, the deterioration of the legal system, which had already begun, contributed to the constitution of monopolist ownership; the illegality of the latter hence served only to aggravate a process already in motion.

The other source resided in the concrete conditions which ultimately gave rise to the Stalinist order. The ownership exercised by the global monopoly merely assimilated the illegality of the generalized expropriation on which it was founded. It had countered legality with repression even to exist, and it used extra-economic constraint in place of the law to function. As far as the law is concerned, the expropriation of the proletariat, the peasantry, and the state are events that never took place, for there are no legal terms to describe them.

The legal regulation of ownership in Stalinist societies is direct testimony to the perversion of the interdependence between law and ownership. Henri Chambre notes: "The essential point which must be stressed is that the instruments and means of production are 'public property,' or property of the state; in other words, 'property of all the people.'"[80] The Khrushchevean utopian formulation aside, what is important is that in these societies legal prescriptions concerning ownership are as precise in what they ignore as they are vague in what they affirm. By assigning ownership of the same means of production to the producers and to the state, the law creates an insoluble dilemma on this vital issue.

Naville says of the USSR that "economic structures, there as elsewhere, give the law its entire meaning."[81] But the converse is just as true, namely, that in these societies what gives the law its entire meaning as regards ownership is not its articulation with economic structures but its separation from them. It buttresses this separation first by concealing real ownership and second by guaranteeing ownership that in reality does not exist. Accordingly, the protection which the law gives to the ownership of the global monopoly consists not in providing it with legal sanction, but in simply ignoring it.

The break down of the law was necessarily transmitted to the state, which is its material embodiment. The strength of the state was inevitably compromised by its having to be the social vehicle of an ineffectual law. But it also suffered the very real consequences of its illusory ownership. The state was the sole institution legally invested with ownership which remained practically inaccessible to it; on the basis of that fact alone, it constituted the most serious potential threat to illegal ownership. And to leave it with no illusions in this regard, the monopoly placed the state under particularly harsh surveillance. The eclipse of law thus in turn contributed to making the state's total subordination to the suprastate authority an inherent component of the social relations that enable this form of ownership to function. But more even than legality, it was the specific way in which the state assumed the functions of management that defined its position within the Stalinist social order.

3. Separation between ownership and management

As it evolved toward monopolist forms, capitalist ownership turned against the laws of the market which had given it birth and enabled it to grow. Joint-stock companies began to appear about the same time as monopolies began to form, and with them the separation between ownership and management as well. Long before it was described as a "managerial revolution," this disjunction, still in its elementary stages, was interpreted by Marx as marking the beginning of the dissolution of capital, brought about as a direct consequence of its own development. Weber called attention to the "separation of managerial functions from appropriated property, especially through limitations of the functions of owners to the appointment of management and to the free appropriation of shares of the profit."[82] Stalinism's assimilation of the monopolist model also included adopting this separation between ownership and management.

Stalinism also introduced certain singularities of its own into this separation, and to understand them more thoroughly it is essential to determine the principal qualities which distinguished the Stalinist monopoly from capitalist monopolies on the one hand and from the state monopoly erected by postrevolutionary society on the other. This raises several crucial questions. How, for example, was the separation between ownership and management assimilated by the structure of the new social order? The answer to this question would in a sense define the nature of the order. A discussion of the specific qualities Stalinism gave to this separation also brings up the question of the role of the bureaucracy in the social order, a topic considered central by many specialists on the subject.

In his restrictive reference to "appointments" above, Weber suggests that capitalist ownership implicitly assumes two new and, in practical terms, complementary functions by foregoing the function of management: that of creating the managerial apparatus and that of controlling it. Under Stalinism, these two complementary functions took on a quite special importance given the extent of the property to be managed and its particular fragility, resulting from its limitations.

In both capitalism and Stalinism, the separation of the attribute of management was indicative of a basic modification in ownership. Its object was broadened. Of course this broadening was infinitely greater under Stalinism. Also, the separation between ownership and management, which enabled capitalist ownership to consolidate itself, enabled the Stalinist monopoly to avoid capitalism. In the specific form of joint-stock companies, the concentration of capitalist property is accompanied by a dilution of its ownership. In De Vroey's terms, "Paradoxically, dispersion of stock thus favors the centralization of capital."[83] In contrast, under Stalinism, centralization of property was accompanied by the centralization of ownership. While resorting to the same process of separating ownership from management—required in both cases by the same process of centralization of ownership—capitalism and Stalinism pursued contrary ends which in turn produced disparate social effects.

To achieve this separation, capitalist ownership apparently had no choice: it had to create a specialized apparatus. But under Stalinism, a choice did exist, at least in principle: it could have done the same as capitalism, or it could have conferred management on the producers. Once again, Stalinism embraced capitalist experience—but with a far different outcome. Instead of encouraging the formation of associations of private property owners, the separation between management and ownership under Stalinism led to the deprivatization of property by taking it out of the social domain entirely, i.e., by "desocializing" it. The corollary was the centralization of ownership, now divested of the function of management, in the hands of a supreme authority situated above society.

Its capitalist surroundings continued to entice under this separation. Stalinism opposed capitalism even as it emulated it. The ambiguity of its methods reflected the ambiguity of its premises: the necessity of capitalist relations survived the abolishment of the social classes that embodied them.

The difference between the two solutions to the problem of ownership and management is reflected in the way the attribute of management correlates with that of appropriation. Capitalist ownership relegates the functions of management to special cadres in order to expand appropriation (if in a modified form); but for the Stalinist monopoly the same act has separated the monopoly from appropriation as well. In capitalist corporations, ownership is collective, but appropriation remains ultimately private.

In its classic form, appropriation, according to Dessai, resides in the fact that "whatever is the difference between total revenue (M') and the cost of production (M) is taken by the capitalist" who "can start the cycle again with M' in his hand—free to hoard it, spend it on consumption, or advance it."[84] What the transformation of individual capitalist ownership into capitalist corporate ownership changes in matters of appropriation is the object over which an owner exercises absolute sovereignty. This object is no longer the overall difference between M' and M, but only a fragment or share thereof, proportional to his contribution to M (the cost of production). The capacity of this share to influence how this difference is utilized is limited by the weight it carries in the ownership of the company, but it is unrestricted with regard to the returns accruing to it on this basis. Thus, whether individual or collective, capitalist ownership always in the end assures those who exercise it one form or another of private appropriation. As Giddens points out, appropriation is a vital economic mechanism of capitalism. What it in effect achieves is to yield profits that are invisible to the producers yet accessible to the owners; it transforms value collectively created into a private possession. Insofar as private appropriation and capitalism are truly inseparable, the effective blocking of appropriation signals in fact the abolishment of capitalism.

To achieve that same end, Stalinism did not merely block the mechanism of appropriation, but replaced it with a surrogate mechanism. That mechanism was centralized allocation, which Stalinism turned into a generalized concessionary process, selectively channeling the goods of social labor by directive from above into the hands of each of society's members. In transforming management into a preeminently bureaucratic activity, the monopoly not only blocked the mechanism of appropriation, it also created the social mechanism for ensuring the controlled distribution of its rewards. Of the two, the first measure was crucial to the constitution of the Stalinist order, the second became and remained of prime importance for its functioning.

In economic terms, the difference of which Dessai speaks between M' and M is in fact the specific object of appropriation, i.e., the surplus. Traditionally, the blocking of appropriation in Stalinist society has been described solely from the standpoint of its presumptive agent: the expropriation of real or potential owners and the impossibility of the global monopoly's engaging in appropriation without dealing a devastating blow to its own legitimacy. In fact, the transformations working against appropriation concerned not only its presumptive agent, but its specific object as well, i.e., the surplus. As Ticktin remarks on Stalinist societies, "Appropriation is impossible since it is not clear where the surplus exists, how big it is, and even what it is."[85] Because of their territorial spread, the production units capable of creating a surplus can only be partially controlled. The control exercised by the managerial apparatus to prevent enterprises from appropriating the surplus is so great that it obstructs production. A portion of what is usually considered surplus remains permanently uncollectable by both the monopoly and its central managerial apparatus.

But the surplus does not merely disappear through dissimulation—the work of individuals. It also simply evaporates as a result of the dissolution of value, which is the work of an economy of ambiguity. As they cannot be exchanged, the means of production produced by the largest enterprises have only the apparent value attached to them by the extra-economic decision of the center. This same apparent value is then passed on to all salable products created with these means of production. The surplus thus ceases to be a relevant economic quantity: the difference between M' and M is no more than a mass of objects whose apparent value, arbitrarily established, conceals the dissolution of their real value. What might in this situation constitute the object of possible appropriation thus in reality is no longer a surplus, but in fact overproduction. The evanescence of the surplus is the ultimate consequence of the original destabilization of property, which under Stalinism became the incomplete but exhaustive property of a super-centralized and absolute monopoly.

But the evanescent quality of the surplus not only obstructed appropriation. With the surplus reduced to overproduction, the functions of management changed their object, and this in turn obliged it to adopt new methods, implicitly altering its general state. Appropriation was relegated to a marginal existence in the form of misuse, waste, and peculation. Yet despite the widespread nature of these practices, true appropriation remained generally inaccessible. This prevented the reprivatization of property and hence a return to the capitalist mode of production. The less confusion there is on this point, the more likely will be the chances of arriving at a correct definition of the nature of this social order.

With the reservations attendant on any classification, three principal schools may be said to exist when it comes to establishing such a definition. One considers the Stalinist social order a socialist society, or—in a widespread critical variant—state socialism. Another regards it as a new form of capitalism, or state capitalism. The third calls it a society in transition from capitalism to socialism—although the real historical process seems slower than the impatient expectations nourished by some scholars would have it.

Especially popular among those theories in which the state is the key to the definition of Stalinist societies are the theories of state capitalism and state socialism. But if, as I have tried to argue, it is true that the separation between ownership and management provides the crucial functional reason for the inferior hierarchical status reserved for the state in these societies, then economic and social primacy does not lie with the state, but with some supreme entity outside and beyond it. It is not true that Stalinist societies are under the domination of the state, nor do they represent a version of capitalism. The term state capitalism therefore is doubly irrelevant, although its intellectual endurance is remarkable. Its sources are perhaps the political prestige of its initial use, the historical development of state ownership in a number of capitalist countries, and the choice of the term "capitalism," which presumably reflects a concern to dispel every illusion as regards the socialist nature of this social order.

The concept of state capitalism or state monopoly is found among apologists and critics of Stalinist society alike, although they of course accent different aspects. Some of Lenin's initial formulations seem to have retained their impact. On the eve of the first self-conceived socialist revolution of the 20th century, its unchallenged leader gave a disquieting definition of what socialism in postrevolutionary society would be like: "Socialism," he notes in his article of September 1917, quoted earlier on, "is nothing other than the stage immediately following state capitalist monopoly. . . . Socialism is merely state monopoly capital put in the services of the entire people and which on that account ceases to be a capitalist monopoly."[86] In this particular vision, state monopoly capitalism is regarded both as a transitional form leading to socialism and as socialism in the strict sense. But so reduced, the socialist project must necessarily ignore two questions: the socialization of the means of production and their management by the producers. Finally, given the role assigned to it, the state, far from withering away, would necessarily assume capital importance. Lenin seems to be looking for a way to reconcile socialism and underdevelopment, with the latter—normally—preponderant. He does not seem to use the term state monopoly capitalism especially rigorously. In "State and Revolution," he refers to "state monopoly capitalism," while in "Left Wing Communism, An Infantile Disorder," "The Tax in Kind," and in his reports to the Third and Fourth Congresses of the Comintern and to the 11th Party Congress, he prefers the simple formula "state capitalism." "All of these waverings in terminology," says Saby, "merely reveal a theoretical inadequacy as regards the term state capitalism, an inadequacy which is easily explained by the simple fact that Lenin was himself in the process of discovering new economic structures." Similar reservations are found in many an author, e.g., Frankel, who notes the "deficiency of notions such as state capitalism,"[87] or Poulantzas, who talks about the "inconsistencies in the Marxist theory of state monopoly capitalism."[88]

In the 1950s, Mao defined the People's Republic of China in largely the same terms. "It is therefore not an ordinary capitalist economy," he remarks, "but a state capitalist economy of a new type."[89] In contrast, on the eve of the victory of October 1917, the left-wing communists called attention to the great dangers entailed in this formula. One of their most preeminent representatives, Ossinskii, wrote in March 1918 in the second issue of the daily *Kommunist*, the organ of the Communist Party of Petrograd: "Socialism and socialist organization will be established by the proletariat itself or not at all; something else will then appear in their place: state capitalism."[90] The Trotskyists took up the term again in the 1930s in their effort to define the new Stalinist society, and later the term state capitalism was used to the same purpose by "Workers' Council Communism" (Korsch, Mattick, Pannekoek, Ruhle, etc.).[91] Further, while Bettelheim expresses his misgivings: "There exists a graver danger, namely, to end up with a kind of bureaucratic state capitalism,"[92] Bahro deplores the de facto situation: "We have all embarked in the same ship of state monopoly capitalism."[93] But put quite simply, the Stalinist mode of production cannot be capitalist because it excludes all the social categories from ownership. It is not state capitalism, (1) because contrary to widespread convictions, no social class possesses either the property or the state, (2) because the state itself, despite its legal titles, is excluded from ownership and reduced to the role of manager, and (3) because it excludes from appropriation not only society but also the supreme entity situated above it. As Leon Blum observed in 1947, "In Soviet Russia, state capitalism is, frankly speaking, a contradiction in terms because the appropriation of the instruments of production by the state does not and cannot bear the essential characteristics of capitalist ownership."[94]

The variations on the concept involve the terms capitalism or monopoly, or their combinations. The constant term is state. This term also occurs in the seemingly contradictory formulation, "state socialism," which is contrasted to both state capitalism and state monopolism. Enshrined by Weber, the term has recently undergone a remarkable revival. It is found with a variety of nuances in Antonio Carlo, Otto Šik, Henri Lefebvre, Branko Horvat, Paul Mattick, Svetozar Stojanović, etc. "The majority of current Marxists," observes Rudi Supek, "speak of 'state socialism' or 'statism' and define Stalinism as a 'state mode of production.'"[95] As it would appear, any attempt to probe into the real nature of Stalinist society must necessarily fall wide of the mark if it concedes a decisive role to the state, regardless of whether the definition is capitalist or socialist. Supek concludes that "It would seem more correct to speak of a system which is distinct from both capitalism and socialism."[96] In her study of Soviet agriculture, Susan Gross Solomon considers that "The choice did not lie between capitalism and socialism."[97] The reduction of Stalinist societies to some formula of capitalism or capitalist monopoly may be irrelevant, but entertaining any notion that includes the term socialism is outright misleading. It criticizes Stalinism in a manner which implicitly defends it.

The separation under Stalinism between ownership and management brought about by the centralization of the former also means a separation between ownership and state. As it took place under capitalism, this separation has been interpreted from Burnham and Rizzi to Bell and Parsons as a transformation in the class structure of these societies. A necessary condition for the Stalinist monopoly to become effective was its effective separation from management. Indeed its global nature depends on its sustaining this separation. In the case of management, therefore, the monopoly is unable either to make it universally inaccessible, as it did with appropriation, or to turn it into a sterile and vacuous attribute, as it did with legality. Even though the separation remains incomplete in that the monopoly reserves for itself its customary unlimited right to interfere when it sees fit; and even though reversible, in the sense that the monopoly is free to change institutions, persons, and powers without any consultation, the lines of division are clear-cut enough that the supreme entity is able to maintain its monopoly and even its primacy in the direct practical tasks of management.

These are then briefly the principal conditions which make the relations of the monopoly with the social entity encharged with management a special case of its relations with society. Its singularity essentially rests in the fact that, to assure its supremacy the monopoly focuses its attention not on the attribute, i.e., the functions of management, but on the social entity invested with those functions. Unable, as has been said, to make management inaccessible, like appropriation, or ineffective, like legality, the monopoly concentrates on exercising the strictest control of its managers and in so doing makes the relationship a preponderantly political one, rather than economic. The result is an unparalleled subordination of the managers, for whom it nourishes an organic mistrust even though it has entrusted its property to them. Thwarted in the exercise of its supremacy in direct economic action, the monopoly recovers it wholly in a paroxystic display of political inequality in its exercise of absolute domination over the managerial group.

The manner in which the monopoly avails itself of its political power to compensate for its economic limitations in matters of management brings to full light one of its principal structural traits—its dual economic and political nature.

4. Compensatory power

The monopoly would have been unable to form, persist, or become relatively functional without having politically unlimited power to compensate for its limitations in the exercise of the functions of ownership. The monopoly became global, its sway extending beyond the whole of the nation's assets to include as well all the extra-economic powers a modern society might conceive.

Ownership and power interact in a more or less synchronized and disguised manner throughout the contemporary world, but nowhere has this confluence of action achieved the degree of globality, integration and—despite the disregard of it that has all but become tradition in the critical literature—transparency that it has in Stalinist societies. The received view is that an excessive power assumed the role of owner. But the converse is more likely the case: it was by assuming that role that power became excessive to the degree it did. Despite its potential, power alone could not have brought about a social change of the scale in question and above all have stabilized its effect. Other factors external to power were necessary. One of these factors was the lamentable state of the object of ownership, i.e., the means of production; another was the social context which made the natural, presumptive agents of ownership even less capable of exercising it in a productive fashion—within that context.

Later this situation changed. The state of the means of production improved remarkably and inverted the dilemma. The working class grew in number and skills and presumably was learning to manage production. But now the continued existence of the dual monopoly specifically required that the working class be excluded from these functions for its continued existence. Under these changed circumstances, with all the other factors which had contributed to the formation of the dual monopoly having disappeared, power was left alone to perpetuate the monopoly. Only then did a substitution which had originally enjoyed plausibility become truly abusive and usurpatory. Thus at the origins of Stalinism was the transformation of the monopoly over the legal exercise of violence into a monopoly over the illegal exercise of ownership.

In the course of history, when ownership of the principal means of production has changed hands, it has passed from one social class to another. In postrevolutionary Russia, however, a part of ownership was shifted from the class structure to the state. To end this unstable situation, Stalinism wrested the whole of ownership from both class and state, i.e., from society. A new agent of ownership, sufficiently separate and, therefore, separable from society became necessary to effect this transfer. It goes without saying that to take the functions of ownership from all the classes and social categories as well as from the state, this agent had itself to be sufficiently separated from those it replaced. Locating ownership outside society required the formation of a supreme authority which was capable of exercising that function precisely by virtue of its own position outside society; hence the vital importance of this unprecedented social architecture, created to ensure the isolation of a dual monopoly over power *and* ownership.

Whereas the attributes of power played a generative role in the formation of the dual monopoly, i.e., they were instrumental in its constitution, their role in the functioning of the monopoly was above all compensatory and reproductive.

Out of the ownership vacuum resulting from the shift of the functions of ownership outside society, Stalinism would create the economic matrix for new social relations and a new social structure. The supercentralized dual monopoly became a new social—or, in reality, extrasocial—agent of ownership. Its principal function on a general level was to transform structurally incomplete ownership into economically functional ownership that would not revert to capitalism. Power ceased to be the protector of property as it is under capitalism. Instead, it became its sole direct possessor as a result of this power-ownership monopoly. Even under capitalism there have been sporadic attempts to effect such fusions of power and ownership in ways that are more often hidden than manifest. From Mussolini to third world dictatorships, history has shown that capitalism at widely varying levels of development has been able to achieve a comparable degree of centralization of power, but not of ownership. Only if this particularity is ignored can a definition of Stalinism that employs the concept of totalitarianism even seem plausible. But aside from evident analogies in the organization of power, what makes the Stalinist social order unique is its extreme centralization of power and ownership and their fusion in a dual global monopoly assuring its non-capitalist nature.

Pursuing the same comparison—or, rather, the incongruities in the concept itself—I would point out that, generally, dictatorships represent circumscribed political episodes, whereas Stalinism assumes the dimensions of a historical epoch wherever it becomes established. The tendency has been to explain its enduring nature by its most spectacular functional accomplishment, industrialization. But the structural mutations which accompanied the implantation of the dual monopoly in its social and economic context were as important. What is essential is that these structures adapted to the dual monopoly, not vice versa. This capacity of the monopoly to constrain its surroundings to adapt to its presence rather than vice versa may at first glance seem surprising. But the crucial point is that the bare act of constitution of the monopoly divested society of its central institution, ownership. This transfer at the same time altered the principal social relations and their hierarchy. Class relations did not disappear, but yielded priority to relations of authority.

All social relations, even the most vital and hence potentially the purest, became fraught with ambiguity under the domination of the monopoly. No relations remained unaffected. Down to the most elementary relations of exchange, there was no economic activity which did not in the final analysis bear the stamp of the monopoly's authority.

Control over the surplus product merged under the monopoly with control over the institutions and individuals that produce it. Under capitalism, separation of these two functions of control implies their complementarity, maintained in large measure by force of law. It is the task of the authorities to ensure respect of the law, and respect of the law is the safeguard of property. But under Stalinism, the separation of these two control functions was eliminated, and with it the necessity of maintaining complementarity and, thus, legal articulation between them. Having merged with ownership, power ceased to embody the law. It replaced it. Incapable of protecting anticapitalist property, power in the end absorbed it.

But the converse could also be argued. The functions of power and ownership having become indissoluble, power was absorbed by the latter and became its decisive attribute. Whenever the loss of certain economic attributes of ownership made itself felt, power moved in to fill the breach. In this respect, the fusion of power and ownership succeeded in making structurally incomplete ownership functional.

V. STRUCTURAL TRANSFORMATIONS IN THE ECONOMY

1. Perpetuation of primitive accumulation

Of all the transformations that Stalinism made in the economy, the most evident was industrialization. But—and this is of cardinal importance—this first instance of anticapitalist industrialization was largely inspired by the capitalist model of primitive accumulation. In those countries where it later recurred, Stalinist industrialization began from different levels of development under historically distinct conditions and achieved varying results. But despite dissimilarities, the methods of primitive accumulation used were the same in each case. An examination of certain particularities of this process as it took place in the USSR should bring out those qualities which make Stalinism an international phenomenon.

According to Marx, primitive accumulation consists essentially of the separation by force of petty producers from their means of production. While agreeing on the inevitability of primitive accumulation, the Bolshevik leaders of the pre-Stalinist era differed on the means to be employed. The conviction that recourse to this shameful model of capitalism was legitimate was never repudiated by the defenders of Stalinism. Thus in his testament, published in the West in 1969, Eugene Varga (whom Trotsky called a "theoretical Polonius") commented: "If the birth of capitalism necessitated a period of primitive accumulation, so too does the birth of socialism in a devastated and backward country."[98] In taking over the historical mission of industrialization which capitalism had failed to carry to completion, these societies seem constrained to avail themselves of its methods as well.

The problem was to pass through the same process of primitive accumulation yet avoid its natural social consequence, i.e., to convert capitalist into anticapitalist primitive accumulation. For postrevolutionary Russia and later for other countries that took this historical path, the need to put an end to technological backwardness was coupled with the necessity of proving the historical legitimacy of anticipatory revolutions and of eliminating the general consequences of anticipation, crystalized in the general disarticulation of postrevolutionary society. The question of pace, irrelevant for past industrializations, became central. Acceleration was necessary to make up for the historical lag and to overcome the effects of the desynchronizations caused by anticipatory revolution. Ranging from the "snake's pace" recommended by Bukharin to the haste called for by Trotsky, all alternatives concerned the scale of the privations that accumulation would impose upon the population.

Stalinist industrialization differed from capitalist industrialization in two principal respects: its specific social function and its social base. Its social function was to surmount the antinomies of pre-industrial anticapitalism, while what was specific to its social base was the absence of a spontaneous economic tendency toward industrialization—in fact, a lack of social actors prepared to initiate it and carry it forward.

This lack in postrevolutionary Russia produced the historical paradox that the victory of the anticipatory revolution engendered social stagnation. With a post-capitalist social organization and predominately capitalist forces of production, this society seemed destined rather to founder than to develop in any direction at all. It possessed neither the spontaneity nor the strategy to overcome this situation nor, implicitly, the social forces to embody the one or the other. Victory in the civil war left it with its principal internal sources of its dynamism exhausted, delaying among other things industrialization.

The project of industrialization therefore found itself suspended in historical space, caught in an intolerable antinomy. Not that some subjective strategy, misbegotten of revolution, existed and was preventing the natural agents of industrialization from seeing it through; it was rather the absence of these agents which made such a strategy necessary but provided no means for creating it. Thus, when Stalinism eventually assumed its mission of industrialization, the resulting industrialization contained an imitative element that made it at once more extreme and more constricted than the capitalist model.

Every strategy involves a series of subjective decisions, but every series of subjective decisions is not necessarily a strategy. For this sort of subjectivized spontaneity, any movement, controlled or not, is preferable to stagnation. What Stalinism in reality abandoned therefore was not a strategy but its sterile search for one or, more precisely, the irresolution and inaction which such a search entails. Absent in society and assumed by the monopoly, spontaneity became pragmatism out of the necessity of adopting an apparent rationale *ex post facto*. From Preobrazhensky to the present, numerous authors have underscored the eclecticism of Stalinist solutions to the fundamental problems that face societies born of anticipatory revolutions. "In fact," observes Cohen, "the revised Bukharinist program adopted as the First Five-year Plan at the 15th Party Congress in December 1927, which called for more ambitious industrial investment as well as partial voluntary collectivization, represented a kind of amalgam of Bukharinist-Trotskyist thinking as it had evolved in the debates of the 1920s."[99]

Alfred Meyer points to "the basic affinity between Trotsky's plans and Stalin's actions" which marked "almost every major item in the political program that Stalin later carried out."[100]

The political conflict among the diverse Bolshevik factions was offset by their compatibility in theory and was based in fact on their common inability to work out an adequate theory and strategy. Despite their lasting effects, the actions of Stalinism bear the mark of this inability; in Lewin's terms, "the elements of a solution were suggested by circumstances rather than by theoretical anticipation."[101] Having transformed anticipation into action before the revolution, the Bolsheviks were unable to construct a theory and strategy of anticipation after victory. In the face of circumstances not covered by theory, past convictions began to acquire the overtones of a faith which, despite their differences, all the leaders reaffirmed, although as individuals they were unable to elaborate it with responsible arguments. Public discourse deteriorated from debate to dogma in a decline best illustrated by Bukharin's famous exhortation: "Here is a country backward, illiterate, and impoverished, with a gigantic predominance of non-proletarian elements, here you will build socialism, here you will prove that even under such unprecedentedly difficult conditions you can lay firmly the foundations of a new world."[102] The principal architects of the first anticipatory revolution were unable to perceive its limits. Their theoretical discomfiture would become the cornerstone of Stalinist ideology.

It is important to appreciate this context to understand that Stalinism—and Stalinist industrialization in particular—did not represent the triumph of one strategic project among others, but rather that of a specific political expression of a lack of strategy among other political expressions of that same lack. Similarly, at the social level, Stalinism marked the victory of a politically structured spontaneity embodied by power over the politically unstructured spontaneity of the productive classes. Neither of the productive classes manifested strong enough spontaneity to reinforce the new social context and to carry it forward to the original objectives of the revolution. On the contrary, in its most clearly defined form, i.e., as seen in the peasantry, social spontaneity was rather inclined toward a resurgence of capitalism.

If it is true that the unique destiny of social spontaneity at this historical juncture was to move ineluctably down the path toward capitalism, the cheerless corollary must be that in the historical scenario bequeathed to it by the anticipatory revolution, power could radically oppose capitalism only by opposing social spontaneity. It also follows that within the unprecedented context of pre-industrial anticapitalism, it is essentially irrelevant whether the Bolshevik leaders, beginning with Lenin and Trotsky, may have underestimated the creative potential of social spontaneity. The truth was that social spontaneity was itself far from able to demonstrate that it did in fact possess that potential.

What power substituted for social spontaneity was a spontaneity of its own which was guided by one overriding objective: to safeguard and consolidate anticapitalism. This is what Stalinism did to the letter: it preserved the pre-industrial structures of this pristine anticapitalism even after industrialization had carried society into the new era.

It is not fatalistic to suggest that even if the outcome of the collision between the principal factions of Bolshevik leadership had been different, the social consequences might not have been essentially different from those of Stalinism. It is no longer the hand of Stalin that has been responsible for the continued existence of the global monopoly in the USSR into the 1980s, and it was not Fidel Castro who decided to establish it in Cuba in the early 1960s. The limits of pre-industrial anticapitalism define the objective conditions placed on the spontaneity of power, regardless of how the latter may be subjectively expressed. The pace and priorities of industrialization can vary from one country to another and even from one period to another within the same country. In these respects the objective conditions are relatively flexible. At the structural level, on the other hand, they display a remarkable inflexibility. Though its orientation may vary, these conditions render inevitable both industrialization and the social and economic structures needed to make it rapid and anticapitalist. At the intersection of these two types of structure, a dual global monopoly virtually defining the Stalinist order thus emerges each time a country fettered by a combination of lingering feudalism, genetically enfeebled capitalism, and international imperialism throws off these fetters through anticipatory revolution and embarks upon anti-capitalist industrialization. The monopoly makes anticapitalist industrialization possible but survives indefinitely after the accomplishment of this end, firmly anchored in the economic and social structures which permitted it to function. The result is a progressive immobilization of the whole of society by structures that have outlived their usefulness, in an antinomic process deriving from the same genetic flaw that was responsible for the lack of social spontaneity and political strategy.

In its classic form, industrialization entails the transformation of both the technological tools of labor and the social relations of production. There is a correspondence between these two transformations. The introduction of industrial technology heralded the genesis of two social classes, each of which then employed it in its own way: the proletariat to make it productive, the bourgeoisie to make it profitable. But in anticapitalist industrialization, whether belated or anticipated, this correspondence breaks down. Societies which have embarked upon this path endeavor to assimilate industrial technology but not its social corollary. They are for the technology of capitalism, but against the capitalist class and capitalist relations of production. The capitalist model is neither wholly assimilated nor wholly rejected.

In fact rejection and assimilation are combined, and resemblances to capitalism are evident across a broad range: in the organization of productive units, in the priorities of technological development, in the specific occupational stratification of the labor force, and in the ways in which resources are mobilized. The dissimilarities concern less the process than the context in which Stalinist industrialization takes place, which while not excluding the capitalist class, leaves vacant the role of the social agent that provides the initiative for industrialization. In most countries with a Stalinist social order, there is one other dissimilarity which nourishes and reinforces the resemblances. Anticapitalist industrialization did not begin from zero. A few timid beginnings had taken place earlier with, of course, an incomplete capitalist character. In these cases anticapitalist industrialization was simply the accelerated continuation of this capitalist prelude, enhancing the similarities that already existed.

The adaptation of economic and social structures directly concerned not so much industrialization in the strict sense, at least in the first phases, but the underlying process of mobilizing resources, i.e., primitive accumulation. Seen in retrospect, the enduring nature of some of the changes brought about demonstrates that they were much more than mere adaptations to circumstances and in fact represented veritable structural mutations. The sobering implication (1) that pre-industrial anticapitalism was unable to fulfill the imperative of industrialization except by assimilating the capitalist model of primitive accumulation and (2) that this assimilation took place with so little control that it in fact became the spontaneous demiurge of a social order which had never been prefigured. The genesis of this social order, therefore, did not represent the realization of a project, but was rather the consequence of blind opposition to the immanent tendency of primitive accumulation to produce its natural sequel—the capitalist social order.

Indeed, Stalinist primitive accumulation had the same content as the capitalist model, expropriation; it employed the same basic instrument, violence; and in principle it embraced the same object, the producers. As striking as they may seem at first glance, these similarities were embedded in a social context which was totally different from that of capitalist accumulation and which thereby gave rise to differences of no less importance. For instance, the social agent of primitive accumulation was not the capitalist class, nor a social class at all, but an anticapitalist political power in the process of acquiring a global monopoly over power and ownership; expropriation affected not only petty producers but the whole of society as well; and its principal social effect was not the polarization of society into a capitalist class, owner of the industrial means of production, and a proletariat reduced to selling its labor, but rather the division of society between a proletariat reduced essentially to that same condition and an anticapitalist monopoly with a proprietary hold on the totality of society's goods.

But in either case, whether under the dominion of capital or the global monopoly, command over industrialization (including primitive accumulation) and ownership of the means of production was in the same hands. There is no question that what prevented primitive accumulation from generating capital was the monopoly or, conversely, that Stalinist primitive accumulation did not give rise to capital precisely because it had given birth to the monopoly. Nonetheless, the beneficiary of accumulation was the agent of the industrialization in either case.

Though initially highlighting the birth of the monopoly, these traits continued to mark the ways in which the monopoly exercised its domination over society. Industrialization required and absorbed so much surplus social labor that its end result was to further the property of the monopoly guiding it. The same excesses which in the short term made possible the accelerated pace of industrialization over the long term prevented the transformation of primitive accumulation into simple accumulation, i.e., accumulation of capital.

Stalinist industrialization is in general more rapid than its capitalist antecedents, but its pace is even further enhanced by two peculiarities of accumulation. First, accumulation opposes production to consumption; and second, it subordinates agriculture totally to the needs of rapidly growing industry. To maintain the rate of accumulation at this inordinately high level, the rate of consumption must be kept at a level much below the needs of the population. The market not only acts as a prohibitive force on these needs, but serves also to define them and in the end risks augmenting the rate of consumption. The systematic disregard of the needs of the population becomes the guiding principle of accumulation and hence of this version of anticapitalist industrialization. In concrete economic terms this principle amounts to a series of what one might call strategic imbalances: between production of the means of production and production of consumer goods; between industry and agriculture; between the presumptive value of the product and the value of labor power, etc. Economic mechanisms alone are insufficient to create these imbalances; extra-economic constraint is essential. But although legalized at the level of the state, such constraint can be effective and stable only if it is exercised by an entity endowed with adequate powers.

In the light of these functional needs, the advantages of the monopoly and its privileges was manifest. Economically excessive accumulation required extreme centralization of ownership and power in the hands of an entity which would thereby be able to replace and subvert the action of economic mechanisms with its own coercive extra-economic action. There was only one plausible way to oppose the needs of the population, and that was to intervene against the action of the mechanisms of the market. But to make that opposition effective, mere intervention was not sufficient. Their action had also to be supplanted by an effective countervailing force. That force was the fundamentally coercive regulation of economic relations by the global monopoly with the market all the while continuing to exist. The Stalinist social order basically structured the relations of extra-economic constraint required by perpetuating primitive accumulation.

Primitive capitalist accumulation had even less regard for the needs of the population than Stalinist accumulation. Limited by the exigencies of accumulation, the market was no more receptive of the needs of the population than was the extra-economic constraint exercised by the global monopoly. It is a historical fact that the primitive accumulation of capital has never witnessed a period where the market was sovereign—on the contrary, extra-economic constraint has played a considerable role, and in particularly brutal forms at that. But, while capital can remain perfectly indifferent to the needs of the population, it cannot be indifferent to the sale of its products. Therefore it has a direct and vital interest in consolidating the role of the market, thereby indirectly bringing a reduction in the role of direct extra-economic constraint. At the point where constraint gives way to the market, capital itself moves from the stage of primitive accumulation to development. And at this point as well, the two processes of accumulation part ways: primitive capitalist accumulation comes gradually to an end, and primitive anticapitalist accumulation continues perpetually.

A functional difference lies at the root of this disjunction. The immediate function of capital is to sell its products; that of the Stalinist monopoly is to accumulate the means of production. For the former, sale is the condition of accumulation, and it is therefore turned toward the market. For the latter, sale is an obstacle to accumulation, and it is therefore turned against the market and toward an available alternative—extra-economic constraint. The functional perpetuation of primitive accumulation had its structural counterpart in the perpetuation of the dual monopoly over power and ownership. Thus, Stalinism provided a lasting structure for the normally transitional relations of extra-economic constraint required by primitive accumulation, which the social context had made insurmountable.

There has long existed a fundamental agreement on the special role of agriculture in anticapitalist industrialization and Stalinist primitive accumulation. But recently views have emerged which show a tendency to reassess the importance of this role. In 1975 Michael Ellman ventured the rhetorical question: "Did the agricultural surplus provide the resources for the increase in investment in the USSR during the First Five-year Plan?" His answer was an emphatic no, the echo of which persists to this day.[103] Of course the opposite opinion persists as well, held, among others, by Alec Nove, who writes: "Agriculture thus made a decisive contribution to the financing of the [First Five-year] Plan." To support this conclusion he makes the following comparison: "In 1933 the grain procurement organization . . . paid roughly 5.70 rubles for a centner of rye and sold this rye to state flour mills at 22.20 rubles."[104] Perhaps the truth in this dispute lies in statistical data which are still relatively accessible. But whatever the case, it is important to keep distinct a number of problems which tend to become intermingled. For example, the volume of agricultural surplus channeled into industry must not be assumed to reflect the degree to which these goods were really converted into effectively productive industrial investments. While it may be acknowledged that a transfer of goods from one sector to the other did in fact take place, there is another and perhaps more essential question: namely, what advantages accrued to industry from this transfer, or what damage did it cause to agriculture? Ellman and others are interested in the first question; the second question is more relevant to the present discussion. For manifold reasons, the general answer to the two questions strikes a negative balance: in the form it took in the USSR during the first Five-year Plan, primitive accumulation did such severe and lasting damage to agriculture that the expansion of industry, spectacular though it was, did not reach commensurate proportions.

There was another, even more important aspect: the principal effects of this transfer were experienced not by industry or agriculture but by the social organization as a whole. The erection of the social order necessary to effect this aspect of primitive accumulation was the lasting historical consequence of this transfer of goods, above and beyond whatever economic effect it may have had.

This momentous historical process was characterized by a number of constant parameters: the paramount objective of all agricultural activity was to serve the needs of industry; the satisfaction of the needs of agriculture was only a subsidiary objective of industry; and agriculture was obliged in its practical activities to sacrifice itself and its own interests to those of industry. a further aggravating circumstance of this inequality was that the economic needs of the respective sectors were defined by the extra-economic decisions of the monopoly, and not as a consequence of their direct relations with one another. The total subordination of agriculture to industry and the consequent total subordination of agriculture to the monopoly could not have been achieved without this mediation of power. To render its mediation more effective and direct, the monopoly transferred the links between the two sectors from the economic sphere to the extra-economic, thereby consolidating its social supremacy. Reciprocity became unilaterality, and free exchange based on consent was replaced by forced sacrifice. Economically, what exists even today between agriculture and industry is not a natural link, but a state of deliberate disarticulation. Once again Stalinism reproduced the general syncretism it believed itself to have shed.

Intended as a measure to have a direct practical effect, the subordination of agriculture and its underdevelopment were in the end transformed from a stimulator into a powerful brake on industrial development. Along with its precarious production—since in reality there was no surplus—agriculture also transferred to industry its suffocating underproductivity. Stalinism wrested the economy from one impasse to plunge it into another. Over the long term, industrial productivity could not be based on underproductivity in agriculture. Although it was not inevitable, as the examples of Hungary and Bulgaria show, Stalinist perpetuation of primitive accumulation also included the perpetuation of nonproductive agriculture.

2. Monopoly on employment

The massive transfer of labor power from agriculture to industry also contributed to consolidating underproduction in agriculture, while at the same time transmitting it to industry. Millions of peasants, stripped of their means of production and of any hope of ever recovering them, were wrenched by the disruptive force of this new condition from their century-old attachment to the countryside. A broad social redistribution of labor took place on a vast scale as a consequence of the reorganization of agrarian property into collective farms and the simultaneous expansion of industry.

The effects of this redistribution were different for the two sectors. For agriculture, it reduced the much-decried pressures of rural overpopulation and thus, implicitly, rural consumption, although at the expense of reducing the size of available able-bodied and skilled labor pool. For industry, this redistribution enabled it to satisfy its immediate needs (multiplied a hundredfold) for labor, but at the price of a general fall in productivity. It was not only that the newcomers were generally unskilled; a growing number of factory managers in fact preferred to hire this unproductive labor, which was willing to accept the worst conditions, in place of higher-paid, skilled workers, with their continual demands for improvement in their living and working conditions. With the absorption of this mass of peasants, the seeds of divergent interest were planted in the working class.

These direct consequences of anticapitalist primitive accumulation, themselves products of special circumstances, did not disappear with the circumstances that had engendered them, but became lasting structural elements of the new social order. From the standpoint of industry, this amounted to a general deterioration in working conditions, sustained by specific hiring practices. The global monopoly possessed a monopoly on employment as well. This monopoly is inherent to all Stalinist societies and has been one of the principal reasons for the perpetuation of primitive accumulation.

Labor enjoys conditions generally similar to those existing in capitalist society insofar as wages are its form of remuneration (with the exception of agriculture). But the similarity is only apparent; the situation is in fact defined by an absolute antinomy specific to the Stalinist order. To be sure, labor is subject to the economic constraint that it must be sold, and to that extent the similarity with capitalism holds; however, the situation is utterly dissimilar by virtue of the fact that there is no real market where this sale can take place. Though it is obliged to offer itself for sale, labor cannot be bought except by the global monopoly, which thereby acquires a general monopoly on employment as well. With only one buyer for labor that must be sold, the millions of individuals forced to sell their labor become a sheer travesty of a market. The labor market itself becomes illusory. The classical meeting place of buyers and sellers, the market nonetheless cannot preserve its crucial function if the possibility of sale is negated by a prohibition on purchase. Therefore, the relation established between those who sold their labor and the monopoly was not an economic relation of exchange but an extra-economic relation of constraint exercised by the monopoly.

A work force that must sell its labor cannot remain indifferent to the fact that it has no access to an effective labor market. On the capitalist labor market, there is a fundamental inequality between the two parties engaged in this specific process of exchange. The presumptive buyers possess the tools necessary to the labor of the sellers, but the sellers have only their labor power, which they can only make use of if they have the tools possessed by the buyers. It is not difficult to see that the factor on which this inequality hinges is the means of production, which belong to the nonproducing owners and not to the productive work force.

Even at the level of simple empirical observation, the organic disunity of the Stalinist economy and the particular way this disunity is reflected by the condition of the producers, particularly wage laborers, is obvious. For example, for workers in the machinery production industry, the production process takes place outside the market (there is no market for its products); the process of reproduction has its specialized consumer goods market, for workers perfectly real; and, finally, their labor is consigned to a market which is wholly and obviously apparent. Thus workers are situated economically outside the real market and within an illusory market at one and the same time.

The fundamental inequality of the capitalist labor market is matched by a formal equality—the economic equality of partners, albeit expressed in legal and political terms, that is inherent in the normal process of exchange. Specifically, the partners have the formally equal freedom to enter into the process of exchange or not; the freedom to choose their partner; the freedom to negotiate and to accept or refuse the conditions of exchange; and, finally, formal freedom in general, based on the cardinal law of the market which presumes that all acts concluded on it represent a free exchange of equivalent goods.

These formal equalities are in general eliminated by Stalinist societies along with the economic and social context which engendered them. But instead of replacing them with real equalities, Stalinism stopped with their elimination. Even the formal freedom of labor to enter or not to enter into the process of its sale is abolished by various laws which, though purporting to combat parasitism, in substance merely give a legal form to forced labor. The freedom to choose one's partner is the exclusive reserve of the monopoly and, both practically and formally, becomes inaccessible to the producers. It is obvious that this polar inequality cannot be a basis for real negotiation.

Thus while preserving and even deepening the inequality specific to capitalism, i.e., inequality with regard to ownership of the means of production, Stalinism went even further to abolish the principal forms of formal equality, i.e., legal and political equality. There can be no legal equality between producers obliged by law to sell their labor and an illegal monopoly which purchases it and which makes such a law. There is no political equality between those who sell their labor, yet are deprived of any autonomous institution for their own defense, and a monopoly which sets the terms for that purchase and, moreover, is able to draw on the totality of social institutions to do so. The capitalist labor market tends to dissimulate a fundamental economic inequality under the guise of certain formal equalities, but the Stalinist monopoly over employment does away with these formal equalities, thereby making the economic inequality more grating and infinitely more transparent.

Where employment is held by a monopoly, the inequality between the seller and the buyer of labor becomes legal, coherent, and comprehensive. Like any other monopoly, this monopoly has as its central function that of imposing non-equivalent exchange within the domain under its sway. The exercise of the functions of the Stalinist monopoly also includes the privilege of establishing the immediate price of labor as well as the price of the goods necessary for its survival. In 1938, Lange and Taylor described this dual function as follows: "as such sole producer, the state maintains exchange relations with its citizens, buying their productive services with money and selling to them the commodities which it produces." But the reality of the situation is decidedly less neutral than it appears from this description. The two price ranges, the prices for which the producers sell their labor and the prices for which they purchase the goods necessary for their own survival, are fixed by the same monopoly. Thus the producers are doubly exposed to the rigors of nonequivalent exchange: the monopoly which is the sole purchaser of their labor power is also the sole seller of their means of production and survival. By its very nature the monopoly takes fullest advantage of this dual evisceration, common to all Stalinist societies, of the value of labor, thereby contributing integrally to the perpetuation of primitive accumulation.

Prices, employed to mystify rather than to measure the value of labor, not only form the link between production and consumption, they also bring together two distinct worlds, that of economic constraint and that of extra-economic constraint. By virtue of this union, the Stalinist economy acquires a coherence beyond its insuperable antinomies and is thus able to function by utilizing basic economic mechanisms for the execution of extra-economic decisions. The entire social edifice is built with a view toward rendering plausible this dissimulation, which thereby becomes merely one more illusion among others.

As a result of these pressures, both the purchase and the sale of labor becomes economically and socially illusory and, because it hosts an illusory process of purchase and sale, the labor market itself is illusory. A totally different relation moves in in its stead.

After having separated the producers from the ownership of the means of production, the monopoly also deprived them of the ownership, i.e., the right to dispose over, their labor. The value of labor was henceforth determined by an extra-economic, coercive decision which in effect severed the relation of labor to the value of both the products of labor and its productivity, the two parameters which regulate real market values. By blocking the action of these parameters, the monopoly transformed the determination of value from an economic process into a bureaucratic decision. But for this bureaucratic decision to have an effective economic impact, its two terms, the monopoly which takes the decision and the producers who suffer its effect, must be linked by relations which enable them to act in consonance, i.e., as two complementary levels of the same bureaucratic structure.

3. From economic motivation to economic pretext

For the capitalist owner, possession of the means of production is motivated by the pursuit of profit. For the Stalinist monopoly, the use of mechanisms of value is motivated by the objective of proliferating the means of production. Whereas the first is concerned with accumulating worth, the paramount interest of the latter is to accumulate things. In the one case, production is the instrument of the economy. In the other, the opposite is true, i.e., the economy is the instrument of production. Consequently under Stalinism the primacy of the extra-economic is not only instrumental, it is also motivational; all economic activity is motivated in the last instance by extra-economic objectives. The priority of the extra-economic in the regulation of production is the perfect counterpart, therefore, to the priority role it plays in motivating that process. Stalinism reduces economic motivations to simple pretexts.

When confronting the rigors of scarcity, Stalinism retained economic mechanisms. Later on, in the endeavor to overcome scarcity through anticapitalist industrialization, it placed economic mechanisms under extra-economic regulation. But the apparatus erected to launch industrialization remained essentially unchanged after it had achieved its goal. Although relations of this kind may have been justified in the early stages of industrialization, they acquired a spontaneous tendency not only to perpetuate themselves, but to become static, take root, and become generalized. The tendency for market relations to become generalized, which is characteristic of capitalism, had its counterpart under Stalinism in the tendency for extra-economic regulations to become generalized.

Instead of transcending the economic, which would have meant the elimination of mechanisms of value, Stalinism regressed to the pre-economic, which means maintaining these mechanisms but distorting their action through the pressures of extra-economic regulation. As long as economic mechanisms were seen to entail the risk of a resurrection of capitalism if they were left to develop on their own momentum, any alternative at all could plausibly be considered preferable. Extra-economic constraint was one such alternative and as such appeared to be endowed with a moral superiority and rationality embodied in its social source, the global monopoly. The logic of constraint carried it from the economy into every other domain of activity with the same moral and rational justification in every case. The generalization of relations of coercion and subordination offered this congenitally disarticulated society a new structure and hence a new homogeneity represented ideologically as monolithism. Insofar as the reversion to capitalism was avoided through the use of coercion, the generalization of coercion appeared both necessary and legitimate.

The rationality of coercion tends, depending on the historical circumstances and the social actors, to become a rationality of repression or to generate new disarticulations. This latter tendency has been preponderant since Khrushchev and is most easily perceptible in the discrepancy between visible social behavior and the secretive awareness of the immorality of that behavior. The generalization of the servile ways of subordination cannot constitute a moral act in our epoch no matter what their motivation, nor can they be felt or professed to be such even by those who promote them. Socially this discrepancy tends constantly toward a break between the claims of official ideology and the day-to-day experience of the population. For individuals and groups, the discrepancy between their outward conduct and their inner thoughts and conscience tends constantly toward conflict. Intellectuals especially have assimilated and expressed this conflict in their creative works, which bear witness to the moral disintegration of the individual brought about by the Stalinist homogenization of society. Stalinism did not surmount the original social disarticulation; it merely concealed it. To prevent this creeping conflict from threatening existing structures, centralized coercion went from the control of conduct to the control of minds, the minds of persons both public and private.

The subordination of the economy to extra-economic constraint and the transformation of relations of production into relations of submission are the operational expression of the fundamental fact that the agent exercising the functions of ownership is in essence extra-economic. Chronologically, the functions of ownership accrued to power, not vice versa. But once invested with those functions, it was inevitable that power become uncontrollable, indisputable, and infallible. It is almost tautological that the direct economic supremacy of power presupposes the primacy of power relations in the economy. From this it follows that class relations must play a secondary role. As it developed over time, this inversion of social priorities reflected the conditions that gave rise to it, which were characterized less by the achievements of power than by the state of the economy and the failures of the social classes.

To be effective, extra-economic constraint requires more than just supercentralization; it must also enjoy the broadest social acceptance. After Stalin's departure from the scene, the predominant tendency in this regard was to avoid the economically unproductive measures of extra-economic constraint and to downgrade the latter to mass repression. Extra-economic regulation of economic activity pays tribute to the basic antinomy in its premises and its functioning by its continual oscillation between two hard-to-reconcile tendencies: one, toward the strengthening of centralization, and the other, toward economic reform—toward the image of unanimity (or quasi-unanimity) and toward a certain relaxing of its institutions, extolled as democratization.

So long as it preserves its global nature, the monolithism of ownership and power will attempt to reproduce that monolithism in the political structures of society. But it is vulnerable at core, and that fact makes it emphatically prefer formal, docile unanimity to real majority support (the possibility of which it seems profoundly to doubt). The antidemocratic nature of these societies is at bottom not a reflection of the political will of its successive leaders—although it is of course not independent of it—but of the unlimited centralization of ownership and power, transformed into a social structure. To the extent that such formal docility is actually achieved, the substance of the relations that ensure it is coercion from above and subordination below. These are relations which are inherent to every bureaucracy, except that in this case their purpose is to ensure the functioning of a society rather than of just an apparatus. It is telling that in none of its historical forms has the direct exercise of ownership been intermingled with the direct exercise of democracy, even in societies with democratic political structures that have since become traditional. The explanation of this incongruity lies in the fact that the exercise of ownership is based on the legal guarantee of the right of *abusus*, which the exercise of democracy would preclude. On the other hand, it is possible for a given power to employ democratic means to protect the nondemocratic exercise of ownership; that is one of the current paradoxes of late capitalism. But insofar as it is dedicated to the systematic distortion of the relations of exchange—which are the economic bedrock of democracy—it will necessarily distort their political consequences.

No nuanced structures of this sort can form under Stalinism where a supercentralized power exercises monopolist ownership over the whole of the nation's assets, and where the distortion of market relations reaches the point of sheer mystification. There is not the least chance in these societies of reconciling dysfunction and its context with the exercise of democracy. Among the rules of democracy most intolerable for the functioning of the monopoly is that which subordinates it to the electoral control of society. On this point the Stalinist monopoly behaves in a way that is essentially no different from that of any financial magnate in the West. Neither would even consider the idea of subjecting his or its economic power to the whims of universal suffrage. The merely formal nature of elections under Stalinism therefore is in fact a functional requirement of the economy. Having assumed the ownership of the whole, power assumes implicitly the antidemocratic nature of that ownership as well. Stalinist society ensures the absolute predominance of relations of coercion and subordination in order to stabilize its distribution of roles and anchor it in a social structure. Efforts to democratize this social order would tend therefore to eliminate these essentially antidemocratic relations, and thus implicitly to eliminate Stalinism itself. It follows then that Stalinism and democracy are organically incompatible; that the antidemocratism of this society is a political phenomenon in its manifestations but not in its substance; and that this being so, Stalinism is susceptible of amelioration only within the limits of a more tolerant antidemocracy. The chance of gaining democracy is contingent on one factor above all else: the abolishment of the global monopoly over ownership.

But neither power nor ownership have survived the process of their fusion without profound transformations. What ownership gave to power in the first instance was its irremediably nondemocratic substance; what power gave to ownership was the preeminence of extra-economic constraint in its exercise.

Beyond its visible manifestations, the primacy of extra-economic constraint is manifested in two traits absolutely specific to this economy. First, with the means of production no longer possessing the quality of commodity, the bulk of production capacity is used to produce products which economically are nonexistent, extra-economic products. Second, and to a large extent as a consequence of the first trait, this society has an unexcelled ability, inscribed in the structures of its economy, to remain indifferent to the economic results of its productive activity. Insofar as it retains economic mechanisms, Stalinist society has had to systematically distort their action in order to acquire these two unique characteristics and maintain them on a continuing basis.

Like any other economy, the Stalinist economy avails itself of market, value, price, wage, and money mechanisms. But unlike any other, the Stalinist economy prevents these mechanisms from fulfilling their general function of articulating production with the market. Even a mere surface comparison between the prescriptions of the economic plans and the eloquent demands of the market will reveal their systematic disarticulation, although it is true that since the 60s this disarticulation has been more differentiated—hence the diversity and sheer number of markets, so often commented upon.

At the one extreme of this spectrum is the totally illusory market for means of production. Although, formally, means of production can be neither bought nor sold, they nonetheless have a nominal value. At the other extreme is the peasant market, generally called free, in which economic mechanisms suffer fewer distortions than in the other markets in this economy. Between these two extremes are markets that are illusory and/or real, to varying degrees: for example, the market for consumer goods at plan prices, the black market at speculative prices, the labor market, the market of obligatory contracts imposed upon agricultural production units and the peasants, etc. Such fragmentation of the market is one more proof of how fragile and even specious is the structural cohesion of these societies.

At the origin of this atomization is the underlying ambiguity an economy such as this, subject as it is to two regulators—the law of value and the decisions of the monopoly—a dualism for which the only possible rationality is that their actions are at least not convergent. They do not overlap but differ from, if not oppose, one another. They are most fundamentally opposed in the production–consumption cycle, the terms of which the market tends to correlate, and extra-economic constraint to keep separate. This is seems to be what Mihaly Vajda had in mind in stating: "However, because the satisfaction of already existing consumer needs has increasingly become a necessary precondition for the proper functioning of the system, certain elements of a market economy must be tolerated. In this manner the system's viability is guaranteed by regulatory mechanisms which are incompatible with its very economic principle." Fluctuating but continuous, the domination of extra-economic constraint over economic mechanisms may be measured in terms of two empirical indicators: the first, easier to observe than to measure directly, is the chronic shortage of consumer goods on the market; the second, more directly measurable, is the rate of growth in the production of means of production, i.e., capital goods, which exist wholly outside the market.

It follows from the foregoing that, unlike in questions of ownership, where it reigns unchallenged, in matters of regulating economic activity the monopoly not only suffers the presence of another force, it even accepts, to a point, being opposed. The common assumption is that the monopoly is not sufficiently powerful to be able to eliminate this rivalry, or that the rivalry is useful to it, or both. Earlier on, I commented on the efforts of Stalinism to assimilate the experience of war communism. That experiment failed because it was an attempt at centralized extra-economic distribution of scarcity without recourse to the traditional mechanisms of the market. Stalinism inherited the principal limitation of the experiment, scarcity, but was determined not to repeat its failure. It therefore resolved to take on this limitation and what followed from it, the necessity of preserving economic mechanisms, yet maintain them under the strictest control. It may be argued that by not eliminating economic mechanisms, the Stalinist monopoly thereby necessarily took on the objective limitation placed on its power by the implantation of a supercentralized form of ownership in an economy of severe scarcity. Its leaning toward economic mechanisms was the material expression of its deference to a need that was beyond its capacity to meet.

The crux of this model is that the global monopoly prevents or obstructs the action of economic mechanisms by simulating them, and what appears to students of societies and, indeed, to those living in them to be such mechanisms at work is in actual fact wholly or partially the disguised economic action of the monopoly. The real relative economic efficacy of such feigned economic action is of decisive importance for this specious economy. The price of a particular product, arbitrarily set by the monopoly, bears largely no relation to value, but for the social actors who need that product and who hence must purchase it, this arbitrary price has the same prohibitive force it would have if it were an adequate expression of value. This faculty of economic mechanisms to lose their substance without thereby losing their functional potential was not discovered by Stalinism; it is at the origin of the constitution of capitalist monopolies as well, with the difference that under capitalism this distortion of economic mechanisms is restricted to certain economic branches and even to within these branches, whereas under Stalinism it is generalized.

To transform economic mechanisms into active agents of extra-economic constraint, the global monopoly invests them with certain special functions to its own advantage. These are the function of amplifying extra-economic constraint, the function of dissimulation, and the function of circumventing the direct application of that constraint. To return to the example of arbitrary prices, it is thanks to the functioning of this skewed economic mechanism that the monopoly, instead of openly and directly subjecting millions of people to a formal act of extra-economic subordination, is able to allow them to retain the illusion that their decision to buy this or that object is a tangible act of economic autonomy. Consequently, one of the functions exercised by economic mechanisms in this particular context is to partly relieve extra-economic constraint of the necessity of direct intervention, thus easing the tensions that such interventions create. Instead of interposing itself in each instance between the needs of individuals and the objects required to satisfy them, the monopoly leaves this concern to the price, money, and exchange mechanisms.

Accordingly, every piece of money and every act of sale and purchase becomes the social vehicle of a coercive decision. More important than the legal texts, the police, and the bureaucracy, it is this combination between the apparent neutrality of such mechanisms and the long habit of members of society of making use of them is able to magnify the impact of extra-economic constraint on economic behavior. This then is a second function through which economic mechanisms benefit the monopoly, i.e., that of amplifying considerably the effects of its decisions.

Finally, a third function, already implied in the first two, is dissimulation. Just as the true social seat of ownership is dissimulated by its fictional ascription to the working class, so is the coercive exercise of its functions largely camouflaged by the delusory use of illusory economic mechanisms. For the individual, the execution of an order under the pressure of constraint and his free decision to purchase or not to purchase a certain object at a certain price have nothing at all in common. In all these cases, which constitute over and over again the living content of economic activity, the dissimulating functions of these mechanisms give the relations of coercion and subordination the appearance of relations of free exchange.

In the light of discussions on the correlation between plan and market which in some Stalinist countries have accompanied attempts at economic reform or reforms themselves, these considerations may appear exaggerated or even outmoded. A discussion of these reforms, however, would take me wide of my purpose, which is to analyze a particular segment of history, the genesis of Stalinist societies, and to describe the principal and most lasting economic transformations that accompanied their birth. Their current state, which represents a different phenomenon, i.e., neo-Stalinism, falls strictly speaking outside of this schema; but just as the radical experience of war communism was assimilated up to a critical point by nascent Stalinism, the experience of nascent Stalinism, which was also radical, has been assimilated up to a critical point by neo-Stalinism. In the first case this critical point was marked by the passage from the abolishment of economic mechanisms to their utilization, and in the second by the transition from their excessive distortion to milder, more flexible forms.

At the present level of their productive forces, the renunciation of economic mechanisms would probably result in economic disaster in the majority of these countries. The historical trend of reforms has been not toward the elimination but toward the reinforcement of these mechanisms. But the essence of a phenomenon is never manifest directly (which does not mean that analysis can disregard it), and the essential point here is that the economic mechanisms in question are largely the mechanisms of a capitalist economy. Their free play is no more and no less than the equivalent of the free development of capitalist ownership; therefore, if capitalist ownership is to be avoided, the free play of these mechanisms must also be avoided or at least limited.

It follows that an anticapitalist social order and an economy based on the action of economic mechanisms are organically incompatible. Extra-economic constraint, most conspicuously embodied in the plan, protects anticapitalism against these capitalism-generating economic mechanisms, embodied in the market. Placed under a dual historical constraint, i.e, the constraint of scarcity, which obliges it to make use of economic mechanisms, and that of its anticipated, premature birth, which impels it to perpetuate itself, this pre-industrial anticapitalism, which has taken the form not of the socialization but the monopolization of ownership, can neither avoid nor tolerate these mechanisms. All it can do is to disrupt their action and in this way transform them into its own instruments.

The evident conclusion is that in this context the distortion of economic mechanisms by extra-economic constraint is by and large inevitable. What can be avoided is not the distortion, but its variability. As historical experience has shown, too much distortion can lead to the catastrophic decline, although perhaps not the utter collapse, of the productivity of social labor. That is the case with mandatory deliveries of agricultural produce to the state in the majority of these countries. Too little distortion risks planting the seeds of the restoration of capitalist ownership—as in the case of *perestroika*, which is essentially merely a resumption under less inauspicious conditions of the Leninist NEP experiment abandoned by Soviet Stalinism.

The upshot is that if it is true that economic mechanisms tend spontaneously to generate or resurrect capitalist ownership, and extra-economic constraints to reproduce pre-industrial anticapitalism, intentions of establishing harmony between the market and the plan have little chances of developing into a realistic strategy. Accommodations between the two are possible and desirable; within certain limits, as has been pointed out, there even exists a margin of potential complementarity of which the global monopoly avails itself liberally. Nonetheless, it is crucial to keep in mind that the relation which links the market to the plan is ultimately one of conflict. A structural conflict can be controlled; it cannot be transformed into harmony or idyllic coexistence. The global monopoly maintains its domination over society most directly more through manipulation than through repression; indeed, this form of subordination may be regarded as Stalinism's identifying trait. Unlike mass repression, the monopoly's forceful and unhesitating interventions to ensure and maintain the universality of relations of coercion and compliance are constant and affect every sphere of society.

What the plan and the market have in common is that each brings together and gives form to a specific type of social relations which extends beyond it and of which it is only the rough expression. The social relations expressed through the market are economic in substance; those expressed through the plan are extra-economic. The former are most faithfully embodied in commodity exchange, the latter in another type of exchange—exchange between centralized coercion and compliant execution. The movement from the manifest level of plan and market to the more basic level of economic and extra-economic constraint brings more clearly to light one of the principal features distinguishing the Stalinist monopoly from capitalist monopolies.

As in any other monopoly, the specific economic function of the Stalinist monopoly resides in its systematic deformation of mercantile exchange. However, this very deformation pushes to its limit the range of action of this general function of monopolies, which Preobrazhensky describes as follows: "The concentration of all big industries of the country in the hands of a single trust . . . increases to an extraordinary extent in comparison with monopoly capitalism the possibility of carrying out . . . a price policy on the basis of monopoly."[105]

Here a fundamental economic difference between Stalinism and war communism appears in full light. Whereas the latter aimed to abolish exchange and the market, Stalinism maintained them, thereby providing the monopoly with its specific field of action and hence its general *raison d'être*. The key was to preserve the market in such a way as to prevent it from functioning; it was this which made the suprastate monopoly a formidable accumulator of means and assigned the Stalinist social order its industrializing mission. With the whole of the economy under its sway, the suprastate monopoly was now able to assume that unique role which distinguishes it from any other monopoly: namely, that of general regulator of relations of exchange. Its global nature enabled it to proceed unencumbered from episodic nonequivalent exchange to its generalization. But in the process, nonequivalent exchange also became illusory. Put more precisely, what was generalized was not exchange, but its nonequivalence, for exchange was in fact rigorously restricted.

The way these mechanisms of exchange function is best and most generally illustrated by the example of the means of production. Simply stated, the same monopoly which prohibits the sale and purchase of the means of production defines their importance to the economy through its powers of extra-economic constraint. It attributes to them a formal economic identity while preventing them from having one that is real. Its extra-economic decision is expressed in the language of economic mechanisms which in reality have been reduced to silence. It prevents the market from setting the value of the means of production and instead assigns to them a price of its own. Clearly this price is no longer a measure of value; it is merely the economic clothing of a coercive extra-economic decision. The case of subsistence goods is quite different; not only can they still be bought and sold, but normally they can only be obtained on the market, or on some market, through direct purchase and sale. Their commodity nature remains wholly unaltered. Between these two extremes in economic status is labor, the sale of which is obligatory, while its purchase forbidden.

As Brus observes, "Monopolies take advantage of their economic strength to restrain the process of adaptation, which rests on reciprocal ties between the conditions of production and conditions of exchange.''[106] But whereas capitalist monopolies only impede this process of mutual adaptation, the Stalinist monopoly effects the total separation of these two terms. In the first case, obstruction represents a functional disturbance in the economic structures requiring this adaptation; in the second, separation represents the regular function of an economic structure in which the essential portion of production is barred *a priori* from the exchange process. This is one more point of utter dissimilarity demonstrating that the Stalinist monopoly is not a capitalist monopoly, just as it is not a state monopoly, contrary to the most long-standing confusions. What defines the Stalinist monopoly and distinguishes it from every other monopoly is its incomparable degree of centralization, concretized in its two fundamental points of reference, its subject and object, and the manner in which they are articulated.

Its subject is an extremely restricted and exclusive supreme authority with a strong tendency toward personalization. It legitimates its monopoly over ownership by its monopoly over power. Its material object is the whole of the nation's assets, comprising directly all the means of production and, indirectly, through the monopoly it holds on employment, labor. The articulation between these two poles has a pronounced unidirectional character: it excludes reciprocity via a one-way exercise of extra-economic constraint.

For a capitalist monopoly, nonequivalent exchange is made possible by the parallel existence of equivalent exchange; for a Stalinist monopoly, nonequivalent exchange is made possible because equivalent exchange is universally impossible. To the extent that Stalinism separates the production of objects from the production of value, it implicitly transforms the exchange of potentially equivalent values into the exchange of objects for which no measure of equivalence exists. In a certain sense, exchange is maintained but equivalence is destroyed. But in effect nonequivalence is also destroyed, since both ultimately rest on the same term of reference which has been eliminated—value. The global monopoly therefore must necessarily replace nonequivalent exchange by coercive exchange. Coercion may be applied to the process of exchange proper or to its mechanisms. It operates on the process when the decision to buy or sell does not belong to the respective actors, but is imposed upon them from without—for example, the "contractual" obligations of the peasants or collective farms to sell to the state certain products in certain amounts at certain prices by a certain time. It operates on the mechanisms of exchange insofar as it does not oblige the individual to purchase a certain object, but merely to credit it with a value which in reality it does not have and which has been attributed to it by a coercive extra-economic decision.

Whereas a capitalist monopoly is a logical development of capitalist ownership, the Stalinist monopoly is the miscreation of its premature abolishment, and this difference in their origins leads to differences in their functioning. The fact is that in establishing its global monopoly, Stalinism opposed the laws of capitalism with the form of ownership they would have generated spontaneously in the course of their natural development as a consequence of the centralization occurring in capitalism's advanced stage. The direct source of the global monopoly under Stalinism, however, was the abolishment of underdeveloped capitalism. Hence, its direct action does not turn on reproducing the capitalist laws of the market, but on replacing them with anticapitalist, centralized, extra-economic coercion. If one can say that the capitalist market is merely the distorted manifestation of the real links between the needs of individuals and their productive capacities, the Stalinist market is but a manifestation of this manifestation and a distortion of this distortion.

Ultimately this ambiguity is reflected in the special situation of the means of production. Their formal exclusion from the market signifies that society is prohibited from purchasing them and that the monopoly is free *not* to sell them. It is essential for an understanding of how this machinery functions to observe its internal logic, which it opposes to the logic that governs the functioning of the economy. A pertinent example of this internal logic is the fact that, by a kind of retroaction, the subjectively imposed exclusion of the means of production from the market thereupon becomes an objective condition of this sham economy. Insofar as their sale is *prohibited*, the means of production cannot have a value, but if they do not have a value they *cannot* be sold. Prohibition is transformed into impossibility, and what is impossible has no need of being prohibited.

Even if stockpiling maneuvers may be used from time to time to corner markets, ultimately every capitalist entrepreneur produces to sell. None of them has the freedom of the Stalinist monopoly, which produces the means of production precisely in order not to sell them. Transmitting their non-value to all the salable objects they produce, these unsellable means of production veritably constitute the extra-economic base of the Stalinist economy. Consequently, it is not only subjective constraint which is extra-economic in this economy; the extra-economic has its objectified form as well, and indeed even its objective embodiment: namely, the means of production. I would argue that this freedom of the global monopoly to produce means of production which it has no need to sell constitutes the secret and principal source of its exceptional industrializing potential and the attraction that this model still has among pre-industrial countries. This freedom, written in Stalinism's genetic code, is a particular manifestation of the general separation between production and the market which the monopoly introduced to take the place of their interaction. This separation extends from their functioning to their results. The systematic adulteration of the market encourages greater production of means of production. But the imbalance that arises is also partly the reflection of the different ways in which production and the market are affected by their separation. Whereas production can remain largely indifferent to market signals, the market cannot remain indifferent to the limitations which production imposes upon it through ignoring it, nor to the fact that it is deprived of the possibility of being able to transmit its signals, or that its signals even if transmitted are disregarded.

The signals of the market consist, first and foremost, of solvent demand. On the market, solvent demand generates a hierarchy of preferences for diverse categories of available goods. In turn this hierarchy is the principal term of reference for the orientation of production. The Stalinist monopoly's freedom from the market also implies that it is free from this hierarchy of preferences, and hence from solvent demand, which it thus need not and in fact does not take into account in its direct actions. But all the mechanisms operating on the market converge on this mechanism of solvent demand with its synthesizing function. If it is blocked, all the other mechanisms are rendered ineffectual as well. The paralysis of solvent demand may therefore be considered a truly original trait, if not indeed an identifying trait, of a Stalinist economy.

The impact of this paralysis of solvent demand is continuous, that is, each economic cycle is vitiated by the effects of the paralysis manifested during the preceding cycle, and in fact all preceding cycles, and solvent demand is further debased. In addition to being paralysed in its action, it is distorted in its expression, for rather than expressing the needs of the population, it expresses the partial ignorance of these needs manifest during the course of the preceding cycle.

Thus at this level the freedom of the monopoly has two complementary consequences: first, that of not producing what the solvent demand of the population would have required if it had been able to manifest itself normally, and second, that of producing what no solvent demand requires. Thus this type of non-capitalist society adopts as its *raison d'être* the discrepancy which Rosa Luxemburg described as ''a universal law of human labor which makes for more and more social labor time being employed in the manufacture of producer goods rather than of consumer goods.'' But rather than a universal law, what seems to be operating here is a specific tendency imprinted on the conduct of these societies by the conditions of their genesis: after having anticipated the possibility of socializing the ownership of the means of production, they plunge headlong into the anticipation of a solvent demand for means of production which their economies do not have the capacity to produce.

The freedom of the monopoly is only a corollary of the lack of freedom of solvent demand, that is, the lack of freedom of the population to express its economically legitimate needs. Once again the lack of freedom of the population inherent in this social order shows itself as the political consequence of its special mode of economic functioning.

Political consequences aside, the paralysis of solvent demand has economic effects of cardinal importance. First, ignorance of solvent demand falsifies value in these societies. According to Marx, value is the socially necessary quantity of labor invested in the production of a particular object, which implies that not all labor-producing objects necessarily produce value. To achieve this dual productivity, labor must also be recognized as socially necessary by the market. It follows that all labor which produces objects that are not matched by a solvent demand is labor which produces use values that do not have an exchange value. In this way, adulteration of solvent demand leads to the general adulteration of value.

Economic mechanisms continue to exist but are drained of their substance. They are unable to fulfill their crucial function, that of regulating the whole of economic activity. Banished from the new economic context created by Stalinist society, this capital function would be largely assumed by the new social context it had also created.

4. The surrogate structure

In proceeding to generalize expropriation, Stalinism was to a great extent reminiscent of the exploits of war communism. But whereas the latter remained but a peculiar episode, Stalinism became an original and viable system of production. Why did Stalinism succeed where war communism had failed?

At a very general level, the answer to this question can be reduced to two cardinal points. The first, discussed in the preceding section, refers to the fact that Stalinism was able to create a workable economic context. The second, which will be dealt with now, is its relative success in putting together an adequate social environment that would permit this economy to be functional within certain limits. Thus a decisive source of the viability of Stalinism was its capacity to give a plausible if not stimulative expression to the economic effects of generalized expropriation. In fact, the generalization of expropriation and the emergence of this social context went hand in hand; one would have been inconceivable without the other. Thus my central hypothesis: The historic achievement of Stalinism—its affirmation as a specific mode of production—is due principally to the fact that it buttressed generalized expropriation with the generalization of relations of extra-economic constraint, crystalized in an appropriate social structure.

To summarize briefly: The most direct result of generalized expropriation with regard to economic relations was the constitution of a new system of ownership, which was given concrete form in the establishment of a global monopoly. With regard to social relations, the most direct effect of the establishment of the monopoly was the emergence of a social context which would ensure its efficacy and hence its rationality within that context.

Perhaps more even than in the case of the economy, the constitution of this new social context was governed by the special requirements of pre-industrial anticapitalism and can only be considered to be part of a strategy by an idle stretch of the imagination. The men in power at the time took decisions whose real long-term effects had nothing in common with the aims they believed themselves to be pursuing. "The machine is rolling," said Lenin at the last Party Congress in which he participated, "not in the direction we are leading it, but in the direction in which some thing is leading it. . . . The machine is in fact rolling in a quite different direction than those at the wheel imagine." Toward the end of the 1920s, even more than at their beginning, spontaneous, unknown, and inscrutible forces were leading postrevolutionary Russia toward that which it was to become. The true problem is not that the significance of this experiment escaped its original actors, nor those who would repeat it in its major outlines following World War II, but that it continues to this day to remain largely opaque to its protagonists and critics alike.

The most powerful and hence most significant of these forces were the general destructuring of postrevolutionary society (its syncretism); the failure of the social classes to assume ownership of the means of production or to exercise the functions of that ownership in an economically productive manner; and the transfer of property through generalized expropriation which transformed ownership from a class prerogative into a privilege of power. Under the joint pressure of these forces, the social classes, class relations, and thus, implicitly, the already declining class structure, ceased to play a determinant role in this society. An intolerable social void was in the process of being created, which other social entities, joined together by other types of relations forming another structure, would have to fill. Consequently, the social basis for the advent of Stalinism is not to be sought in the action of a new class (the bureaucracy) but in the powerlessness of the traditional productive classes—and especially the working class—to fulfill their social role.

For a valid analysis of Stalinism, therefore, recognition that it is not a class society is fundamental. That is not to say that classes as a specific form of social structuring have disappeared but that their mutual relations have ceased to be the principal molder of other social relations. What are the surrogate relations which assume this indispensable role in Stalinist society, assuring its cohesion and its capacity to perpetuate itself? Obviously, the answer to this crucial question necessarily depends on the definition one gives to the social nature of the Stalinist mode of production.

Some writers prefer to trace the general regression of class relations to a decline in the traditional classes, replaced by other new classes immune to this decline and thus capable of acquiring or maintaining a dominant position in Stalinist societies. For Djilas this class is the bureaucracy; for Konrad and Szelenyi it is the intelligentsia. Hegedus makes a different diagnosis: "Though classes in the classic sense no longer exist, this society still has a structural character grounded in production relations."[107] According to this argument, classes have disappeared, but a structure exists, which implicitly assumes the existence of some other binding element for class relations. Hegedus goes on to say, "Private ownership basically no longer exists in socialist societies; a peculiar new structure has, however, developed, based on the division of labor."[108] A study of the connections between ownership and social structure could certain give important insights for the critical analysis of Stalinism.

But if one seeks the rudiments of this new structural edifice in the division of labor, one risks—if the concept is taken in its strict sense—being left with an element that is too general and attributing the role of dominant social relations to relations which are basically occupational or technical. There is no human society which does not have division of labor; it is a basic concept. Therefore, the likelihood is greater of uncovering the similarities between the Stalinist social order and every other modern society than of unearthing what it is precisely that makes Stalinism unique.

It is not easy to see precisely what the connection between the abolishment of private ownership, which Hegedus takes as a basic point of departure, and the division of labor could be. The difficulty is that, because of the transformations wrought in the system of ownership, not only did class relations regress but other social relations ascended to positions of dominance. Generalized expropriation effected under Stalinism abolished private ownership and made its object the property of the state, and so effectively barred the way to the future evolution of socialized forms of ownership.

Once separated from class relations, relations of ownership acquired a new content; they became power relations. By reducing class relations and class structure to a secondary role, Stalinism conferred the predominant social role on power relations, and so on the specific social structure built up around them. The point on which all these changes converged was the emergence of an global monopoly and its corollary, a society totally stripped of effective access to ownership or to power and, moreover, of every practical possibility of even attaining them. Generalized expropriation and the stabilization of its results signaled first and foremost the economic victory of political power over the productive classes.

Power relations were elevated to their preeminent role by centralized repression and were maintained in that role by integrating them into a structure carved out to fit them. As they were integrated into the social structure, relations of power gradually become relations of authority i.e., bureaucratic-type relations (to use Weber's distinction). Once this took place, centralized mass repression could be replaced by its mere threat. The domination of bureaucratic-type social relations—very often interpreted as the domination of the bureaucracy—was thus established.

Bureaucratic-type relations have always had a broad appeal, from earliest antiquity to modern industrial societies. Their perennial quality speaks for itself: bureaucratic social relations can accommodate themselves to the most diverse modes of production. Unlike class relations, they are compatible with the most dissimilar productive forces.

It therefore becomes clear that, by reducing the class structure to a subaltern role, Stalinism blunted the consequences of the incompatibility between the latter and the state of the productive forces. With bureaucratic-type relations the mainstay of its power, Stalinism was grounded in a structure that was equally indifferent both to the initial backwardness of the productive forces and to their later development by industrialization.

A bureaucratic structure separates the economic sphere and social sphere, whereas a class structure links them together. But this did not violate the law of correspondence as in postrevolutionary society; rather that law was circumvented, and the genetic syncretism of the system was absorbed rather than superseded. The bureaucratic structure was independent of the productive forces and obstructed rather than stimulated their development.

This is why the rapid transformation of the productive forces would leave the mechanisms of the bureaucratic structure intact. To take Vajda's description, "Since there is no longer any private ownership and, at the same time, genuine communal ownership has not been realized, the dynamics of production are not internally safeguarded. The bureaucratic structure of domination does not encourage any expanded form of economic production."

Bureaucratic relations as Weber defines them are a category of stable social relations the substance of which is authority exercised in one direction. Whereas political authority presumes the possibility of control and resistance from below, bureaucratic authority excludes it. For this reason acceptance of political authority assumes the form of adherence, buttressed by deliberation and the exchange of views, while acceptance of bureaucratic authority is manifested in subordination and excludes any real exchange of views.

Translated broadly into political terms, class relations form structures, while bureaucratic relations, which are disinclined to acknowledge class differences, normally only form organizations, generally called bureaucracies. In human society as in any other sphere, structures appear and function quite spontaneously, while organizations constantly require deliberate human intervention. These are in fact two widely differing forms of the social aggregation of inequality. In class structures, social inequality between individuals is produced principally by objective mechanisms and is the consequence of their action. In organizations, inequality between individuals is imposed and accepted by the individuals themselves and, what is more, represents an inherent goal of their action. Social inequality is itself unequal in the two cases.

Reflecting on variations in social inequality from one mode of production to another in his book on historical materialism, Bukharin concludes: "The *specific* form of this relation of economic exploitation and servitude determines the form of the given class society."[109] For Stalinist societies, the specific form taken by relations of servitude is defined by the interworkings of factors that may be aggregately characterized as follows:

1. The principal content of these relations no longer has a class character; their main terms are not social classes.

2. This content has a bureaucratic character.

3. Unlike every other social formation past or present, under Stalinism,

bureaucratic-type relations regulate the activity not of one circumscribed segment of society, but of the whole of society; this is indeed the prime aspect of their generalization.

4. The other aspect of the generalization of bureaucratic relations resides in the fact that they subordinate to themselves not only the whole of society, but also all other social relations. The predominance of bureaucratic relations in Stalinist society is thus both extensive and all-encompassing.

5. Under this double weight of bureaucratic relations society acts less as a functional structure than as a hierarchical organization.

6. To the extent that this whole is capable of perpetuating itself and ensuring plausibly productive social labor and a plausible level of culture, it may be deemed functional. This means implicitly that the bureaucratic-type organization of society will assume and fulfill a number functions proper to the class structure. Given this transfer of functions the bureaucratic organization of Stalinist societies may be considered to be the predominant structure of this social order.

7. Unlike bureaucratic organizations in the narrow sense, a bureaucratic organization that embraces the whole of society does not necessarily break down into several bureaucracies or fragments of bureaucracies.

Weber mentions the industrial enterprise among his examples of bureaucratic organizations. In it bureaucratic relations assume two principal forms. In the most deep-rooted form, which is also indirect, the owners of the means of production enjoy total and unlimited disposal over the surplus product, while the producers, who have created the surplus, have no say on this matter nor are they even consulted. In the second form, which is direct and perfectly apparent, labor relations are frozen in a strict vertical hierarchy of different gradations of authority, requiring the unconditional subordination of each level to each other level above it. At the base of this scaffolding are the direct producers, reduced to the role of executors acting exclusively on orders.

Except for the social locus of the owner these characteristics are also found in industrial enterprises of Stalinist societies. Their fundamental dissimilarity from capitalist enterprises comes to light where the enterprise proper intermeshes with its social context, i.e., where the general social form of production relations which extends beyond the enterprise intermeshes with the specific form of labor relations, operative only within the enterprise. In capitalist democracies, the same workers who are unconditionally subordinated to the owner and his representatives in the labor process become their partners in negotiations and their adversaries in the political process of setting the economic and social conditions of their participation in the labor process. The bureaucratic relations which regulate the labor process become class relations outside the firm, where they regulate the general relations of production external to the work process.

In Stalinist societies this metamorphosis has been practically eliminated. The relations of subordination which govern the work process are extrapolated to relations of production in their totality. Because of the monopoly on hiring and the divestiture of the proletariat of its class organizations, all collisions and even all genuine negotiations have been excluded. The same principle of indisputable authority that regulates the labor process also regulates the definition of the economic and social conditions in which it takes place.

This discussion should make clear that unlike the situation in other dictatorial regimes, the antidemocracy of the Stalinist social order has its deepest roots not in its political system but in its social and economic structures. Bureaucracy feeds on the exclusion of democracy. As long as the bureaucratic structure persists, and hence as long as relations of subordination constitute the decisive binding element of social coexistence, any attempt to democratize the political system will in the end achieve very little at best. A society cannot be based on a bureaucratic-type social structure and on democratic political institutions at the same time. But it is equally so that in our epoch—as the facts amply demonstrate—even the most advanced democracies cannot dispense completely with bureaucratic apparatuses. What makes Stalinist societies impervious to democratization, therefore, is not the weight of their bureaucratic apparatuses but the fact that bureaucratic-type relations have become a fundamental social structure. This is why mass protest movements can only succeed in these societies on condition that they do not limit themselves solely to political objectives.

Like class structure, the Stalinist bureaucratic structure socially validates a specific distribution of ownership of the means of production. In this respect, the generalization of bureaucratic-type relations is the social continuation of the generalized expropriation effected on the economic plane. While its substance remains the same as that of the class structure, a bureaucratic structure also has a number of distinctive traits specific to it. Thus the groups it engages in the distribution of ownership are not homogeneous social classes as such, but composite and socially heterogeneous social entities. Thanks in broad measure to this heterogeneity, the elements of the bureaucratic structure are linked by relations of subordination rather than of competition. The ultimate function of this structure is to validate a particular distribution of property by preventing it from taking place. Indeed, numerous students of these societies, noting this ambiguity, conclude that their structure cannot be studied in terms of relations of ownership. "In some of the Eastern countries," observe, for example, Konrad and Szelenyi, "sociologists should have begun to justify the old suspicions by calling into question the relevance of relations of ownership to any analyses of the structure of socialist societies."[110] Despite the above singularities, which give Stalinist societies their specificity, if ownership has ceased to be the principal molder of the class structure, it is because it has become the principal molder of the surrogate bureaucratic structure that replaced it.

The changes that took place in the social machinery for the distribution of ownership reflect transformations in ownership itself. The assertion that the function of the bureaucratic structure was more to prevent than to ensure the social distribution of ownership rests on two considerations. First, the existence of the global monopoly transformed access to ownership from a selective privilege to a general interdiction. Second, the functions of ownership had already undergone such profound deterioration that ownership had hardly more than a vestigial character.

Hegedus, in an effort to describe the substance of the basic structure of these societies, proposes a mathematical model containing "three independent variables: relations of ownership, position in the division of labor, and sector of the economy," to which he adds a series of "supplementary variables such as place of residence, educational level, income, social prestige, age, sex, literary taste."[111] In an effort to be exhaustive, such an approach risks submerging the specificity of the social order in a torrent of facts which, although they may be correct, are as a whole of little relevance for determining the nature of the Stalinist mode of production. In the end, one independent variable, relations of ownership, remains decisive and central to any attempt to analyze the nature of this social order.

Under capitalism, the class structure may be seen as the social crystalization of the distribution of a limited number of generally complete forms of ownership. By contrast, under Stalinism the bureaucratic structure is the social crystalization of the interdiction of the redistribution of one single form of incomplete ownership. One crucial substitution was at the root of this abrupt paralysis: social distribution no longer concerned ownership, but only some of its attributes. Accordingly, the mechanism of distribution also underwent a modification. From a dynamic, expansive mechanism based on competition, it became a mechanism of self-perpetuation based on coercion. Finally, the social agents of ownership and the relations uniting them underwent corresponding modifications to complete the permutation. Subordination established itself as the predominant social relation to protect the new system of ownership—which in effective terms meant no more no less than adapting society to its dispossession.

Generalized expropriation was burdened by certain antinomies, manifested in the uneven way it affected the different segments of the social structure. The extent of their dispossession varied, but this inequality merely reflected inequalities among the attributes of incomplete ownership, distributed via relations of coercion and subordination and fixed in the bureaucratic structure.

From the macrosocial perspective, this strange new structure appears as a vertical ladder with three levels. At the top is the supreme authority, which is the sole possessor of the monopoly over absolute power and incomplete ownership and can only perpetuate itself by restricting the other levels to the exercise of the attributes conferred upon them. At the middle level is the state and nonstate bureaucracy exercising the function of management under the strict control of this supreme entity. Its object is ownership, power, and, in part, the inoperative attribute of legality (which is the possession of the state). Finally, at the base, is the vast majority of society, and first and foremost the producers, excluded equally from ownership and management and possessing solely the attribute of legality, in this context perfectly inoperative.

The geometry of social inequality is sustained essentially by the generalization of one-way relations of subordination. The supreme authority, itself subject to no age-old sway (but in fact subordinated to a historical necessity which it believes it controls), stands over both the productive classes and the managerial bureaucracy. Finally, itself rigorously subordinated, the bureaucracy in turn subordinates the productive classes in the most direct manner. Imposed by repression, these relations came with time to be accepted and even courted by some of those who must bear them.

Once this structure had been erected and set into operation, its functioning and perpetuation were contingent on the relations of subordination it expressed being able to mold the wants and actions of the members of society as extensively and thoroughly as possible. This pervasiveness was achieved through an edifice of domination structured with utmost rigor. The supreme entity exerts its dual monopoly from above in the most absolute fashion; the bureaucracy pursues its managerial functions without the least infringement on the functioning of the monopoly; and the productive classes, through their perfect submission, serve only to enhance further the property and power of the entity at the pinnacle of the pyramid.

The *raison d'être* of this structure with regard to relations of ownership was to transfer the separation between the producers and the industrial means of production proper to capitalism to a noncapitalist social context. As in class society, this separation took the social form of specific structural differentiations; but unlike class society, in this new context the structural differentiations divided not classes, but social entities. For it to assume a lasting structural character, this differentiation must reflect and delimit specialization and at the same time assure their functional articulation.

Utterly free of the objective constraints of correspondence, bureaucratic relations became dominant in the new society because they formed the structure most adaptable to its syncretism, i.e., to a society that was destructured at birth. Under Stalinism specifically, this freedom was able to effect the separation of the normally interdependent social and economic spheres in order to separate ownership from society. The most intricately regulated articulation, and hence the most clear-cut differentiation within this context, marked the separation between the top level, which possessed the monopoly, and the other social groupings. In the end the practical result of this entire vast edifice was to adapt the very foundations of society to the existence and functioning of the monopoly.

The differentiations between the diverse levels making up this structure vary in depth just as they do in class societies. The clear purpose of these variations is to provide social sanction for the degree of functional specialization distinguishing each level from each of the others. But Stalinist societies are unique in that they show a marked tendency toward asymmetry in this respect. For instance, the functional division between the level which possesses the monopoly and the bureaucracy which manages it lacks reciprocity. Whereas the exercise of ownership is absolutely barred to the managerial level, the exercise of the functions of management remains totally accessible to the level holding the monopoly. The asymmetry in the functional division between the managerial level and the level of production is less rigorous but just as real. The debarment of the producers from management is just as absolute as that of the managers from the functions of ownership. In exchange, the interference of management in production proper encounters limits, at least in principle—something which the interference of ownership in management never experiences. The bureaucracy projects downward the same kind of nonreciprocal constraint to which it must submit from above.

These asymmetries played a crucial role in the whole in which they acquired form; they laid the structural and functional foundations for the generalization of relations of subordination. For the bureaucracy, wedged between them, they became the objective condition of its own social ambiguity. The bureaucracy in turn became the principal vehicle for the diffusion of relations of subordination throughout society, giving the structure of the whole the verticality inherent to every bureaucratic organization. Caught between the two opposite extremes in this structure, the middle level was crucially instrumental to the separation between property and producers in the original form it assumed in the Stalinist social order. Oppressed from above and oppressor to those beneath, the bureaucracy gives the structure as a whole the verticality inherent in any bureaucratic relations.

This unique structure has profound implications for the subjective sphere as well. For the two other levels, bureaucratic relations represented merely their principal link with the external environment. For the bureaucracy, however, these relations were both external and internal. By virtue of having internalized these relations, the bureaucracy was the sole level also to internalize the stratification these relations brought about wherever they were instituted.

As regards the productive stratum at the base of this structure, bureaucratic relations were merely imposed from without; they were not internalized. Reduced to this impersonal state, bureaucratic relations did not give rise to stratification, but on the contrary resulted in a unique homogenization of this bottom level, and hence its dual social identity: while for its external environment it was an undifferentiated mass of producers, internally it comprised basically two classes which, despite their convergence, remained permanently distinct. To this must be added the fact that by definition bureaucratic work is not directly productive. On the other hand, insofar as it continued to do work that was directly productive, the stratum at the base could not become part of a bureaucracy, although it might reach an accommodation with a bureaucratic structure. The objective boundaries of the bureaucracy therefore were power and ownership above and productive labor below. The existence of these boundaries made possible the generalization of bureaucratic relations without that bringing about a generalization of the bureaucracy. Instead, a differentiation was created such as is common in principle to every social structure. Further, it was by virtue of these same limits that it was not the bureaucracy but an ambiguous supreme authority which rose to ascendancy on the strength of the predominance achieved by bureaucratic structures throughout society.

The deterioration of the class structure paved the way for the primacy of the bureaucratic structure. The transfer of functions to the bureaucratic structures was not so much imposed by the latter as it was necessitated by the functional failings of the class structure and ultimately was but the indirect consequence of the destructuring of society caused by the anticipatory revolution and the syncretism that was its product.

The significance of the initial comparison between war communism and Stalinism will perhaps now be clearer. In this general context of syncretism, the monopoly instituted by war communism was able to consign class structure to a mere subsidiary role as the Stalinist monopoly did later, but unlike Stalinism war communism did not succeed in establishing an alternative structure with sufficient integrative capacity in its place. Limited to this one negative achievement on the social plane, war communism rested on a social void—a grave handicap that was crucially responsible for its inability to outlive the special circumstances that had made it possible. In contrast, the Stalinist monopoly owed its vitality largely to its support structure, or, if one prefers, the specific relations it embodied.

5. The supreme entity

One of the points in the critical theory of Stalinism that has most resisted explanation is its extreme degree of centralization. There have been lamentations enough over its consequences, but the specific institutional form which centralization assumed under Stalinism have suffered rather from neglect. For totalitarian theory, for instance—or for its diverse offshoots—this form is principally political, with few notable links to the social or economic organization of society. Even where it is acknowledged that these societies have a pyramidal structure, the summit of the pyramid usually remains enveloped in a thick mist. More often than not, this position is ascribed to a class or to the state—sometimes even by scholars who lean toward the thesis of *étatisation* in untroubled disregard of the question of how the state can represent the pinnacle of the social pyramid and absorb the whole of society at one and the same time.

Castoriadis provides a good illustration of the difficulties encountered by attempts to identify this summit. He observes: "There is no domination by the state as such over society. . . , nor absorption of civil society by the state. The state is itself dominated by a separate 'political' body, in the typical case all-prevailing: relative to the Party, it is the ultimate seat of decision and power, and in the Party itself, it is the summit of the apparatus."[112] Contrary to totalitarianism theory, for Castoriadis the state, far from absorbing civil society, is itself dominated. As regards the source of domination, it is attributed to three entities at once: the Party, its apparatus, and the summit of this apparatus.

So long as theory continues to confuse the summit which dominates this society with the apparatus or any other entity within society, the vision it is able to provide of the Stalinist social order will remain clouded. In fact a rigorous and total separation from every other social entity and from society in general is an indispensable premise for the absolute and undivided domination of this supreme entity. Once the functional separation became entrenched and unbridgeable, it underwent a crucial mutation and became a structural differentiation. Henceforth the supreme entity could control the whole of society without being subject to control from below. The defining trait of Stalinism is not so much the antidemocratism of its political system as the ademocratism of its social structure.

Every totality based on authority relations has two inseparable terms: an active term which exercises the authority and a passive term which is molded to submit to it. Of course, in reality such organizations are somewhat more complicated that this simple dichotomy: there exists also a third term whose function it is to convey the impulses of authority from one term to the other. In Stalinist society the active term is the supreme entity, the only entity sanctioned to exercise this role. The authoritarian structure derives its rationality not from the qualities which are demonstrated by the supreme entity in fulfilling this role, but merely from the fact that it exists. But this form of supercentralization is not a political extrusion; in fact, under the given conditions it represents a necessity of a structural nature, that of extricating the society from its destructured state.

The active term in these relations is of vital importance for any structure or organization based on authority relations. The role remains inseparable from the structure, independent of the actors called upon to fill it. One cannot exist without the other. Consequently, its continued existence is not exclusively its own work; it is also the work of the context in which it is situated and which demands it. The sheer force of the status quo, inherent in every functioning social structure, is one external source of the perpetuation of this active term in authority relations. The uncontrolled sway exercised by the supreme entity, excessive in terms of the abstract principles of democracy, appears as legitimate and necessary relative to the functional necessity of the bureaucratic structure it crowns.

A number of specific problems stand out within the vaguely defined parameters of this social context. For example, to what extent is the supreme entity under Stalinism itself integrated into these social and bureaucratic structures it was meant to dominate? And, if it is integrated, then to what extent is it able to retain its initial political character?

With regard to the first problem, the irrepressible inclination of the supreme entity to place itself above the law and society in general had empirical antecedents. Similar inclinations, institutionalized or merely personified, have punctuated different societies over the course of history. Most often they have been embodied by the state. Merle Fainsod points out that Peter the Great ''recognized that the state was a political entity separate from the person of the ruler, and he provided that his subjects take two oaths, one to the state and the other to the ruler.''[113] Marx observed of the political power of officials in Germany that ''the autonomy of this caste seems to be situated outside or even, so to speak, above society.''[114]

Other episodes of this sort over the course of history may perhaps help to diminish the deep reluctance to accept or even acknowledge the fact that Stalinist societies are under the absolute domination of a supreme authority reduced to a handful of people or even a single person. What is historically unprecedented is not the reappearance of such a supreme entity in itself, but its lasting implantation in a modern society and the erection of a social structure able on the basis of generalized relations of subordination to ensure its functioning. As the sole subject in these relations, the structure of which is its general object, the supreme entity is both incorporated into this structure and external to it.

All the elements of the bureaucratic structure are complete and integral parts of it, with the exception of the supreme entity which is its principal beneficiary. The ambiguity of its position in this respect was pointed out by Weber: ''At the top of a bureaucratic organization there is necessarily an element which is at least not purely bureaucratic.'' He then gives the example of ministers and presidents who, while situated at the top of state bureaucracies, are ''officials only in a formal sense, and not substantively, as is true of the managing director or president of a large business corporation.''[114]

This ambiguity is tolerable up to a point for a state bureaucracy; but it becomes intolerable in a social structure in which relations of authority perform the vital function of demarcating the separation between ownership and nonownership. Such is the case in Stalinist society. A profound differentiation developed between the base of this structure and the other two levels—between producers and nonproducers—a differentiation far more profound than between the supreme entity and the bureaucracy, which merely separated the two categories of nonproducers (although it was no less vital on that account).

It therefore necessarily became more formalized, introducing between these two levels a veritable social abyss to compensate for their deficient economic differentiation. Once again, the one-way exercise of relations of authority reduced the effective links between the supreme entity and society exclusively to those of domination, and the condition of society to that of utter submission. The links between these two terms existed solely to realize that domination and to shield the supreme entity from all social control. Because of the total absence of reciprocation, the limits on the action of the supreme entity remained essentially undefined—hence the perpetual ambiguity of its position vis-à-vis the bureaucratic structure and society at large.

Was it possible for power to rise to the summit of a bureaucratic structure and at the same time preserve its political character? This is by no means an abstract question. It was in fact at the center of the great political confrontations which shook the Bolshevik Party and its leadership during the 1920s. There was no critical position taken against the rising Stalinist faction which did not touch on the process of bureaucratization of the Party. To the extent that the picture provided by the documents that have come down to us is accurate, it seems that the bureaucratization of the Party was not just a part of the process of generalization of bureaucratic relations; it was both instrument and premise. In the end it was irresistible and irreversible. Like the relations of production, political relations became merely bureaucratic. The supreme entity began the process of subjugating the whole of society to it by destroying the social relations most capable of opposing it; but what it destroyed in fact was not a political organization but the system of political relations as a whole. The practical advantage that ensued from this operation was to free the supreme entity from the social control that its own periodic election would have exercised but which, in the given context, would have been so paralyzing.

Stalin had for all practical purposes abolished the Congresses, Plenums of the Central Committee, etc., with brutal straightforwardness. Although they began again to be held regularly after his death, their real function remained as before: to serve as an electoral facade for the fact that every movement in the workings of the supreme entity is regulated by mechanisms which are archetypically bureaucratic and, moreover, are meticulously tuned not to impugn its supremacy to the least degree. To protect itself against the potential threat contained in political relations, the supreme entity itself became bureaucratized, and as bureaucratic procedures invaded the whole of its inner workings, they became the principal molder of its relations with the rest of society.

These changes gained in depth with the passage from mass repression to mass oppression, i.e., from classic Stalinism to contemporary neo-Stalinism. All power avails itself of bureaucratic relations, but none to the degree in Stalinist countries, where it has transformed its instrument into its model.

Despite the thoroughness with which the supreme entity became bureaucratized, it could not as power completely lose its political character. As with the productive classes, the bare fact that it was part of a bureaucratic structure did not suffice to transform it into a bureaucracy.

To obtain a relatively undistorted picture of how this social order functions, it is necessary to be absolutely clear about the real identity of its most active element. In other words, the supreme entity must not be confused with the Party, the state, or even the bureaucracy in general; on the contrary, it was its complete autonomy vis-à-vis all these elements which conferred upon it its veritable social identity and, moreover, was the crucial factor which enabled it to maintain them in a state of absolute dependency. With the advent of Stalinism, it was inevitable that the former Party and state leadership should be superseded by an entity which separated itself rigorously from both in order to achieve their subjugation. The execution of the immense majority of the former leaders of the Revolution followed with cruel inevitability; more even than their political destruction, their physical liquidation rendered irreversible the separation between the recently constituted supreme entity and the social institutions (the Party and the state) from which it came. The process itself, which began with polemics, went on to exclusions and expulsions, and ended with executions, engaged the leading actors of the epoch in a most direct fashion. It in fact marked the transition from political to structural transformations which subsequently proved all but permanent. To the extent that these remarks may be considered at least plausible, the critical history of Stalinism can only benefit by shifting its focus from these political episodes to the structural permutations which they made possible.

Once it had physically annihilated the most important leaders of the Revolution, the supreme entity settled into the political void which its isolation from the rest of society required. The reorganization of ownership (generalized expropriation in early 1929) chronologically preceded the reorganization of power (the great trials of Kamenev, Zinoviev, Bukharin, etc., took place in 1936–1937). As the specific form assumed by power, the supreme entity was not only the demiurge of the new economic and social context, it was also its product. To oversimplify, its genesis may be seen as a historical process which spread from one sphere of social life to another. It began in the sphere of the economy, with generalized expropriation and the constitution of the global monopoly, continued into the political sphere, where the attachment of supercentralized ownership by power led to its own supercentralization, and ended at the structural level with the formation of a supreme entity beyond society, seated at summit of a bureaucratic-type structure which embraced all of society. The immediate content of all these events, which of course were far less schematic in their actual unfolding, was a growing separation between the supreme entity as it took shape and the political and state bureaucracy of which it had originally been been a part.

In immediately postrevolutionary society, with its social distribution of ownership and the relative diffusion of power, the leadership and its apparatus, while distinct, were not two autonomous entities. A proof of this is that the deep dissension within the leadership was largely fueled by pressures from different groups within the bureaucracy, while the various leadership factions regularly sought support in one or another sector of the bureaucracy (as, for example, in the trade union debate). The less united the leadership, the greater was its dependence on its own apparatus; conversely, the tighter this conflict-producing interdependence, the clearer it became that only a united leadership would be able to bring the bureaucracy under its domination. Though their interaction was political in substance, relations between the leadership and the bureaucracy impelled the former increasingly to take unilateral actions which were primarily bureaucratic in substance. The propagation of bureaucratic relations signaled not the triumph but the enslavement of the bureaucracy.

The separation between ownership and management, with a corollary separation between command and execution, completely abolished the former cooperation and community of action, and on the debris of the latter arose an absolutely autonomous authority and a new bureaucracy capable of transmitting its own condition of servitude to the rest of society.

The first barrier erected between the supreme entity and society was its absolute separation from the bureaucracy from which it had come. This separation ultimately assumed all the qualities of a structural differentiation as the new roles became fixed in the new relational context that was gradually encroaching on the whole of society. This structural differentiation between the supreme entity and the bureaucracy was first and foremost a reflection of the functional division between the exercise of power and ownership and the exercise management.

Analyses of Stalinism routinely offer comparisons with similar phenomena under capitalism when they deal with this question. But the similarities are intermingled with differences, and one of these differences is the inordinate tension which reigns in relations between owners and managers under Stalinism. This special tension is due to more than just the social position of the supreme entity, the global nature of its monopoly, or the fact that the latter embraces both ownership and power alike; in fact, it results from differences in the origin of ownership and management.

Under capitalism, the birth of monopolies preceded the birth of management; under Stalinism, the managerial bureaucracy, with its vague proprietary aspirations, preceded the formation of the global monopoly on ownership. Under capitalism, management was instituted by ownership which prescribed its powers; under Stalinism, ownership established itself at the expense of the managerial bureaucracy, the powers of which it thereupon severely reduced. In the first case, relations between ownership and management were based fundamentally on continuity; in the second, on discontinuity. Thus a potential for revolt against the supreme entity is inscribed in the genetic code of the Stalinist bureaucracy. Actualized in the hidden form of imperceptible but formidable daily pressures, this potential has drawn the bureaucracy into all the major conflicts which, from 1956 to the present, have shaken Stalinist societies. On each of these occasions, its inherent ambiguity has regularly divided its ranks into one segment which defended the supreme entity and another which contested it. But even the protest has invariably been directed toward the functioning of the suprastate authority, and not the bureaucratic structure which renders it perpetual.

Brought into the open by events of this kind, this potential for revolt nourishes the organic mistrust the supreme entity has of its bureaucracy, which in turn nourishes the historical tendency to transform their separation into conflict. This is one more reason why the absolute subordination of the managerial bureaucracy to the supreme entity is one of the principal conditions for the regular functioning of the broader structure of which they are both a part.

It is of crucial importance, therefore, to the supreme entity to underscore incessantly its distinctness from the bureaucracy—its "leading role"—as a warning to the managers against any temptation to interfere with its property. It is illuminating that in these societies the legal systems, which make no mention of this ownership, provide extremely severe punishment for those who violate it. To take a concrete and suggestive example, in his *Legal Works*, Vyshinsky tells us that before the great political trials of the 1930s, he had been the prosecutor in the trials of the canned goods trust, the motor combines, the electric power stations, etc. Even today, in Europe, the countries with this social system are the only ones in which peculation and the misappropriation of state property can receive capital punishment and where such sentences are carried out with particular public fanfare.

Of course this degree of severity is manifested only sporadically. It cannot be said to reflect the tone of daily relations between the two levels, but it does show their substance and their difference from relations between owners and managers in capitalist corporations. Much more thorough under Stalinism, the subordination of the managerial bureaucracy to the seat of ownership exhibits a number of particularities, the most conspicuous of which are the conditions of hiring and employment, the criteria for promotion and dismissal, and surveillance.

The monopoly over employment is in the hands of the supreme entity. It extends over the entire work force, including the bureaucracy, where it acquires several peculiar traits. Employment in the bureaucracy has a special social significance different from anywhere else in the labor force; it confers upon a person the social status of nondirect producer, signifying his separation from the grand army of producers. There are always more people striving to enter into the ranks of this privileged category than there are positions available, to say nothing of those striving to keep their positions or to be promoted. Consequently the supreme entity has no need to attract or recruit candidates; they are already waiting at the doors, and it is up to them to gain favor.

This practically inexhaustible "reserve army" waiting to enter the bureaucracy exerts considerable and continuous pressure on those already working in it. It is a relative commonplace that in Stalinist societies promotion to a position in the bureaucracy is not blocked by any social or occupational barriers comparable to those in capitalist societies. This democratization of the bureaucracy at its base multiplies a hundredfold the pressure which the reserve army is able to bring to bear on it. Under these multiple pressures coming simultaneously from within its own ranks and from the rest of society, the position of the bureaucracy with its single employer prevents it from achieving the degree of cohesion that would permit it to function and act autonomously.

The bureaucracy's social condition of subordination to the supreme entity is abundantly enhanced by the employment criteria practiced by the latter in its regard. A hybrid set of criteria govern both the accession of new workers to the bureaucratic hierarchy and the careers of those who have long been in it. The ambiguity of these criteria further amplifies the ambiguity of the bureaucracy with regard to its functions. Unlike in the case of capitalism, the criterion of professional competence functions only in conjunction with the criterion of personal loyalty, although the converse is not always true. Of course loyalty is infinitely more difficult to demonstrate than competence. It is therefore generally expressed in the form of political fidelity—which may in fact be authentic during the formative phases of these societies, but is no longer more than mystification and dissimulation once they have attained relative maturity and stability. The higher the position in the bureaucracy, the more weight carried by personal loyalty relative to that of competence. One of the most delicate actions of *perestroika* is the promotion of persons committed to it as well as the mass dismissal of devotees of stagnation.

By making professional competence an elective addendum to the criterion of personal loyalty, the supreme entity adapts the social scale of values to its own tendency toward personification. In fact, the very function of the supreme entity, that of directing all social or individual activities from a single center, precludes even the possibility of competence. With competence excluded, it claims infallibility, independent of the individuals who exercise it. It is hardly any wonder that the supreme entity should not wish to encourage in the bureaucracy a competence to which it itself has no access. An incompetent and loyal bureaucracy can do nothing but ratify this infallibility, while a competent bureaucracy would be tempted to contest it.

After the appointments system, surveillance is a third means utilized by the supreme entity to ensure the bureaucracy's total subordination. Ownership, as defined earlier on, implies control over the surplus product and exclusion of the rest of society from access to certain objects or goods. But the supreme entity in Stalinism possesses only incomplete ownership and, accordingly, only incomplete control over the surplus product, and it is able to exclude the rest of society from its possessions only incompletely. To reduce the threat these two limitations pose for its monopoly on ownership, the supreme entity tends to compensate for its incomplete control over the surplus product by exercising the most complete surveillance over society. In its role as manager of the bureaucracy, it is the principal beneficiary of the incompleteness of this exclusion, and, accordingly, it is against the bureaucracy that the transformation of control into surveillance is primarily directed. These same limitations add an element of uncertainty to the irreversibility of the results of generalized expropriation, and sensing that uncertainty, the supreme entity attempts to consolidate those results by the generalization of surveillance. Surveillance may be considered a paroxysmal form of social control; if subordination is the substance of bureaucratic relations, the substance of subordination is in good measure surveillance. Police excesses and their corollary, the inefficacy of legal guarantees, are consequently structurally inherent to these societies. Although it is directed against the whole of society, surveillance nonetheless implicates the bureaucracy in a special way: the bureaucracy is at once its principal target and its principal executor, which enhances further its ambiguity. Surveillance thus reveals itself to be a functional and therefore plausible manifestation of the relations of subordination characteristic of this social order, rather than merely an excessive expansion of police activity.

The supreme entity's main concern in maintaining its surveillance over the bureaucracy is not the latter's efficiency, but its loyalty; it follows therefore that it is less interested in activities than in individuals. It follows further that privacy must necessarily be regarded as an obstacle to the smooth functioning of society. An official must renounce his individuality not only in the exercise of his function, but also in the whole of his existence; even his inner life belongs in fact to the public domain. It is only by placing his individuality totally in the hands of the supreme entity that he is vouchsafed the right to serve it.

Saint-Simon dreamed of a society in which the government of persons would give way to the administration of things. Stalinism effected the opposite transition: from the control of activities to the surveillance of persons. It was logically consistent if not inevitable that this transition should be accompanied by another: when judgements were rendered, the presumption of the innocence of these persons was replaced by the presumption of their guilt. To achieve its end, however, the presumption of guilt must be internalized by the suspects themselves. Quite obviously, a genuine rule of law, i.e., the rule of effective legal guarantees, would represent a serious obstacle to the generalization of an *a priori* presentiment of guilt throughout the whole of society—with one exception, the infallible leader. The outstanding point is not only that a legal system incapable of guaranteeing ownership is also incapable of guaranteeing the freedoms of the propertyless, but that such individual guarantees are regarded as socially harmful. This form of oppression is translated into ideological language by the catchword the "flourishing of the human personality." Formally, the model person whom the supreme entity holds up to society, and to the bureaucracy especially, is a perfect being in terms of the established scale of values. If the bureaucrat were endowed with the set of virtues programmed into this model, he would be free of any flaw; he would in these terms be infallible. But his infallibility, implying the presumption of his innocence, would be an attempt on the legitimacy of the supreme entity, which alone has the license, and is even obliged, to be infallible. To sustain its infallibility, the supreme entity requires fallible servants. Such once again is the ambiguity of the bureaucracy's position vis-à-vis the institution to which it must answer, and such is the quality of the distance which separates them.

The theoretical assimilation of the fact of this separation has important implications for the critical analysis of Stalinism in its present state. If one agrees that management is a functional specialization of the bureaucracy, one also implicitly accepts that management does not own of the means of production. And if it is not the owner, it is difficult to maintain that it is the dominant class, or even a class at all. Its economic status would be incompatible with its social status. Further, if one accepts the idea of a nonowning bureaucracy, one is thereby implicitly committed to showing where this ownership is situated, which means acknowledging explicitly and unreservedly the existence and role of a supreme entity.

Usually, the question is approached very diffidently if it is approached at all. But one author who has attempted to face it squarely is Brus, who states clearly: "It is beyond a doubt that the high degree of separation between management and ownership which we observe in contemporary capitalism constitutes . . . an important premise of socialism as well.''[115] There is a key truth in this which is crucial to an understanding of the role of the Stalinist bureaucracy and the Stalinist social order in general. If it is admitted that under Stalinism, as under capitalism, the bureaucracy is specialized in the management of property which it does not possess and that under capitalism this property belongs to the capitalist class, then the question is to determine to whom under Stalinism this property belongs when it is forbidden to both the bureaucracy and the producers and must therefore be distinct from both.

Sanctioned by law, the separation between ownership and management is based in capitalism on the distinction between the economic mechanisms employed by the two to participate in the distribution of the surplus product. These mechanisms are appropriation for the owners and salary for managers. Under Stalinism this distinction disappears. It is largely the same mechanism, salary, which enables both to participate in this process. With access to neither appropriation nor to legal sanction, ownership is insufficiently delimited from management and its apparatus; their separation must acquire new content. Essentially this content consists of a set of crucial powers which the supreme entity reserves utterly and exclusively for itself and which it exercises in the most total liberty vis-à-vis the bureaucracy and the rest of society.

For this structure to function at least acceptably, the exclusivity of its powers and prerogatives is obviously more important than their actual performance. In fact the powers which the supreme entity in Stalinist countries claims for itself may vary from country to country and from period to period. According to Brus, this apparent flexibility is sufficiently great that in fact two different ''models of functioning'' for socialist economies have emerged, which he calls ''centralized'' and ''decentralized.'' But a closer examination will show that the two are both variations on the degree of centralization. Even in the ''decentralized model'' which Brus proposes, ''the distribution of the national income, which [also] determines . . . the distribution of centralized funds between collective consumption and accumulation [as well as the] choice of principal areas for investment'' is handled at the same ''central level.'' For the economy overall, the distribution of decision-making powers shows, according to Brus, lines of demarcation between three major categories of economic decisions: ''basic macroeconomic decisions,'' ''individual'' decisions, and ''current economic decisions.'' ''The question at issue [i.e., whether centralized or decentralized] is thus limited in fact to this last group; the models of functioning of socialist economies, if they are truly to remain faithful to the principles of the regime, can only differ on the question of centralization or decentralization of the third category of decisions.''[116] The upshot of these observations for the present discussion is that: discussion is that:

1. The Stalinist organization of ownership is defined by a strict yet flexible functional division between the supreme entity which holds the monopoly and the

bureaucracy which only administers the monopoly's possessions.

2. The monopoly over incomplete ownership is manifested essentially as a monopoly on macro-economic decisions. The supercentralization of these decisions is the principal means by which supercentralized ownership ensures its effectiveness. It is the constant in this division. If this category of decisions were to become the object of decentralization, what would change would be not only the condition of the supreme entity, but also the mode of production itself.

3. On the other hand, the reproduction of this social order can tolerate a certain variation in the distribution of powers and prerogatives for "current economic decisions." The potential for flexibility in this system, therefore, is confined within particularly rigid limits.

In fact the various attempts at economic reform that have been undertaken down through the years have concerned exclusively current and individual economic decisions, with a view to curbing excessive interference from above, and have refrained from tampering with the fundamental macro-economic decisions which are the exclusive domain of the supreme entity. The law on enterprises, long put off by Gorbachev's adversaries, seems to call this limit into question.

Certain regularities have been revealed in the general functioning of the Stalinist social order by the successes and limitations of these reform attempts:

1. Unlike macro-economic decisions, current and individual decisions are variable in both directions, i.e., their domain may be alternately expanded or narrowed.

2. With few exceptions, and regardless of their direction, these variations are not imposed by the bureaucracy or the population, but permitted by the supreme entity;

3. Should the supreme entity decide to redefine the rights and prerogatives of the bureaucracy and the population, it nonetheless would preserve the prerogative not only to go back on that decision, but also to interfere in the exercise of these newly defined rights and prerogatives.

4. No macro-economic decision is transferable; every current economic decision is reversible.

5. Any interference of the bureaucracy in the domain of prerogatives reserved for the supreme entity is considered a crime; every interference of the supreme entity in the domain of prerogatives reserved for the bureaucracy is considered absolutely legitimate.

6. Any modification in the distribution of powers and prerogatives with regard to current economic decisions is a matter between the supreme entity and the bureaucracy; the producers are totally excluded and have no choice but to submit to its consequences. The upshot of all such modifications is that the more unpracticable the economic separation between ownership and management, the more rigid the social separation between the seat of ownership and the managing bureaucracy. What ownership lost owing to its incomplete nature only reinforced the domination, already all but absolute, of the supreme entity. Even the way the

monopoly shed some of its attributes in the end contributed to its consolidation.

Thus, by denying itself appropriation, the supreme entity also denied it to the rest of society. Its procedure in this respect was almost a rule of conduct: society cannot enjoy any prerogative which was barred to the monopoly. Similarly, the attribute of legality bestowed on the producers was devoid of any real impact. Not only did it not ground ownership in law, but it was also powerless in its capacity as general regulator of social behavior. Another rule of conduct may hence be inferred: a prerogative which is inaccessible to the supreme entity cannot be assumed by society except if it is totally formalized. The attribute of management, on the other hand, was conceded on the presumption that it would be effective; it was therefore only natural that the social entity encharged with this function should be subject to the harshest subordination. Finally, a third rule of conduct was that no segment of society can enjoy a prerogative that is inaccessible to the supreme entity unless it has been entrusted to it by that authority itself and is under its strictest surveillance.

The supreme entity defends its ownership either by vitiating its functions or by incapacitating the social agent encharged with their exercise. For instance, the formalization of legality is as total as the subordination of management. The one certain manner to guarantee that the separation between ownership and management could become economic effective without being socially destructive was through the total subjugation of the bureaucracy.

The three levels of the bureaucratic structure function to a certain extent in concert; it is in this way that the separations among them are integrated into the social order and rendered functional, as long as no violent crisis erupts. With no internal dynamic of their own or forces capable of stimulating them, the implication is that there must be some external constraint for them to function at all, and hence a social entity capable of exercising that constraint. Further, if functioning, in the sense of carrying on a productive activity, is a vital necessity, it follows that the social entity which makes this activity possible is also vitally necessary in this context. That is why, beyond the profound divergence of interests between the productive classes and the bureaucracy, they nonetheless still have a common interest in preserving a supreme entity that is a source of commands to action. And, while particular commands may be contested, the source of those commands cannot; it remains everlastingly indispensable.

This social apparatus created the premises for industrialization by transforming relations of ownership. Stalinism made the transition from an ownership vacuum and constant turmoil that paralyzed economic activity to a functional form of incomplete ownership that temporarily put an end to this paralysis. But generalized expropriation and the advent of an entity which assumed the exercise of the global monopoly did not eliminate this ownership vacuum. It merely reorganized it. Ownership passed from a state of continual turbulence to a stationary condition. The global monopoly arrested the breakdown of ownership through the positive integration of its effects into an appropriate social structure.

Henceforth wielded exclusively by an authority beyond society, ownership nonetheless remained utterly inaccessible to the latter, for which the ownership vacuum not only persisted but became institutionalized.

How specifically the role of the supreme entity is exercised depends on the circumstances and, especially, on the actors. For instance, from the fact that the attribution of infallibility to its leaders is inherently necessary to these societies it does not follow that they will also produce such leaders. In Stalinist dictatorships, unlike non-Stalinist ones, it is not necessarily the leader who enforces the myth of his infallibility; rather, the society requires it. In creating a necessity it has no possibility of fulfilling, Stalinist society in fact created a permanent point of crisis in its most sensitive mechanism, the regulator of all of its activity, namely, the supreme entity. It cannot avoid this crisis; therefore it endeavors to conceal it. Yet the crisis surfaces regularly nonetheless in two manifest forms: either the leader proves himself in fact fallible, with extremely grave consequences for the society until he is ultimately disposed of; or his fallibility is discovered post mortem by the same actors who had affirmed his infallibility while he was was alive and well. So long as, under the impact of these variables, the dysfunctions of the supreme entity do not lead to open conflict and the bureaucratic relations on which it is based can maintain a working balance among the principal social agents, the supreme entity is able to make use of its monopoly on ownership and power to play a unifying role for the whole of society. After having created a unified society of the dispossessed by generalized expropriation, the supreme entity went on to create unity in subordination, first imposed and later accepted. If Stalinist societies place the principal institutions and symbols of their cohesion outside the state (which traditionally plays this unifying role) in the extrasocial realm created by the supreme entity, it does this not simply to emphasize their importance but also to consolidate this function. The cult of the personality and the exaltation of ''monolithism'' and the ''leading role of the party'' are the ideological expression of this transfer—the former sporadic, the latter continual; in both cases they imply that ownership and power are situated beyond society. As the principal forces giving society its cohesiveness, ownership and power are no longer a part of the social context bequeathed by the revolution. Now outside society, they have built a new social context better equipped to assimilate this transfer. Once this environment was established and began to function, the ownership vacuum (actually a vacuum of the social agents of ownership) was structurally assimilated.

Having debarred all potential social agents from the exercise of ownership over the means of production, it became objectively impossible for Stalinism to socialize them directly. Therefore, to avoid the alternative of their reprivatization, it proceeded to desocialize their ownership. The vitality and relative productivity of this accommodation were owed to the bureaucratic structure which ratified, justified, and perpetuated the division between a society divested of all effective ownership and a supreme entity standing over society, in possession of a monopoly on power and of the whole of the nation's assets. Later, after industrialization, this stabilized structure would perpetuate the absence of the social agents of ownership that had made this structure necessary in the first place.

The more extreme the centralization, the greater will be the temptation to legitimate the objectively determined prerogatives of the supreme entity in terms of the subjective qualities of the individual incarnating it. Most of the Stalinist countries have manifested due reservations with regard to this transference after the tragic experiences of classic Stalinism. But the inclination to produce a "cult of personality" might in fact be necessary to the functioning of the supreme entity, in view of the continual waverings between its repudiation and its outright cultivation.

In their book on comparative history, William Rosenberg and Marilyn Young comment on the celebration of Stalin's 70th birthday in 1949 by quoting the dithyrambs uttered on this occasion: "Dear father, genius, teacher, savior of the fatherland. . . ." Only four years later, the person who recited this hymn would change his style radically. His name: Khrushchev. The authors go on to observe that "This cult was the totally unnecessary consequence of necessary historical and political circumstances."[117] Quite apart from his striking inconsistency in the matter, Khrushchev had the not inconsiderable historical merit to have suggested publicly the futility and perniciousness of this penchant to travesty the historical necessity of a suprasocietal supreme authority by investing the person who represents it at a particular moment with superhuman qualities.

History has subsequently demonstrated that it is imperative to Stalinist societies to maintain a type of social structure which will permit and require even their domination by a supreme authority and that the cult of the individual personifying that authority is merely a nonnecessary consequence of this necessity that can always be revived on demand.

After thirty years, official Soviet analysis of this phenomenon has remained doggedly superficial and has become perceptibly less explicit. At the 27th Party Congress, Gorbachev protested against the cult of personality—to be sure, in terms incomparably less blunt than Khrushchev at the 20th Congress—but remained silent on the persistence of a supreme authority and the general tendency toward its personification.

The difference between the cultivation of the cult of the leader and its abandonment is in political terms enormous. But in sociological terms, the fact remains that in Stalinist societies, the effective functioning of the supreme entity invariably requires a supreme leader unanimously recognized as such. With the cult or without it, and irrespective of whether he is called Kim Il Sung or János Kádár, every Stalinist society has a supreme leader whose role is anchored in at least two principles:

1. His appointment to this role is tacitly understood to be for life, which means that in reality he cannot be contested and therefore cannot be elected to that role.

2. His opinions and his decisions are not subject to critical review; unconditional compliance alone is permitted.

Though capable of such extreme centralization, society is nonetheless incapable of providing it with rational legitimation. And it is for this reason that it must inevitably justify—if less in words than in deeds—the unparalleled privileges of this entity on the basis of the virtues of the individual embodying it; all it can avoid is the most nefarious manifestations of such an explanation. Even in its less fulsome forms, this transference has at least two troublesome consequences. One is the profound tendency toward gerontocracy; the other is the inevitability of recurrent crises of succession. North Korea has already dealt with the question, and the other Stalinist countries seem to be preparing themselves for it. The concern to protect the supreme entity against this type of crisis can even go as far as to transform the function of supreme leader into a dynastic institution. In this respect, the supreme entity contributes substantially to the total discrediting of a social order which is prepared to renounce its illusory doctrinal legitimacy only to replace it with a personal or familial legitimacy that is even more illusory.

Stalinism's paradoxical achievement of preserving and even consolidating the noncapitalist context it inherited rested on two pillars: the creation of the supreme entity and the erection of a structure which gave it social legitimacy. A second paradox, complementary to the first, was the global yet incomplete character of the monopolist ownership exercised by the supreme entity. The monopoly did not become capitalist because it had no access to appropriation, and it ceased to be a state monopoly because it had divested itself of the attributes of legality and management.

For a time the restructuring of society was able to attenuate the consequences of the original syncretism by virtue of having placed ownership outside the class structure. But in doing so it created a new syncretism, the long-term consequences of which proved insuperable. The initial project of socialization was abandoned and replaced by a lasting reality of complete desocialization. The same entity which abolished the most elementary premise of the capitalist class when it eliminated the last vestiges of private property in the end assumed the role of that class itself by rigorously separating the productive classes from their means of production. The groping and hesitant anticapitalism of postrevolutionary society became riveted to this formula of noncapitalism; the chaotic pursuit of a socialist project whose realization lay far in the future was supplanted by an unexpected version of antisocialism. The socialist project thereupon acquired a new function, that of legitimating a monopolist entity, which virtually signified its abandonment. The illegality of the monopoly was compounded by its becoming legitimate.

Condemned perpetually to both ostentation and dissimulation, the supreme entity is a virtual defining element of the Stalinist social order and is key to the critical efforts to understand it.

POSTSCRIPT

The astonishing vitality of Stalinism does not come from its indifference to the rules of democracy, but from its ability to offer a plausible solution to the terrible problem of underdevelopment. Despite the immense toll it exacts, this solution has an immediate, historically demonstrated efficacy. Contemporary capitalism proposes a model of its own—which it then prevents others from adopting. It has not succeeded in finding a competitive alternative solution other than by exception, and then in special circumstances. Even worse, in perpetuating the present organization of the world, it continues also to perpetuate and, in certain respects, even to aggravate underdevelopment. Imperialism has not proven that it can subsist without generating underdevelopment. As long as it continues to exist it will continue to provide Stalinism, which purports to be a countermodel, with the historical premises for its survival and spread throughout the world.

There is a distinctive division of the world in respect of the phenomenon of Stalinism. On the one hand, there is the center of the imperialist system engaged in its unceasing crusade against Stalinism yet stubbornly maintaining the conditions which keep it attractive; and on the other, there is the periphery of the system which, with some reservations—and in some cases none at all—directs its hopes toward the Stalinist model; finally, there is that segment of the world which originally was determined to free itself from the imperialist system yet has done its utmost to imitate it and which today, from China to Cuba, experiences Stalinism as an everyday reality that it now aspires to surmount without sacrificing what it has achieved. This part of the world possesses a direct existential awareness of the extent to which the Stalinist solution to the problem of underdevelopment in the end gives rise to new problems that are as intolerable as they are insoluble.

It was the destiny of this book to be received by that part of the world which lives to the lee of underdevelopment and Stalinism, but which continues unceasingly to nourish them. Nonetheless, it is addressed in principle to the two other divisions of the world: that part for which Stalinism represents a hope yet to be realized and that part for which it is a reality to move beyond. How can underdevelopment be eradicated without plunging into Stalinism? Where Stalinism is a reality, what is the way beyond it?

The fundamental presumption throughout this book has been that the chances of preventing or of transcending Stalinism will remain diffuse and uncrystalized so long as the circumstances of its birth and genesis are not clearly understood. A viable strategy for its demise must incorporate the historical experience of its coming and its stay among us.

NOTES

1. F. G. Casals [Pavel Campeanu], *The Syncretic Society* (Armonk, NY: M. E. Sharpe, 1980), p. 63: 3.

2. Ferencz Fehér, Agnes Heller, and Gyorgy Markus, *Dictatorship over Needs* (New York: St. Martin's Press, 1983), p. 58.

3. Hillel Ticktin, "Rudolf Bahro: A Socialist Without a Working Class," in *Critique*, 10-11, Winter–Spring 1978-1979, p. 134; Donald Filtzer, "Preobrazhensky and the Problem of the Soviet Transition," in *Critique 9*, Spring-Summer 1977, p. 73.

4. Talcott Parsons, "Structural-Functional Theory in Sociology," in *The Idea of Social Structure*, ed. Lewis A. Coser (New York: Harcourt Brace Jovanovich, 1975), p. 68.

5. Ernest Mandel, *Traité d'économie marxiste*, Julliard, vol. 4, p. 10.

6. Frank Parkin, "System Contradiction and Political Transformation," in *Classes, Power and Conflict*, ed. Anthony Giddens and David Held (Berkeley/Los Angeles: University of California Press, 1982), p. 578.

7. Quoted in Boris Souvarine, *Stalin: A Critical Survey of Bolshevism* (New York, 1939), p. 695.

8. Milovan Djilas, *The New Class* (New York: Frederick A. Praeger, 1957), p. 45.

9. Ivan Szelenyi, "The Position of the Intelligentsia in the Class Structure of State Socialist Societies," in *Critique*, 10-11, p. 61.

10. Charles Bettelheim, *Les Luttes de Classes en URSS, 1ère Période 1917-1923* (Paris: Seuil/Maspéro, 1974), p. 125.

11. Edward Hallett Carr, *The Bolshevik Revolution 1917-1923* (New York: Macmillan, 1968), vol. 2, pp. 68, 69.

12. *Ibid.*, p. 69.

13. *Ibid.*, p. 32.

14. Leon Trotsky, *Histoire de la Révolution Russe* (Paris: Ed. du Seuil, 1950), vol. 2, *October*, p. 712.

15. Quoted in Carr, , p. 35.

16. Trotsky, *op. cit.*

17. Gilles Martinet, *Les Cinq Communismes* (Paris: Seuil, 1971), p. 41.

18. Trotsky, *op. cit.*

19. Carr, *op. cit.*

20. Hélène Carrère d'Encausse, *Une révolution—une victoire—L'Union Soviétique de Lénine à Staline, 1917-1953* (Paris: Ed. Richelieu, 1972), p. 77.

21. William Henry Chamberlin, *The Russian Revolution* (New York: The Universal Library, Grosset & Dunlap, 1963), vol. II, p. 255.

22. *Ibid.*, p. 256.

23. *Ibid.*, p. 481.
24. *Ibid.*, p. 481.
25. Erik Olin Wright, "Class Boundaries and Contradictory Class Locations," in *Classes, Power and Conflict*, p. 119.
26. C.B. Macpherson, "A Political Theory of Property," in *Democratic Theory: Essays in Retrieval* (Oxford University Press, 1973).
27. Branko Horvat, *The Political Economy of Socialism* (Armonk, NY: M. E. Sharpe, 1982), p. 235.
28. Emile Durkheim, *Professional Ethics and Civic Morals* (London: Routledge, 1957), p. 142.
29. Agnes Heller, *Esprit*, no. 7–8, July-August 1978.
30. Montesquieu, *L'esprit des lois*, book XXVI, chapter 15.
31. Jeremy Bentham, *Traité de Législation*, vol. II, p. 33.
32. Robert Linhart, *Lénine, les paysans, Taylor* (Paris: Ed. du Seuil, 1976), pp. 39–40.
33. Quoted in Bettelheim, *Les Luttes de Classes en URSS*, vol. II, p. 137.
34. Ernest Mandel, *Traite d'économie marxiste*, vol. 4, p. 8.
35. S. N. Prokopowicz, *Histoire économique de l'URSS* (Paris: Flammarion, 1952), p. 282.
36. E. H. Carr and R. W. Davies, *Foundations of a Planned Economy (1926–1929)* (London: Macmillan), vol. 1, p. 955.
37. Charles Bettelheim, *Les Luttes de classes en URSS—2ème période 1923–1930* (Paris: Seuil/Maspéro, 1977), p. 279.
38. Carr and Davies, *op. cit.*, p. 456.
39. Mandel, *op. cit.*, p. 8.
40. Pierre Broué, *Le Parti Bolchévique* (Ed. de Minuit, 1963), p. 327.
41. Rosa Luxemburg, *La Révolution Russe* (Ed. Spartacus, 1947), p. 47.
42. Mandel, *op. cit.*, vol. 3, p. 67.
43. Szelenyi, *op. cit.*, p. 73.
44. "Plateforme de l'opposition de gauche (1927)," in *Les bolchéviks contre Stalin* (Paris: Publications de la Quatrième Internationale, 1957), p. 93.
45. Quoted in Isaac Deutscher, *Le Prophète Armé* (Paris: Julliard, 1962), p. 493.
46. Broué, *op. cit.*, p. 141.
47. E. H. Carr, *The Interregnum*, 1954, p. 328.
48. "Plateforme de l'opposition de gauche," *op. cit.*, pp. 81, 82.
49. *Ibid.*
50. Rudi Supek, "Expériences et problèmes de l'autogestion yougoslave," in *L'autogestion, un système économique?* (Paris: Dunod, Bordas, 1981), p. 67.
51. Nikolai Bukharin, "Burzhauznaia revoliutsiia i revoliutsiia proletarskaia, 1922," quoted in S. Heitman, *Bukharin—A Bibliography with Annotations* (Stanford, CA: Stanford University Press, 1969), p. 168.
52. Pavel Campeanu, *The Origins of Stalinism* (Armonk, NY: M. E. Sharpe, 1986), p. 86.
53. Michel Löwy, *La bureaucratie staliniènne comme "état" social*, Rapport no. 15 au Congrès de l'Association Française de Sciences Politiques, Table Ronde no. 3.
54. Bettelheim, p. 359.
55. Nikolai Bukharin, *O novoi ekonomicheskoi politike i nashikh zadachakh*, IIb, June 1, 1925, pp. 3–4.
56. Barrington Moore Jr., *Social Origins of Dictatorship and Democracy* (Boston: Beacon Press, 1966), p. 474.
57. Roy Medvedev, *Le Stalinisme* (Paris: Ed. du Seuil, 1972), pp. 136, 147.

58. Stephen F. Cohen, *Bukharin and the Bolshevik Revolution* (New York: Knopf, 1973), p. 330.

59. Leonard Shapiro, *The Communist Party of the Soviet Union* (New York: Vintage Books, 1960), pp. 393, 394.

60. Robert C. Tucker, "Stalinism as Revolution from Above," in *Stalinism, Essays in Historical Interpretation*, ed. Robert C. Tucker (New York: W.W. Norton, 1977), p. 78.

61. E.H. Carr, "Revolution from Above: The Road to Collectivization," in *The October Revolution, Before and After* (New York, 1969).

62. Moshe Lewin, *The Making of the Soviet System* (New York: Pantheon Books, 1985), p. 45.

63. Quoted in Merle Fainsod, *Smolensk à l'heure de Staline* (Paris: Fayard, 1958), p. 167.

64. Medvedev, p. 137.

65. Marie Lavigne, *Les Economies Socialistes* (Paris: Ed. Armand Collin, 1970), p. 158.

66. Fehér, Heller, and Markus, p. 55.

67. Djilas, p. 207.

68. Ernest Mandel, *Critique de l'Eurocommunisme* (Paris: Petite Collection Maspéro, 1978), pp. 144–145.

69. Rudolf Bahro, *L'Alternative* (Paris: Stock, 1979), p. 124.

70. Quoted in Cohen, p. 178.

71. Poulantzas, vol. II, p. 104.

72. Edwin Mansfield, *Economics—Principles, Problems, Decisions*, 3rd ed. (New York: W.W. Norton, 1980), pp. 634, 635.

73. Arkady N. Shevchenko, *Breaking With Moscow* (New York: Ballantine Books, 1985), p. 233.

74. Hannah Arendt, *The Origins of Totalitarianism* (New York: Harcourt Brace Jovanovich, 1973), p. 397.

75. Pierre Naville, *Le nouveau leviathan, 5, La bureaucratie et la révolution* (Paris: Ed. Anthropos, 1972), p. 202.

76. Feher, Heller, and Markus, p. 56.

77. Karl Marx, *Oeuvres* (Paris: Gallimard, 1963), vol. I, p. 256.

78. Alfred G. Meyer, *Communism*, 3rd ed. (New York: Random House, 1967), p. 110.

79. Harry Braverman, *The Future of Russia* (New York: Grosset & Dunlap, 1966), p. 110.

80. Henri Chambre, *L'économie planifiée* (Paris: PUF, 1975), p. 19.

81. Naville, p. 138.

82. Max Weber, *The Theory of Social and Economic Organization* (New York: The Free Press, 1964), p. 249.

83. Michael De Vroey, "The Separation of Ownership and Control in Large Corporations," *The Review of Radical Political Economics*, vol. 7, no. 2, 1975.

84. Meghnad Dessai, *Marxian Economics* (Oxford: Basil Blackwell, 1979), p. 30.

85. Hillen Ticktin, "The Class Structure of the USSR and the Elite," in *Critique*, no. 9, Spring-Summer 1978, p. 49.

86. Lénine, *Oeuvres complètes*, Edition en langues étrangères (Moscow), vol. 25, p. 389.

87. Poulantzas, p. 96.

88. *Ibid.*

89. Mao Tse Tung, *Oeuvres choisies*, Edition en langues étrangères (Peking, 1977), vol. V, p. 104.

90. Maurice Brinton, "Les bolchéviks et le contrôle ouvrier," in *Autogestion et socialisme*, September-December 1972, p. 111.

91. Korsch, Mattick, Pennekoek, Ruhle, et al., *La contre-révolution bureaucratique* (Paris: Julliard, 1973), pp. 49, 61, 280.

92. Bettelheim, *Planification et croissance acélérée*, p. 55.

93. Bahro, p. 248.

94. Quoted in Meyer, p. 41.

95. Supek, p. 119.

96. *Ibid.*, p. 120.

97. Susan Gross Solomon, *The Soviet Agrarian Debate* (Boulder, CO: Westview, 1977), p. 83.

98. Quoted in Naville, p. 114.

99. Cohen, p. 61.

100. Alfred G. Meyer, "Lev Davidovich Trotsky," in *Problems of Communism*, November-December 1967.

101. Lewin, p. 260.

102. Nikolai Bukharin, "Nashi zadachi," in *Bolshevik*, no. 11, 1924.

103. Michael Ellman, "Did the Agricultural Surplus Provide the Resources for the Increase in Investment in the USSR during the First Five Year Plan?" in *The Economic Journal*, December 1975, p. 844.

104. Alec Nove, *An Economic History of the USSR* (Harmondsworth: Penguin, 1975), p. 210.

105. Evgeny Preobrazhensky, "Khoziaistvennoe ravnovesie v sisteme SSSR," in *Vestnik Kommunist Akademii*, XXII, 1927.

106. Włodimierz Brus, *Problèmes généraux du fonctionnement de l'économie socialiste* (Paris: Maspéro, 1968), p. 120.

107. Andras Hegedus, *The Structure of Socialist Society* (New York: St. Martin's Press, 1977), p. 45.

108. *Ibid.*, p. 48.

109. Nikolai Bukharin, *Historical Materialism* (Ann Arbor: The University of Michigan Press, 1969), p. 282.

110. George Konrad and Ivan Szelenyi, *The Intellectuals on the Road to Class Power* (New York: Harcourt Brace Jovanovich, 1979), p. 42.

111. Hegedus, p. 70.

112. Cornelius Castoriadis, *La société bureaucratique* (Paris, 1973), p. 20.

113. Merle Fainsod, "The Russian and Soviet Case," in *Bureaucracy and Political Development*, ed. Joseph La Palombrara (Princeton, NJ: Princeton University Press, 1971), p. 243.

114. Weber, p. 335.

115. Brus, p. 53.

116. *Ibid*, pp. 86, 87.

117. William G. Rosenberg and Marilyn B. Young, *Transforming Russia and China* (Oxford: Oxford University Press, 1982), pp. 214, 215.

ABOUT THE AUTHOR

PAVEL CAMPEANU was born in Bucharest, Romania, in 1920. He joined the Communist Youth League in 1935 and the Romanian Communist Party in 1940. From 1941 until 1944 he was imprisoned for antifascist activity.

In 1960 Campeanu received a Ph.D. in sociology from the Stefan Gheorghiu Academy and from that year until 1980 was head of the Opinion-Polling Department of Romanian television. He was appointed Professor of Social Sciences at the Bucharest Polytechnic Institute in 1950, then joined the Institute of Social Sciences at Stefan Gheorghiu Academy in 1956 and the journalism faculty in 1976. He has served as a communications expert with UNESCO, is a member of several international mass-communications associations, and has lectured widely in North America and Eastern and Western Europe. He was awarded the Prize of the Romanian Academy in 1964 and again in 1977.

Campeanu is the author of numerous articles published in Romania and elsewhere, and of several books, among which is a trilogy on audiences: *People and the Theatre, People and TV*, and (in collaboration with Stefana Steriade) *People and the Movies*. His comprehensive examination of Stalinism, first outlined in *The Syncretic Society* (M. E. Sharpe, 1980), begins in *The Origins of Stalinism* (M. E. Sharpe, 1986) and continues in the present volume.